Doing
Philosophy
Comparatively

Doing Philosophy Comparatively

Foundations, Problems, and Methods of Cross-Cultural Inquiry

Second Edition

Tim Connolly

BLOOMSBURY ACADEMIC
LONDON • NEW YORK • OXFORD • NEW DELHI • SYDNEY

BLOOMSBURY ACADEMIC
Bloomsbury Publishing Plc
50 Bedford Square, London, WC1B 3DP, UK
1385 Broadway, New York, NY 10018, USA
29 Earlsfort Terrace, Dublin 2, Ireland

BLOOMSBURY, BLOOMSBURY ACADEMIC and the Diana logo are trademarks of
Bloomsbury Publishing Plc

First published in Great Britain 2023

Cover design by Louise Dugdale
Cover image: wacomka / iStock

A catalogue record for this book is available from the British Library.

A catalog record for this book is available from the Library of Congress.

ISBN: HB: 978-1-3501-7755-0
        PB: 978-1-3501-7754-3
        ePDF: 978-1-3501-7756-7
        eBook: 978-1-3501-7757-4

Typeset by RefineCatch Limited, Bungay, Suffolk
Printed and bound in Great Britain

To find out more about our authors and books visit www.bloomsbury.com
and sign up for our newsletters.

Contents

Tables

Preface to the Second Edition

The period since the first edition of this book was published in 2015 has been an exciting one in the field of comparative philosophy. There have been more books about the basic problems and methods of cross-cultural comparison than ever before, including works like *Fundamentals of Comparative and Intercultural Philosophy*, by Lin Ma and Jaap van Brakel (SUNY, 2016); *Cross-Tradition Engagement in Philosophy: A Constructive-Engagement Account*, by Bo Mou (Routledge, 2020); and *Comparative Philosophy and Method: Contemporary Practices and Future Possibilities*, edited by Steven Burik, Robert Smid, and Ralph Weber (Bloomsbury, 2022). The push for the inclusion of non-Western traditions in mainstream contemporary philosophy has spread into the public arena, reaching venues such the *New York Times* and *The Guardian*. And comparativists continue to contest the future of the field, with a growing number arguing that it is time to replace "comparative philosophy" with new forms of inquiry. In this new edition, I have tried to capture the ongoing debates and emerging approaches that continue to make cross-cultural philosophy a dynamic field.

For helpful comments or gracious sharing of their work in my preparation of the material for this edition, I am grateful to Cameron Brewer, Brian Bruya, Paul D'Ambrosio, Mat Foust, Massimiliano Lacertosa, Joshua Mason, Bo Mou, James Roe, Sor-hoon Tan, Bryan W. Van Norden, and others I may have forgotten.

I also thank Becky Holland and Suzie Nash at Bloomsbury for their help and guidance in every stage of the process of preparing this edition. Finally, I have benefitted greatly from five anonymous readers who gave feedback on the first edition (and especially from one of these readers, who gave extensive comments on every chapter); and two anonymous readers who gave comments on a draft of the second edition.

Introduction

Imagine researchers from the future want to study how different philosophical systems develop over long periods of time. To do so, they run a computer simulation in which groups of artificially intelligent humanoids are dispersed throughout the regions of a formerly uninhabited planet, affectionately referred to by the experimenters as Planet Phi. While Planet Phi's environment is set up to be hospitable to life, it takes plenty of effort on the part of its new denizens to secure the goods necessary for survival. Some of the humanoid tribes die out, some barely subsist, and a few flourish.

After many generations, the surviving tribes begin to develop self-conscious reflection on how humanoids ought to act, what they should care about, their place in the surrounding cosmos, what happens when they die—the sorts of things the experimenters recognize as the beginnings of philosophy. Discussion of these problems grows quite intricate, and the team assigned to a tribe has to track a particular debate's evolution across multiple generations to understand what is being said. Distinctive ways of thinking begin to emerge, patterns of thought that gradually become engrained in the consciousness of the tribe's members and interwoven with other aspects of its emerging culture: politics, literature, art, religion. The experiment is a great success.

Further along, however, vast changes begin to occur. The technological systems available on Planet Phi are now advanced enough that intertribal communication is possible. While there had been some interaction among the different tribes before, now it begins to take place on an unprecedented scale. Waves of immigration occur; political alliances are formed; wars are fought across rapidly shifting boundaries. It is still possible for the researchers to tell the tribes apart, but more difficult than before.

Seeing an opportunity, the experimenters obtain further grant money enabling them to study the sorts of interactions taking place in "Phase II" of the simulation. What happens to philosophy, they want to know, when all the different tribes begin to come together?

While comparative philosophers inhabit a very different world from the one just described, they share some important features with the researchers in the story. Like the experiment on Planet Phi, comparative philosophy begins in a kind of wonder about the development and interactive potential of philosophical traditions that have emerged largely in isolation from one another. If you have spent some time studying a philosopher like Socrates, you may be curious about foundational thinkers in other parts of the world. Did Confucius and the Buddha have the same motivation for philosophizing? Did they ask similar questions? Would they believe that Socrates is practicing philosophy in the right way? What about the whole traditions founded by these thinkers? What is unique about Western, or Chinese, or Indian (or African, or Japanese, or Middle Eastern) philosophy? Are there insights common to all these philosophies? Do thinkers in other cultures worry about the same basic problems that arise in the Western tradition: mind and personal identity, knowledge and reality, the principles of our ethical and political life? Can they offer us new ways to think about these problems?

The more we become aware of the existence of other "tribes" who have developed their own ways of thinking about the major issues of philosophy in depth and detail, the more such questions press on us. In studying culturally distinct philosophical traditions alongside one another, comparative philosophy attempts to satisfy our curiosity.

Yet comparing our own ways of thinking with those of others is more difficult than it first appears. To begin, how do we know that different cultural traditions are talking about the same things? To engage in cross-cultural comparison, we will have to translate terms and concepts from one language into another. But is such translation really possible? If it is true, as some theorists have argued, that *language determines thought*, then philosophers who are fluent in one language will not be able to understand the thoughts expressed by those writing in another. The language barrier will be especially significant in the case of the historically and culturally distant realms of thought which comparative philosophy tries to bring together. Can twenty-first-century English speakers really understand what classical Chinese philosophers meant? When we read English translations of texts like the *Analects* or *Daodejing*, are we simply misled into thinking we have understood? How serious a boundary is language in our attempts to understand other cultures' ways of thinking?

Secondly, what standards should we use to understand and evaluate culturally distinct philosophies? Suppose the tribes in the experiment develop fundamentally different ways of understanding the world around them and their place within it, and these ways become entrenched over many generations. As long as the tribes are separate, this is no problem. But when members of one tribe try to understand and evaluate the philosophy of another, they will be caught in a dilemma. If they use their own standards as means for grasping the other tribe's philosophy, will they really comprehend it? Will their assessment be impartial? But what other standards are available? How do we avoid our comparisons being biased from the very start?

Thirdly, what is the goal of comparison? Even if we are confident that we have resolved the first two problems, there is still the question of where to go from there. When we compare, are we looking for philosophical universals—a "table of elements" of human thinking, as it were? Or are we looking to discover alternative conceptions of the good life? When we do encounter what appear to be significant differences, what is the appropriate response? Is it to try to reconcile them, or find a minimal agreement between them, or just let them be? Or suppose the goal is not to point out similarities and differences between the different philosophical-cultural traditions, but to enable productive interaction between them. What is the best means of doing this? These are just a few of the issues we will need to think about.

Engagement with unfamiliar ways of thinking and living can help a society advance. As John Stuart Mill wrote in the mid-nineteenth century, "It is hardly possible to overstate the value, in the present low state of human improvement, of placing human beings in contact with other persons dissimilar to themselves, and with modes of thought and action unlike those with which they are familiar."[1] Our virtues may turn into vices if they are never challenged, and since no single society has a complete set of virtues, encounters with other societies' values can expand our moral range. It was for these reasons, Mill concluded, that it is indispensable for people "to be perpetually comparing their own notions and customs with the experience and example of persons in different circumstances from themselves."[2]

Today we do not need to go very far to encounter people with ideas and practices vastly different from our own. Advocates of cross-cultural education point to the changing demographic make-ups of Western countries, as well as the growth of political and economic power in non-Western countries such as China and India. Contact with other ways of life is increasingly inescapable.

Yet mere exposure to different ways of life will not necessarily lead to any improvement in oneself or one's society. The ability to compare is a skill that needs to be cultivated through reflection and practice. We must learn not only to make fine-grained observations regarding similarity and difference, but also to render qualitative judgments regarding the numerous conflicting ethical and metaphysical worldviews that surround us today. As Lee Yearley, a scholar of comparative religious ethics at Stanford University, writes:

> We must develop those abilities that allow us to compare different visions of the world, and we must engage in the normative analysis that such comparisons involve if we are to thrive, or perhaps even survive, in the present world. We live in a world where we often find radically diverse ideals of human flourishing.... [W]e need a particular set of intellectual skills and virtues to do the comparative philosophy of human flourishing.... [A]cquiring them is critical if we are to meet the personal and social challenges we all face.[3]

If we lack the ability to compare, putting ourselves in contact with others will be of little benefit for us or them.

One of the traditional aims of philosophy has been to reflect on philosophical method: not what to think about this or that particular issue, but how to think well in general. Philosophers have recognized that the process of inquiry is important in its own regard, independently of whatever conclusions are reached. The comparative branch of philosophy is no different. We must take the time to consider the challenges involved in extending philosophy across cultural boundaries and how to overcome them, or else all our efforts may be wasted. We can distinguish this focus on comparative methodology, the *how* of comparison, from the actual content of comparative studies, the *results* of particular Chinese-Western or Chinese-Indian or African-Western comparisons. Reflection on the problems that arise in making cross-cultural comparisons has become an increasingly visible component of the field of comparative philosophy.

Often minor methodological mistakes can result in vast misunderstanding. Take a common Western view of African philosophy, in which a stark divide is made between Western rationalism and the "primitive" and "superstitious" characteristics of African thought. The contrast feeds outsiders' perceptions of Africa as the "dark continent," with even some African intellectuals themselves beginning to identify "African philosophy" with prescientific traditional thought. Yet what if the whole idea is simply the result of a mistake in scope? Western societies, as the Ghanaian-born philosopher Kwasi Wiredu points out, have gone through prescientific stages in their intellectual evolution, and one still sees remnants of these stages in large segments of the population in some Western countries. If we want to make an adequate comparison, we should be placing traditional African thought alongside Western folk beliefs rather than the philosophy produced at modern universities.[4] Here and elsewhere, some advance thinking about what we are doing when we make our comparisons can go a long way.

Just as a little training in logic can help us to detect and avoid basic argumentative fallacies, training in the foundations of comparison may help us to avoid basic mistakes in making cross-cultural judgments. Comparison can go wrong in many ways. We can put too much stock in our translations of other cultures' texts, or fail to see particular passages within the broader context of the traditions in which they were written, or use values and concepts from our own background as the standards by which to measure everything else, or exaggerate the similarities between the philosophies being compared (or make facile contrasts between them), or not be clear about what our assumptions are. Without some prior reflection on the methodology involved in extending philosophy across the vast linguistic, cultural, and historical gaps involved in the subject, comparison may do little more than reinforce one's prior ways of thinking.

The ability to compare is not something that is simply given to us the moment we encounter someone with a different way of life, but rather the result of prior reflection and practice. Working through the basics of comparison can help us to develop the virtues of thought necessary to understand other cultures' philosophical traditions, and to navigate an increasingly diverse world.

How this book works

In this book, we will discuss the many challenges involved in extending philosophy across cultural boundaries and the various strategies that comparative philosophers have developed to resolve them. But before beginning, I should say something about the material the book covers and how it is organized.

Our discussion incorporates many examples of contemporary work in comparative philosophy while discussing questions of methodology, as well as some historical examples of Western engagement with non-Western cultures when these are necessary to understand the full scope of the issues at stake. Nonetheless, this book is not meant to be a *survey* of contemporary research in comparative philosophy or a *history* of comparative philosophy. Those interested in the history of Western engagement with Asian traditions may consult J.J. Clarke's *Oriental Enlightenment: The Encounter Between Western and Asian Thought*. While a survey of contemporary work in comparative philosophy is yet to be written, one can look at publications such as *Comparative Philosophy, Dao: A Journal of Comparative Philosophy, Journal of World Philosophies*, and *Philosophy East and West* to see some of the latest work in the field.

My own background is in ancient Greek philosophy and classical Chinese philosophy, and many of the examples I use to illustrate methodological issues are drawn from these fields. But because the challenges of working across the aforementioned boundaries are not unique to Chinese-Western comparison, I have incorporated methodological reflections not only from comparativists working in this area, but also from those engaged with Indian philosophy, African philosophy, Islamic philosophy, and other cultural traditions. I also discuss work in philosophy of language, philosophy of social science, experimental philosophy, and other parts of philosophy that have bearing on the cross-cultural kind. Finally, I incorporate some material from other disciplines that deal with cross-cultural comparison, including anthropology, political science, postcolonial studies, psychology, and religious studies. The primary focus of the book is not on the theoretical contributions of these philosophical areas or disciplines, however, but rather on the two main methodological dimensions of cross-cultural philosophy: how to understand other cultures' philosophical texts and traditions, and how to make constructive philosophical progress in light of the independently developed views found in these texts and traditions.

Comparison, as the scholar Wilhelm Halbfass writes, "means different things to different people.... It is done for different reasons, based upon different cultural and historical conditions, and pursued with different methods."[5] This book does not defend a single theory of comparative philosophy and try to fit all of the different aspects of the field under that theory. Rather, I incorporate a plurality of views regarding comparative methodology, arranging them for the majority of the book under certain issues and problems. When in the last part of the work the discussion turns to some main approaches to comparison, I try to give a sense of the strengths and weaknesses of each rather than argue for the primacy of one.

This book is divided into four parts. Part I covers the definition of comparative philosophy and its central concepts. Critics have challenged both the comparative and the philosophical aspects of the field, and we begin by considering whether these criticisms are justified, focusing first on the definition of "philosophy" in comparative philosophy (Chapter 1). From there we turn our focus to the meaning of "comparison," examining two main ways in which the study of thinkers and texts from culturally distinct traditions has been thought to be philosophically fruitful (Chapter 2). Finally, we look at the meaning of "culture" and "tradition" themselves and how they are related to the practice of comparative philosophy (Chapter 3).

Part II focuses on the central methodological problems of comparative philosophy. Because the thinkers or texts being compared have been formed according to the languages, concepts, and standards of justification of their distinctive cultures and traditions, there is the issue of whether it is possible for philosophers from one tradition to understand and evaluate those from another—the problem of incommensurability (Chapters 4 and 5). Even if it is possible, the forced or unequal application of one tradition's categories can lead to a distorted image of the other—the problem of one-sidedness (Chapter 6). Finally, there is the difficulty of situating the items compared within the larger cultural traditions of which they are part—the problem of generalization (Chapter 7). We will consider the various challenges each problem poses as well as the main strategies that comparative philosophers have developed to overcome them.

Part III gives brief discussions of four approaches to comparative philosophy: universalism (Chapter 8), pluralism (Chapter 9), consensus (Chapter 10), and global philosophy (Chapter 11). While in reality there are as many approaches to comparative philosophy as there are comparative philosophers, I focus on these four because they illustrate basic orientations toward similarity and difference. Universalism emphasizes points of convergence between different philosophical-cultural traditions; pluralism, points of divergence; consensus, a means of balancing points of convergence and divergence; and global philosophy, a rejection of the convergence-divergence model of comparison in favor of creative interaction between traditions at specific points. I hope that this section of the book not only gives readers some sense of the competing models under which productive work in comparative philosophy has taken place, but also encourages them to think about how to improve or go beyond these models.

For the second edition of the book, I have added a Part IV, which includes exercises that are intended to engage readers in further reflection on the issues in Parts I–III. Some of the exercises are meant to help you apply the ideas and concepts discussed in the main part of the text; others take a debate in more depth and ask you to take a position; still others provide tools by which you can begin to develop your own projects in comparative philosophy. My hope is that the addition of this new part will help the book live up to its title, which suggests that comparative philosophy (like philosophy itself) is not merely something you study, but something you must work at *doing*.

Part I

The Nature of Comparative Philosophy

1

Is There Such a Thing as Comparative Philosophy?

A number of critics have argued that the idea of comparative philosophy does not make sense. They focus either on the "philosophy" aspect, claiming that there is something problematic about extending the term to non-Western contexts, or on the "comparative" aspect, alleging that the concept is too broad to be meaningful. In this opening chapter, we will give a hearing to these challenges to the existence of comparative philosophy. Though I do not think the challenges are successful (as you may guess from the fact that there are many more chapters in the book after this one), they can still help us better understand what comparative philosophy is. We must not avoid these objections but confront them head-on if we are to make progress in the rest of the work.

The legitimacy of "non-Western philosophy"

Let us begin with the philosophy aspect of the criticism. To engage in cross-cultural comparison we must think that there is philosophy in non-Western cultural traditions. Otherwise, there would be nothing to compare. But can we make this assumption? What reason is there to think that philosophy exists outside the West?

Is philosophy universal?

The term "philosophy" has roots in ancient Greece, and philosophers in the subsequent Western tradition have been aware of themselves *as philosophers*. Boethius wrote about "The Consolations of Philosophy," Aquinas about the distinction between philosophy and theology, and Nietzsche about the prejudices of philosophers. The same cannot be said for the most prominent thinkers in non-Western traditions. In East Asia, for instance, the term did not become widely known until the late nineteenth century, and new words were coined in Japanese and Chinese to translate it. Given that well-known thinkers from other cultures—Confucius, Laozi, the Buddha, etc.—had not heard of the term "philosophy" and did not think of themselves as "philosophers," does it make sense to apply the term to them? Is "non-Western philosophy" a legitimate category?

The view that there is no such thing as non-Western philosophy arises from two main sources. On the one hand, some Western philosophers have claimed that non-Western thought does not rise to the level of philosophy. On the other, many outside the West have been skeptical of the attempt to make a Western cultural product the standard for the rest of the world. What both sides share in common is the idea that there is something problematic about extending philosophy to non-Western contexts. In their view, the word "Western" in "Western philosophy" is redundant because philosophy is inherently Western. It makes no sense to speak of "African philosophy," "Chinese philosophy," and the like.

If we have studied the great philosophers in the Western tradition, we may be under the impression that philosophy is something universal. When Socrates says that "The unexamined life is not worth living," or Aristotle that "All human beings by nature desire to know," these claims have implications that go beyond a certain sector of the Greek population circa the fifth and fourth centuries BCE. Why should they be relevant only in certain parts of the Western hemisphere? Isn't there something terribly biased about thinking that the ideal of the examined life does not apply to people living in other parts of the world?

Still, the assumption that a form of inquiry developed in fifth- and fourth-century BCE Athens must be practiced everywhere is equally problematic. If it is wrong to think that no other cultures are capable of philosophy, isn't it just as bad to take it for granted that they are doing whatever Western thinkers are doing?[1]

Excluding non-Western thought

Some of the major philosophers in the Western tradition have held deeply prejudiced views about the philosophical capacities of other cultures. Kant wrote that "Philosophy is not to be found in the whole Orient."[2] Hegel denied that Africans possessed any moral or intellectual development: "The Negro, as already observed, exhibits the natural man in his completely wild and untamed state. . . . What we properly understand by Africa, is the Unhistorical, Undeveloped Spirit, still involved in the conditions of mere nature."[3] And then there is Hume, who claimed that there was nothing of value outside to be found anywhere outside of white civilization: "I am apt to suspect the negroes, and in general all the other species of men (for there are four or five different kinds) to be naturally inferior to the whites. There never was a civilized nation of any other complexion than white, nor even any individual eminent either in action or speculation. No ingenious manufactures amongst them, no arts, no sciences."[4]

Though such blatant statements of racial and cultural prejudice are less common today, one still encounters the view that non-Western cultures lack philosophy. Recently there was a prominent contemporary philosopher who conceded that the Confucian, Daoist, and Buddhist traditions had produced some fascinating texts; yet he maintained that these texts were more like Western religion mystical writings, since they (apparently he had read them all) do not rely on logic and evidence. "Eastern thought," he concluded, "— whatever it is, and however useful it may be—is not philosophy."[5]

The exclusionary position is a much broader issue in contemporary philosophy. In her 2012 essay, "How Is This Paper Philosophy?", Kristie Dotson points out that diverse practitioners of the discipline—those who favor non-mainstream approaches or come from under-represented populations—are often confronted by their fellow philosophers with questions like the one in her title. Behind such questions is the assumption that there are commonly held norms that can help us to determine whether a given project is philosophy, with the expectation that one must show that their project fits the mold if they want to be granted status in the discipline. Often left unstated, these norms are self-reinforcing in that they exclude the very practices that would challenge them.[6]

Even when the prejudice against non-Western philosophy isn't announced in such a straightforward manner, it is often taken for granted. Think for a moment of the core philosophy courses you have taken: Introduction to Philosophy, Ancient Philosophy, Modern Philosophy, etc. Even if you studied only Western texts and thinkers in these courses, there was no effort to incorporate this fact into their descriptions. The same goes for courses in ethics, metaphysics, epistemology, and the like. If the term "Western" added something meaningful to the course title, then we would add it—but it doesn't, so we don't. On the other hand, courses and textbooks that deal with non-Western philosophical traditions always advertise this fact: World Philosophy, Classical Chinese Philosophy, Africana Philosophy, and so on.[7]

If you look at a map and attempt to find the locations of all the philosophers you have studied so far, chances are you will end up looking only at certain parts of Europe and North America. Why is this? Introductory courses on history, art, or religion are seldom limited to Europe and North America; those in philosophy, on the other hand, rarely include philosophers outside of the Western tradition. Few philosophy professors seem to think this is any big deal.

It is in fact quite a thing to exclude, whether explicitly or implicitly, philosophical contributions from other parts of the world. Even if we claim that we are not making any value judgment in focusing on Western philosophers, but simply relying on what we take to be the fact of philosophy's Western origins, this claim may ring hollow to members of the cultures who are left out of the conversation. As one observer puts it, "To deny a people a philosophy is to deny them any kind of intellectual activity, a system of thought, culture, and civilization."[8]

Critics of Western philosophical chauvinism also point out that its practitioners apply an uneven standard of what counts as philosophy. "[F]or long stretches of time," one Indian philosopher writes, "what passes for philosophy in the West could not be characterized as such if the definition were to be as strictly enforced there as it usually is in the case of non-Western cultures."[9] Any definition of philosophy narrow enough to exclude the thought of an entire culture will probably exclude at least one or two canonical Western thinkers as well. Philosophy in the West has changed a great deal since the ancient Greeks. Plato's *Phaedo*, for instance, contains assumptions about the soul, the afterlife, and the physical universe which are well outside the philosophical and scientific mainstream today. We also find a conception of philosophy itself—as purification of the soul from the influence of the body—that few contemporary thinkers would accept. Yet many professors and students make great efforts to understand the nuances of Plato's views in that dialogue, rather than writing it off from the beginning because it does not match our conceptions of philosophy.

The most important problem with the exclusionary position is that it lacks evidence. We have no way of telling whether a culture possesses philosophy comparable to our own until we examine the relevant data from that culture. Without such an examination our claims amount to ignorance justifying ignorance: we don't know anything about whether other cultures have philosophy, and there isn't any need to learn about them because for all we know they don't.[10]

Pushing back against exclusionism

While many cross-cultural philosophers have criticized the exclusionary tendencies of Western philosophy, in the past few years the argument has gained momentum, moving beyond philosophy into the public square.

In 2016, two leading scholars of non-Western philosophy, Jay L. Garfield and Bryan W. Van Norden, published an editorial in the New York Times entitled "If Philosophy Won't Diversify, Let's Call It What It Really Is." They note that very few philosophy programs in the US and Canada teach courses in non-European philosophical traditions, and that of the top 50 philosophy departments in the English-speaking world, only 15 percent have faculty who teach non-Western philosophy. In spite of many arguments in favor of broadening the diversity of philosophy, few philosophy programs have opted to do so, fostering the perception that these programs are mere "temples to the achievement of males of European descent." To discourage false advertising, the authors suggest any philosophy program that teaches only Western thinkers and texts rename itself as the "Department of European and American Philosophy."

In a book published the following year, *Taking Back Philosophy: A Multicultural Manifesto*, Van Norden criticizes contemporary philosophers for "building walls" around a Western canon of philosophy. In doing so, they place themselves in the company of demagogues in the U.S. who want to drive wedges between people on the basis of race and religion as well as nationalists in China who want to keep Chinese culture untainted by external influence. "Almost all philosophers," Van Norden writes,

> would categorically reject *explicit* racism. But I ask my fellow philosophers to recognize whom you are implicitly aligning yourself with when you reject—without genuinely investigating—philosophy from outside the Anglo-European tradition. You are helping those who build and maintain walls: walls between races, walls between religions, walls between civilizations.[11]

If the discipline of philosophy wants to speak to the increasingly complex and diverse world that we inhabit, the first step will be to tear down these walls.

The argument has also been taken up by students. In 2017, members of the student union at SOAS University of London attracted attention for their attempts at "decolonizing the curriculum" at their school. In keeping with the university's historic focus on Asia, Africa, and the Near and Middle East, the students wanted the majority of philosophers included in their courses to be the Global South. They also requested that if European Enlightenment philosophers were required reading, their professors address the colonial context in which these philosophers were writing.[12] These initiatives attracted backlash from the popular press in the UK, with headlines labeling the students "barmy" and proclaiming "They Kant be serious!"[13]

As Meera Sabaratnam, a professor of International Relations at SOAS, pointed out in defense of the students, the initiative was not merely about which philosophers are taught, but also aimed at challenging racist ideology. She writes that

> in the past, assumptions regarding racial and civilizational hierarchy informed a lot of thinking about how the world worked, what was worth studying in it and how it should be studied. Such assumptions also informed and justified the expansion of colonial rule in Asia, Africa and the Middle East until the mid-twentieth century. Whilst many of these assumptions have been challenged with the dismantling of colonial rule, many persist in public discourse as well as academic study.[14]

Challenging such assumptions is not a break from what we do in philosophy or in the university more generally, but rather aims at continuing the tradition of confronting entrenched views about the world.

As these examples illustrate, philosophy's culture of exclusion has been an important area of battle in the past few years. Those interested in non-Western philosophy do not always have to play defense against those who would exclude it from the philosophical arena; they can take the argument to the exclusionists as well.

Is comparative philosophy just Western philosophy in disguise?

On the other side, critics from non-Western cultures have claimed that in spite of its cross-cultural pretensions, comparative philosophy is merely a means for the global expansion of Western philosophy. As the Indian philosopher Daya Krishna sees it, the comparative enterprise from the beginning has meant "the comparison of all other societies and cultures in terms of standards provided by the Western societies and cultures." As a result, he claims:

> The scholars who belonged to these other societies and cultures, instead of looking at Western society and culture from their own perspectives, accepted the norms provided by Western scholars and tried to show that the achievements in various fields within their cultures paralleled those in the West, so that they could not be regarded as inferior in any way.[15]

When we ask about the "philosophy" of a non-Western tradition, we judge that tradition by a category imposed from without. The other tradition is forced to conform to an external standard of philosophy, at the expense of the identity and values it has developed on its own.

Much of modern African thought, for example, has been taken over by "the question of African philosophy," namely, whether there is such a thing.[16] Critics note that the debate often takes place exclusively on Western terms, and that attempts to sort out the philosophical from the nonphilosophical leave out longstanding elements of African thought. The ultimate result of such cross-cultural encounters is that a single conception of philosophy comes to dominate the world over.[17]

In short, the objection is that comparative philosophy is *one-sided*: that it fails to treat all cultures as equal contributors to the comparative enterprise, instead using Western categories to interpret everything else. While professing to be a cross-cultural dialogue, it is really just a monologue delivered by Westerners, broken up only by occasional declarations of affirmation from their non-Western interlocutors. Even the name of the discipline, with its inclusion of the term "philosophy," appears to exhibit a Western bias.

The criticism of "one-sidedness" is important enough that I have devoted a whole chapter of the book to it (Chapter 6). For now, there are a couple of points to be made. The first is that it would be mistaken to think that because the term is a Western one, the practice of philosophy is something limited to the West as well. The words "history" and "poetry" are also derived from the ancient Greeks, but this does not mean that there have not been historians or poets in other parts of the world. The term is not the same as the thing it names. Perhaps other cultures have possessed practices similar to philosophy, but under different designations.

Additionally, the criticisms of Western bias often assume that there is some agreed-upon set of norms common to all Western philosophers that is now being imposed on the thought of other cultures under the guise of comparative philosophy. But there is not one uniform conception of "philosophy" in the history of Western philosophy. Even today there is plenty of disagreement about the proper aims and methods of philosophy. If we go and ask five or six different philosophers about these things, we will probably get as many answers. Comparative philosophers are just as varied in their ideas as any group of philosophers. Often they employ texts and thinkers from other traditions to challenge Western notions of what philosophy is supposed to be. The goal is not to take a single idea, Philosophy, and stamp it onto other cultures, but to enrich an already diverse set of conceptions of philosophy and philosophical practices.

While we do have to be careful of using comparative philosophy merely as a way of viewing non-Western texts through fixed Western categories, the criticism does not rule out the possibility of comparative philosophy from the very beginning. Again, there is no way of knowing whether other cultures possess something similar to Western philosophy without looking at the evidence from those cultures.

What is "philosophy" in comparative philosophy?

Even if we do not believe that philosophy is an essentially Western phenomenon, we still need to think about how the concept applies to non-Western cultures. We have to begin with some idea of what philosophy is, or else we will not know what to look for. Comparative philosophers have used a number of approaches to define philosophy in a global context.

A familiar definition

Consider Wilfred Sellars' famous definition of philosophy, as the attempt "to understand how things in the broadest sense of the term hang together in the broadest sense of that term."[18] The conception of philosophy as thinking about the "big picture," familiar to us in one version or another, has some appeal to comparative philosophers. The editors of the *Oxford Handbook of World Philosophy*, for instance, quote Sellars' definition in the opening line of their introduction, going on to claim that "Any reasonably impartial view that surveys the world's cultures finds this kind of reasoned inquiry into who we are, our experience, and the nature of reality widely distributed."[19] If this is so, then Sellars' definition is sufficient for cross-cultural comparison.

One potential problem, however, is that the definition is too broad to be helpful. Philosophers from different historical periods have disagreed on which "things" are the proper objects of philosophical investigation. If we compare Aristotle, Kant, and Wittgenstein, we get three very different views of the matter; even more so when we begin to incorporate ideas from non-Western traditions. Some contemporary philosophers have thought that philosophy can't tell us anything about "big questions" such as the nature of reality. If you want to learn about such things, they would advise you to ask a physicist or chemist.[20] And without some further specification, rational inquiry into human nature and human experience could just as well describe disciplines like psychology or biology.

Some comparativists have also worried that in lumping together multiple traditions under the generic heading of "reasoned inquiry into fundamental questions" we run the risk of leveling out significant differences between those traditions. A preestablished notion of philosophy can lead us to fixate on the features of another culture's thought that look familiar to us, while ignoring less familiar but perhaps equally significant features. Carine Defoort, a professor of Sinology at the University of Leuven, expresses this point well when she writes that

> Westerners who search for maxims and universal principles in ancient Chinese texts are like Chinese masters who would sift through the whole corpus of Western texts—from political manifestos to philosophical treatises—in search of prescriptions for coffins, without taking into account our current intellectual categories or philosophical interests. . . . A pernicious result of such intellectual mutilation is that the Chinese insights are exposed as primitive or naïve forms of familiar Western concepts, insights, and discussions that are themselves never called into question.[21]

Because of their interest in ritual, the Chinese masters heavily debated issues surrounding coffins, like how deep they should be buried, or how thick their lids should be. If we were to look only for grand theories amid such teachings we would miss out on the issues they considered important.[22]

Critics might object that Defoort exaggerates the significance of an unfamiliar feature of the discourse of Chinese masters in order to make her case. The attempt to look for insights into the big philosophical questions in ancient Chinese texts may in fact uncover sophisticated and novel approaches to those questions alongside whatever else may be present in these texts. Still, Defoort's overall point is an important one. In approaching works from other cultural traditions, we need to be aware of the ways in which our prior conceptions of philosophy can lead to a distorted picture of those works.

Expanded definitions

Skepticism about Western-based definitions has led some comparative philosophers to formulate new definitions of philosophy. The goal is to set forth a definition that is broad enough to encompass the thought of non-Western traditions, while at the same time retaining what has made philosophy in the West distinctive from other practices.

One recent proposal, formulated by Rein Raud of Tallinn University, attempts to describe philosophy solely from an external point of view, without committing us to any particular ideas about the content of individual philosophies. The result is the following definition:

1 The content of philosophy is provided by individual thinkers, rather than by divine revelation or folklore.
2 Philosophy attempts to explain the nature of things in general.
3 Philosophical work engages in dialogue with the work of other philosophers.
4 Philosophy is a cumulative enterprise.
5 Philosophers are independent of worldly authority.
6 Philosophy is socially tolerant—opposing views are not punished.[23]

Raud maintains that these are the features that have made philosophers in the Western tradition different from politicians, novelists, scientists, and theologians. At the same time, he thinks they can be applied to the seminal figures in other cultural traditions.

However, this expanded definition also has faces some objections. Feature (1) excludes conceptions of African philosophy that incorporate folk beliefs; (3) and (4) will not apply to philosophers who initiated philosophical traditions; and we have already considered some problems with (2). The list also fails to tell us what counts as philosophical methodology; it mentions "dialogue," but does not tell us what sort of dialogue. Perhaps the biggest issue for present purposes is that the six characteristics are derived from a Western frame of reference, reflecting what has made philosophers in one part of the world distinct from their counterparts in other fields. But why think that these distinctions map onto other cultures?

As these criticisms illustrate, expanding the definition of philosophy for comparative purposes is quite a challenge. The definition will have to start from somewhere; supposing it starts from Western philosophy, it will be subject to the same objections as the first definition we considered. We will probably be able to find plenty of significant counterexamples from both Western and non-Western cultures. Of course, we have only examined one such definition here. Are there other viable alternatives?

Family resemblance

A third approach to the definition issue is to think of philosophy as a "family resemblance" concept. In opposition to the Socratic view that a concept can be analyzed in terms of some essential element common to all the individuals to which it applies, the twentieth-century Austrian philosopher Ludwig Wittgenstein argued that a concept word instead covers an extremely complicated nexus of various similarities of different kinds. He used the concept of "game" as an illustration:

> Consider for example the proceedings that we call "games." I mean board-games, card-games, ball-games, Olympic games, and so on. What is common to them all?
> —Don't say: "There *must* be something common, or they would not be called 'games'"—but *look and see* whether there is anything common to all.—For if you look at them you will not see something that is common to *all*, but similarities, relationships, and a whole series of them at that.[24]

Wittgenstein referred to the multiplicity of overlapping similarities and relationships between all the different types of games as *family resemblances*. For a concept like "game," it is pointless to try to give a single characteristic or set of characteristics that will apply to all the instances.

Is the same true of "philosophy"? A main justification for family resemblance in comparative philosophy is that it helps us to avoid a one-sided approach to candidates from other traditions. As one proponent writes, the family resemblance approach "opens the way for the practice of global philosophy by allowing us to recognize different traditions as *philosophical* without requiring us to give any one of them a preeminent position as the paradigm case against which to judge all others."[25]

To see this, consider the two attempts at definition above. The first attempt says "philosophy is *A*"—if some other culture has *A*, then it is philosophy; if not, then it isn't. The second says "philosophy is *A*, *B*, *C*, *D*, *E*, and *F*," and argues that this definition can encompass multiple traditions. What both attempts have in common is that they suppose that there are certain features that are *essential* to philosophy. The problem, as we have seen, is that these features may exclude some worthwhile candidates from comparative study.

The family resemblance model in turn supposes that philosophy has no essential features. What we call "philosophy" is similar to what we call "games." There is not a shared feature or list of features exhibited by each and every instance, but rather an overarching web of family resemblances:

Western Philosopher 1: *A C D F*
Western Philosopher 2: *A B E F*
Western Philosopher 3: *B C D F*
Western Philosopher 4: *B C D G*

Now suppose that we look at some hypothetical candidates for the title of philosophy from other traditions:

Non-Western Philosopher 1: *A D G H*
Non-Western Philosopher 2: *A G H I*
Non-Western Philosopher 3: *B C D I*
Non-Western Philosopher 4: *H I J K*

If we took feature "D" to be essential to the definition of philosophy, we would end up excluding other traditions on this basis while missing out on other resemblances they may bear to our own. The family resemblance model may also lead us to re-examine neglected features of our own tradition, like feature "G," if they are more prominent in other traditions.

For example, suppose that we are comparing Western *philosophia* that originated in Greece with the Chinese term *zhexue* that is used to refer to the texts of thinkers such as Confucius and Laozi. We might ask whether these different concepts point to the same pursuit. However, as the comparative scholars Lin Ma and Jaap van Brakel argue, the answer to this question is not relevant—

There is no need for *philosophia* to be *zhexue*, and vice versa, there is no need for *zhexue* to be *philosophia*. Nonetheless, the family resemblance-concept *zhexue* can be extended to include parts of *philosophia* and the family resemblance-concept *philosophia* can be extended to include parts of *zhexue*. Suppose two scholars X and Y encounter one another, coming from the traditions of *philosophia* and *zhexue* respectively. They can always find some similarities, apart from differences, between their traditions. That is to say, they can recognize each other's tradition as, to some extent, in certain respects, a part or extension of *philosophia* or of *zhexue* respectively.[26]

In other words, the family resemblance model allows productive cross-cultural engagement to take place without having to determine that the pursuits on either side are "the same." Ma and van Brakel argue that we should use this model not just with regard to *philosophia* and *zhexue*, but with all the other concepts we are comparing us well.

The idea of family resemblance is useful because it allows us to retain some of the distinctive features of the Western philosophical tradition while still being open to the challenges other cultures may provide to the philosophical enterprise. Suppose that a lover of board games sees two people sitting in the park playing a game that they have never seen before. What initially draws this enthusiast is that they recognize certain features of the games they already know: it is played with some sort of pieces on some kind of board, it looks to be highly competitive, and so on. What sustains their interest, however, is the idea that there is something unfamiliar about it that is worth mastering.

A typical reproach to the notion of family resemblances is that it leaves the application of a concept too unrestricted, since there is no mechanism for determining which family resemblances are essential and which are accidental. The same might be said for its comparative version: how do we know which cross-cultural resemblances are meaningful, and ought to be explored further? While the family resemblance approach is often thought to be more promising than the other two approaches, this question will need to be carefully worked out.

The need for balance

A successful approach to defining philosophy in a global context—whatever that approach may be—will have to avoid two extremes.[27] At one end of the spectrum is the view that says, "if it isn't exactly like what we are doing, it isn't philosophy." While such a view offers a clear definition, it may lead us to exclude many interesting non-Western thinkers from the discussion. Think of the diversity of philosophers within the Western tradition: Socrates, Augustine, Nietzsche, Wittgenstein, Arendt. Would we want to exclude any of them?

At the other end of the spectrum is the broad view: "however different it seems, it's still philosophy." While this may not seem as bad as its narrow-minded counterpart, it is potentially just as dangerous. While narrow definitions of philosophy cut us off from fruitful engagement with other traditions, overly broad definitions let all that is unique about another culture's thinking drift into an ever-expanding and increasingly meaningless category.

As we shall see many times in what follows, this kind of balance is a general requirement of comparative work. Without openness to what other philosophical traditions have to teach us, comparative philosophy would not be possible. But this attitude of openness does not mean giving up our critical abilities.[28] We need to be able to say where philosophy ends and some new enterprise begins, or else we will lose what makes philosophy unique.

The "Comparative" aspect

Let's turn now to the other aspect of our subject matter. Why distinguish *comparative* philosophy from all the other kinds? What is so special about the comparing that comparative philosophers do? Whereas the first objection was that "philosophy" is too narrow to cover what comparative philosophy aims to cover, the second says the word "comparative" is too broad to refer to a specific area of study.

Isn't all philosophy comparative?

Studying philosophy means exploring multiple points of view, weighing these points of view against one another to see which best explains the phenomena. When we study philosophy of mind, we consider dualist theories of mind alongside materialist ones, or different types of materialist or dualist theories alongside one another. When we study key figures in the history of philosophy, we understand them in light of similarities and differences with their predecessors. To understand Aristotle's political philosophy, we must be able to say something about Plato's *Republic*; in order to understand Kant, we must know how he differs from Hume. Even when we are not comparing a philosophical text with works by other philosophers, we are measuring it against what we ourselves regard to be the right answer about the issue the text addresses.

One place where professors of philosophy delight in the comparative nature of their discipline is in handing out essay assignments to their students:

1 *Compare the accounts of such-and-such issue offered by famous philosophers x and y. What distinguishes x's account from y's?*

2 *Which is author x's view of _____? Do you think this view is compelling? If so, defend it against some potential criticisms. If not, what is a better alternative, and why?*

3 *Discuss three different responses that philosophers have offered to problem p. Which response is the best, in your view? Justify your answer.*

Even when these essay topics do not use the word "compare," the goal is to get students to look at multiple sides of an issue. The reason for this is clear enough. Philosophy professors want their students to get in the habit of defending their views, rather than simply asserting them; a straightforward way to accomplish this goal is to make students place their own views alongside competing ones and challenge them to say why their own views are better. Learning any philosophy at all means learning to make comparative judgments.

So why mark off a special branch of philosophy as the "comparative" kind? Robert Allinson takes up this line of reasoning in his provocative essay "The Myth of Comparative Philosophy":

> In short, is it possible to find an example of philosophy, whether Eastern or Western, which does not make use of comparison, nay, this is far too mild a statement, which is not based on a key comparison or contrast as the source of its inspiration and consequent development? All philosophy arises in reaction either as a revolution against or as completion to previous philosophy.[29]

The objection here is not that other traditions do not possess philosophy, but rather that because all types of philosophy everywhere involve comparison, the adjective "comparative" adds nothing to the concept of philosophy. In that case, it is a "myth" that there is a special branch of philosophy called "comparative philosophy."

Any difference between comparative philosophy and philosophy proper, Allinson goes on to argue, is merely one of degree. Most philosophy is restricted in the range of its comparison to a single culture, or language group, or continent. All comparative philosophers are doing is broadening this range to include philosophers in places such as China or India. As he writes, "The only difference that arises is constituted by the inclusion of a wider data base. Thus, a global philosophy, which makes use of the developments from both Chinese and Western philosophy is no more comparative than the previous philosophy of either the West or China."[30]

According to this view, what we count as comparative philosophy depends on historical accident rather than on a well-defined notion of the discipline in question. Before the Chinese and Western traditions became aware of each other's existence, a number of philosophers negotiated different traditions *within* either China or the West. Think of Aquinas' fusion of Aristotelian philosophy with Christian theology. For Aquinas' time, wouldn't this count as an exercise in comparative philosophy? Is the term "comparative" too broad to be useful?

What makes comparative philosophy distinctly comparative?

Allinson is right insofar as he emphasizes the continuity between comparative philosophy and philosophy proper. I have tried to draw attention to this continuity with the title of the book, which suggests that comparative philosophy is a method of doing what philosophers have always tried to do.

Yet this method is unique enough that the term "comparative" is still justified as a designation. First, there is the difference in the *scope* or *degree* of the comparison. Comparative philosophers make comparisons across *culturally distinct philosophical traditions*. As we shall see, this element is a key feature in definitions of the discipline. This feature separates comparative philosophy from the vast majority of philosophy, however much the latter may rely on comparative judgments.

While Allinson challenges the coherence of this notion, arguing that it arbitrarily excludes philosophers such as Aquinas, this is not the problem that he makes it out to be. Different philosophical traditions develop and encounter one another during specific periods in history, so it should be no surprise that the range of materials considered comparative philosophy changes over time. Of course, the scope of comparative philosophy needs to be clarified further. We need to say more about the idea of a *philosophical tradition*, and also about what it means for such traditions to be *culturally distinct*. For the moment, let us consider this work to be done, and return to these issues in Chapter 3 below.

Secondly, the attempt to compare philosophies from different cultures gives rise to a unique set of problems: issues concerning incommensurability, one-sidedness, and cultural generalizations, to name a few. For the comparative philosopher, these issues and problems become an explicit topic of discussion and investigation. Philosophers who work within one cultural tradition do not usually have to think about such things.

A third point of divergence is that comparative philosophers have a distinctive *approach* to similarity and difference. They are not trying to differentiate their own philosophies, which they take to have reached the correct conclusions by the appropriate method, from those of their predecessors or current competitors, whom they take to have faulty methods or conclusions. Rather, the comparative philosopher is trying to approach the other tradition with the goal of understanding or learning something from it.

When Allinson says that "all philosophy is comparative," he is using the term "comparative" in a very general sense. But when it is used in the phrase "comparative philosophy," it encompasses a distinct scope, set of methodological problems, and approach. For this reason, his argument that comparative philosophy is a "myth" is not a compelling one, since it plays on an ambiguity in the term in question. We will examine the meaning of comparison in more detail in the next chapter.

Conclusion

So far we haven't shown that comparative philosophy is free from problems. All we have done is discuss several potential objections to its existence, and how these objections might be addressed.

What these "existential" objections tend to have in common is that they set forth an idealized version of comparative philosophy, and then criticize comparative philosophers for failing to live up to this ideal. The "philosophy" objection criticizes comparative philosophers for failing to find a neutral point of departure for studying non-Western thought. The "comparative" objection in turn requires that the comparison be defined independently of historical circumstances; otherwise, what we call "comparative philosophy" is arbitrary.

The problem with both objections is that comparative philosophy is by its very nature dependent on historical circumstances and rooted in some tradition. To see this point, recall the researchers from the Introduction who study how the different tribes on Planet Phi interact. Unlike those researchers, real-world comparative philosophers are part of the experiment which they are attempting to observe. They always belong to one tribe or another, and inherit that tribe's language and history and standards of philosophy. They do not have the luxury of watching many generations of simulated philosophical interaction unfold within a few weeks or months, but carry out their investigations in real time. To demand that comparative philosophy be completely independent of one tradition or another, or isolated from any particular historical era, is to demand the impossible. There is no ideal comparative philosophy.

Yet even though all comparative philosophy is less-than-ideal, there are varying degrees in which it can fall short. While our image of another culture's philosophy will inevitably be shaped by our own preconceptions, we can take steps to correct for this. These steps will never bring us to the ideal, but that is no objection to taking them.

2

The Goals of Comparison

In the early stages of the discipline, comparative philosophers often made broad claims about what they hoped to accomplish. One of the field's first proponents wrote that comparative philosophy is "the general examination of the ways in which human beings of all races and cultures reflect upon their actions and act upon their reflections," and stated that its scope is "universal history and the cosmos."[1] Others imagined it would produce a worldwide philosophy that united all humanity under its banner.

As practitioners have grown increasingly cognizant of the difficulties of cross-cultural comparison, the aims of their work have become more refined. Work in comparative philosophy today can be sorted into two main dimensions: one that uses comparison to understand particular philosophers and texts or the traditions of which these are part, the other to make constructive progress on a specific philosophical problem or issue. Since philosophy proper also aims at understanding thinkers and texts and making progress on problems and issues, a central challenge of each dimension is to explain why it is fruitful to approach these goals comparatively.

In this chapter we will look at each of these two dimensions in detail, examining the justifications for each kind of comparison as well as its main difficulties. In doing so, we will further develop our understanding of the "comparative" aspect of our subject matter.

A first look at the two dimensions

To begin to make sense of the many different shapes comparative philosophy can take, we must learn to recognize two distinct ways of comparing things.

Descriptive comparison versus evaluative comparison

In one sense, comparison can involve *describing* similarities or differences between the things compared. For instance, someone might say that

> "*Inception* and *The Matrix* are both films that explore the notion of alternate realities, but in different ways,"
> or that
> "The United States spends more on its military than the combined total of the next ten highest-spending countries,"
> or that
> "Both Jesus Christ and the Buddha are believed by their followers to be the products of virgin birth."

The purpose of making these kinds of statements is not merely to point out similarities and differences, but to gain some further comprehension of the items in question. We don't just pick any two items to compare, but rather those that seem to lend themselves to mutual clarification. Our choice of items in and of itself can be insightful or provocative or dull. The whole comparative statements of which they are part can be subject to intense debate.

In a second sense, comparing can mean *evaluating* the relative merits of the objects of comparison. For example,

> "*Inception* has a more sophisticated, original, and interesting take on the notion of alternate realities than *The Matrix* does,"
> or
> "The United States' military expenditures are excessive in comparison to other world powers,"
> or
> "Jesus' birth-story is more credible than the Buddha's."

Here we are not merely trying to understand the items in question, but to make judgments of better and worse. Such judgments not only help us to see the things compared in a new light, but also to enhance our ideas about the subject matter under consideration. What makes for a good science-fiction film, ideal military spending, or believable religious story?

The interpretive and constructive dimensions

Connected with these different senses of the word "compare," comparative philosophy has two potentially related but theoretically distinct aspects:

1 Using terms, ideas, or concepts from one philosophical tradition to help *understand* or *interpret* another philosophical tradition.
2 Seeking to *advance* or *develop* philosophy through cross-tradition engagement.[2]

The *interpretive* dimension looks at the philosophies compared as historical objects, trying to get a sense of why they developed the way they did. The comparison is supported with evidence from particular philosophical texts or from the cultural contexts in which they were composed. The measure of a successful comparison is whether it aids our understanding of the texts or traditions in question.

The *constructive* dimension is oriented toward the future rather than the past. Different cultural-philosophical traditions engage one another to make constructive philosophical progress. This dimension is what distinguishes comparative philosophy from comparative literature or comparative religion. Whereas the latter enterprises may help us to understand and interpret texts or religious practices, they do not themselves count as instances of literature or religion, but rather as the study of literature or the study of religion. Comparative philosophy, on the other hand, *is* philosophy.[3]

To help us see the two dimensions in practice, here are several passages pulled from different works of comparative philosophy in which the authors discuss what they hope to accomplish. The authors in the first column use comparison as a means of reaching a better understanding of different culturally bound philosophies, whereas the authors in the second use it to advance our work on problems or issues:

Table 2.1. The interpretive and constructive dimensions of comparison

"By submitting the basic philosophical suppositions of Indian civilization to a careful comparison with the basic suppositions of a civilization close and familiar to us [i.e. Western civilization], we might obtain a more lucid and reliable picture of the civilization we are trying to unravel."[4]	"The goal of a global philosophy-inspired approach is not necessarily to inspect and comprehend every possible school of thought. Instead, our goal is to further develop our own tradition through engagement with others. We need not come to any definitive views about alternative traditions. What matters is how their ideas may be put to good philosophical use within our tradition."[7]
"I take the project of comparative philosophy as an integral part of cross-cultural conversation that might . . . allow us to reconsider the manner in which thought-traditions have been represented."[5]	"[M]y goal is not so much to juxtapose texts from distinct traditions to notice similarities and differences as it is to *do philosophy*."[8]
"Aristotelian and Confucian ethics can be viewed as mirrors for each other. . . . [W]e must read the original works of Aristotle and Confucius to understand them, but a comparison could help have them better understood."[6]	"Comparative philosophy . . . is a subfield of philosophy in which philosophers work on problems by intentionally setting into dialogue sources from across cultural, linguistic, and philosophical streams."[9]

Definitions of comparative philosophy may emphasize one of these aspects, and particular comparative studies often fit comfortably into the first dimension or the second.

Yet the two dimensions are closely related. If we understand very little about another culture's philosophy, we will not be able to take full advantage of the constructive contributions it can offer. Comparative philosophers are cognizant of the influence that a tradition exerts on the individual philosophers within it and tend to be wary of isolating particular pieces of that tradition without some understanding of their relation to the whole. On the other side, when we are trying to understand a text that deals with certain philosophical issues, we need to be fully aware of the nature of those issues and the sort of thinking it takes to work through them.[10] If we fail to evaluate the merits of the claims made by a philosopher from another tradition, we will not do full justice to the philosopher in question, who in all likelihood understood those claims to be true. In short, the interpretive and constructive dimensions complement, and may even require, one another.

The reflective dimension

Before moving on, we should note that beyond the interpretive and constructive dimensions there is a third, second-order dimension of the discipline:

3 To *reflect* on the nature of comparison itself, where the primary focus is the development of a philosophic account of what comparison is and how it is best carried out.[11]

This dimension includes thinking about the problems inherent in crossing cultural boundaries, as well as attempting to build a framework through which meaningful comparative work can take place.[12] Since works that engage in the interpretive or constructive dimensions of comparison often begin with some discussion of the methodological framework to be employed, we must be able to recognize this dimension of comparative philosophy as well. In the past decade, there has been a growing number of books and articles in comparative philosophy devoted exclusively to methodological issues.

One reason that the reflective dimension matters to comparative philosophy is because reflection about method is fundamental to any philosophy. We can characterize philosophy as much in terms of its methods—Socratic dialogue, logic and critical thinking, analysis, thought experiments, Cartesian doubt—as in terms of its content matter. Comparative philosophy aims at a similar transparency and sophistication when it comes to method. "Comparative philosophy is philosophy," Wilhelm Halbfass writes, "insofar as it aims at self-understanding. It has to be ready to bring its own standpoint, and the conditions and the horizon of comparison itself, into the process of comparison which thus assumes the reflexive, self-referring dimension which constitutes philosophy."[13] The puzzles involved in doing philosophy comparatively are of considerable interest in their own right.

Without paying attention to issues of methodology, it is too easy to arrive at superficial comparisons that say little or nothing about the philosophies in question. A poorly made comparison is like a conversation where we leave thinking we have understood the other person, while in reality we have failed to grasp their meaning. To avoid such a failure of meaningful engagement we need to pay attention to what we are doing in advance, becoming aware of the basic mistakes that can occur in comparative philosophy and some of the strategies that we can take to avoid them.

The reflective dimension also matters because comparative philosophy is a discipline in transition. As a well-known comparativist once quipped, "comparative philosophy has a dubious past, a very bright present, and, hopefully, no future."[14] Those working in the field recognize the many failures that have plagued Western philosophers' past encounters with non-Western traditions, while at the same aspiring to move beyond boundaries in philosophy that make labels like "Western" and "non-Western" necessary. As we will see later in the book (especially Chapter 11), many practitioners even reject the label "comparative philosophy" itself, hoping to push into something new. What is the future of comparative philosophy?

This book itself is an exercise in comparative reflection. I hope the discussion in its entirety will convince readers that thinking about the process of comparison will make our own attempts at cross-cultural philosophy better founded. Let us say no more about this aspect of comparison here but consider each of the first two dimensions at greater length.

The interpretive dimension: comparing to understand

One way of engaging in the first dimension of comparative philosophy is to use concepts from one's own tradition to approach thinkers and texts from other parts of the world. Are Confucius and Mencius best understood as virtue ethicists? Is Buddhism a variety of consequentialism? We can also read thinkers and texts from different traditions alongside one another: the *Nicomachean Ethics* and *Analects*, Zhuangzi and Kierkegaard, Vasubandhu and Berkeley. Whichever strategy we use, the hope is that comparative interpretation will open up interesting and previously unexplored aspects of the philosophies in question.

Still, many observers are skeptical about the possibility of reaching genuine cross-cultural understanding. The process of interpreting across cultural boundaries, they say, is at best highly problematic and at worst impossible. Can we really understand classical Chinese or Indian texts using the concepts of twenty-first-century Western philosophy? Are we merely distracting ourselves with superficial similarities?

The inevitability of comparison

We can begin by thinking about why we need comparison at all. To understand Chinese philosophy or Indian philosophy or African philosophy, we could simply take courses on "Chinese Philosophy" or "Indian Philosophy" or "African Philosophy." What do we have to gain by adding a comparative dimension to the work of understanding other traditions? Why make it a "Comparative Philosophy" course instead?

One answer is that learning philosophy from another tradition always takes place through the lens of one's own. If we have mastered the three main contemporary Western ethical theories—virtue ethics, deontology, and utilitarianism—then we may inevitably end up thinking of those theories when we study non-Western views of how to live. If we have just read the *Phaedo*, we may have trouble putting it out of our mind when we are reading the Buddha's sermons. Since some degree of comparison is inevitable when we learn a new tradition, it is important to be aware of this fact and think about the process through which this comparison takes place.

Comparative interpretation begins with the process of translating another culture's texts. Believe it or not, when you are reading a classic non-Western text in English, the translator has already worked out some of the most difficult comparative issues for us in advance.

The best way to see the influence of this process is to play "dueling translations." Compare the following renderings of a single passage from Confucius' *Analects*:

1 The Master said, "Acquiring Virtue by applying the mean—is this not best? And yet among the common people few are able to practice this virtue for long."[15]

2 The Master said, "The excellence required to hit the mark in the everyday is of the highest order. That it is rare among the people is an old story."[16]

3 The Master said, "How transcendent is the moral power of the Middle Use! That it is but rarely found among the common people is a fact long admitted."[17]

Much of the disagreement centers on how to translate two of the Chinese characters found in the original text: *de* 德 and *zhong* 中. If you happen to be reading the first translation, which renders them as "Virtue" and "mean" respectively, you may naturally end up thinking of Aristotle's famous definition of virtue as a mean between two extremes. The second translation, however, takes special care to avoid the translation of *zhong* as mean, since the translator believes that the term has nothing to do with Aristotle's concept of the mean and wants readers to avoid the comparison. The third in turn renders *de* as "moral force," in this case because the translator thinks that rendering it as "virtue" will make readers think of it in opposition to vice, and he believes that Chinese thinkers did not use the term this way.

As you can see from just this short passage, the process of translation of Chinese texts is anything but a simple one, in which we mechanically match each character with the single word in English that translates it. When scholars translate philosophically significant terms such as *de* and *zhong*, they are necessarily involved in a heavy element of cross-cultural comparison. Innocent first-time readers of texts like the *Analects* will probably not realize the degree to which a particular translation emphasizes certain points of comparison while downplaying others.

The difficulty of translating the above passage lies in figuring out which of our concepts is most like *de* or *zhong*. To make this determination, the translator will need to know a lot about the context in which Confucius used the term *de*, as well as quite a bit about virtue and other relevant concepts in the Western tradition. They will need to be able to justify why one way of understanding each term is better than competing ways of understanding it. Since what Confucius means by *de* might be similar to what we mean by "virtue" in some respects but resemble "moral force" or "excellence" in others, it is possible that each of these translations has something to recommend it.[18]

One way you can become involved in the process of translation is by looking at the introductory material to the text you are reading. Often the translator will explain why they chose to render a certain term the way they did. As you read the translated text more carefully, becoming gradually familiar with its author's way of thinking, you should decide whether you agree with the translator's way of understanding that term. You can always scribble out the translator's interpretation and write in your own if you think it is more accurate!

Universalism and differentialism

How we understand the items we are comparing will also depend on what we are looking for. Philosophers like Plato and Hegel have conceived of philosophy as the attempt to see the "one-in-many," the universal in the particular. Should we follow them in our comparisons of thinkers and texts from different cultures? Or should we rather try to emulate someone like Wittgenstein, who was interested in uncovering significant differences between phenomena? (Wittgenstein once summed up the distinction between himself and Hegel this way: "Hegel seems to me to be always wanting to say that things which look different are really the same. Whereas my interest is in showing that things which look the same are really different."[19])

In contemporary comparative philosophy we find two default positions for understanding the thought of other cultures. Take a look at the two sets of claims in the columns below:

Table 2.2. Universalism and differentialism in comparative philosophy

"[H]uman beings live in the same world, possess the same psychic capacities, and share many of the same basic relationships and institutions. . . . Hence, there is a set of basic desires, feelings, beliefs, and needs which all human beings share and which are necessary for living a human life. This forms the common ground for comparative studies of different cultures."[20]	"The usual approach to comparative philosophy involves finding parallel philosophical concepts, issues, problems, and theories in two cultures. Frequently, however, this approach yields little result. . . . Contrastive analysis must replace comparative analysis in comparative philosophy. . . . [W]e ought to abandon the frenzied search for forced parallels between Chinese and Western thought."[23]
"[T]here is much family relatedness and much overlap among societies. . . . Not without a sensitive awareness that we are speaking of something that is experienced differently in different contexts, we can nonetheless identify certain features of our common humanity . . . from which our debate might proceed."[21]	"[I]n the enterprise of comparative philosophy, difference is more interesting than similarity. That is, the contrasting presuppositions of the Chinese and Anglo-European traditions are . . . a presently more fruitful subject of philosophic reflection than are the shared assumptions."[24]
"[I]f the [European, Chinese, and Indian philosophical traditions] are learned together, it is easier to explore the possibility that there are philosophical positions that are truly universal."[22]	"The task of comparative studies is precisely to make the texts more comprehensible by contrastively 'dispelling' them of seemingly similar 'ideas.'"[25]

Whereas the philosophers in the first column take common features to be the starting point for comparative engagement, the approaches in the second column seek to uncover significant areas of difference. These two approaches are called *universalism* and *differentialism* (the latter is also sometimes known as *particularism*). The universalist tends to appeal to human nature or shared experiences that transcend cultural differences as the basis for philosophical similarities, whereas the differentialist believes that thinking within culturally bounded traditions develops in unique directions.

Comparative studies often begin with the sense that there is some commonality between thinkers or texts from different cultures—otherwise, why compare them? This sense may be based on a shared term, a similar example or argument, or on the presumption that the texts are dealing with similar questions. But this similarity can turn out to be mere appearance.[26] Translations of terms may be misleading, and not tell us much of anything about the concepts the terms are supposed to express; apparently similar examples or arguments may be used in completely different contexts; the presumption of similar questions may be imported entirely by the person doing the comparing. We will not know whether our initial perception of commonality is well-founded until we look more closely at the items being compared. On the other hand, there may be texts that strike us at first to have nothing in common but show deep similarities on a closer look.

Both universalism and differentialism can turn into interpretive vices.[27] If we assume that others are too much like us, we may end up glossing over significant differences and consequently fail to understand the others as they are. This can lead to *descriptive chauvinism*, in which we grant recognition only to those aspects of other cultures which match up with elements of our own. Such an attitude is not just a lazy and arrogant way of relating to others, but also prevents us from learning anything new. Recognition of some important areas of difference seems to be a precondition for serious engagement with another culture's philosophy; otherwise, we would have nothing to gain from the conversation.

If we look only for contrasts, however, we may end up seeing the other tradition as everything we are not. In practice, cultural differences have often been framed in terms of oversimplified oppositions: Western culture is *x*, whereas the non-Western culture is not-x. The counterpart to descriptive chauvinism is *romanticism*: seeing philosophy from other cultures as exotic and mysteriously fascinating. In Western pop culture there is a tendency to see "Eastern philosophy" as interested solely in mystical and nonrational modes of experience. As one critic sums things up, "would-be 'New Age' gurus play fast and loose with terms such as *dao* and *chakra* and with Tarot cards, guaranteeing that non-Western philosophy is presented as a hodgepodge of magic and pseudo-wisdom."[28] This understanding not only downplays the practical and this-worldly orientation of philosophers such as Confucius or the Buddha, but also leads us to miss what might be considered "mystical" in our own philosophical tradition.

Many comparative philosophers may be sympathetic to both universalism and differentialism, but suspicious of either one when taken to an extreme.[29] Lee Yearley puts it well when he says comparative philosophy is about finding "similarities in differences and differences in similarities."[30] If we see a broad similarity in how thinkers from different cultural traditions approach a topic, our next step should be to figure out what is different about their approaches. Yet we shouldn't stop at this point, but instead look for further respects in which their approaches are similar. If we repeat this process several times, we will find ourselves getting to more fine-tuned and interesting discoveries about the thinkers in question.

Over the years my students and I have determined that comparative interpretation has three main rules:

1 Be careful of thinking other cultures' philosophies are too much like our own.
2 Be careful of thinking they are too different.
3 Just be careful!

Many of the strategies we will discuss later attempt to strike a balance between the universalist and differentialist positions.

Self-understanding and other-understanding

Comparativists have found a useful model for cross-cultural understanding in what the twentieth-century German philosopher Hans-Georg Gadamer referred to as "fusion of horizons." A horizon is all that our gaze takes in from the particular place where we are situated. When we read a work of philosophy from a historically or culturally distant setting, the issues we see in that text and the questions we ask of it will depend on our own location in time and space. Yet understanding the text cannot be a matter of remaining where we are, trying to fit the other into our current field of vision, and giving up if it does not fit. Rather, we must shift or expand our own horizon in order to meet what is other. As the philosopher Charles Taylor explains it in a helpful essay on Gadamer's theory of interpretation: "[I]n coming to see the other correctly, we inescapably alter our understanding of ourselves. Taking in the other will involve *an identity shift in us.*"[31]

Products of other cultures come with varying degrees of familiarity. Some of them we will be able to relate to without too much difficulty because we have some basis for understanding them in our own culture. Others will cause us trouble. I first became curious about Peking Opera, a traditional Chinese form of musical performance that began in the late eighteenth century, while I was taking a course in aesthetics. The professor, who was not only highly regarded in the field but a genuine appreciator of all things beautiful, told us one day that Peking Opera is the one form of art that he found impossible to enjoy. Upon tracking down a video of a performance, I found I had the same reaction. The performers were dressed in oddly colored costumes and used a style of acting that was unrecognizable to me; the music was so bizarre that I could hardly think of it as music. How could this be one of China's cultural treasures?

The challenge arises from the fact that it is we ourselves who have to undergo fundamental changes in order to understand what is different. To appreciate Peking Opera, I would not only have to learn a lot about the background of the art form, view many different performances of it, and so on, but also, more significantly, need to change my conception of what music should sound like, recognizing that what I think of as beautiful music is just as much a product of my particular upbringing as it is for someone who loves Peking Opera. Which particular genres of music in my own collection would sound bizarre to someone from another culture? How would this person have to expand their views to appreciate these particular genres?

Taylor's own example is the Aztec practice of ripping out their sacrificial victims' hearts. When the conquistadores encountered this custom, their first reaction was to think of it in contrast with their own civilized religion: "While we worship God, these people worship the devil."[32] At some point, however, it dawned on them that the Aztec custom had a parallel in Spanish society in the ritualistic consumption of Jesus' body and blood during the celebration of the Catholic mass. The conquistadores could use this feature of their own experience as an entry point for understanding what would otherwise be a totally incomprehensible practice, but in doing so, they would have to understand their own practice in a new way.

Similar challenges arise in comparing philosophical texts. First-time students of Indian philosophy may be confused by the doctrines of karma and rebirth that are presupposed in the different schools of Indian thought. How is it possible that philosophical systems could be based on these kinds of beliefs? Isn't this religion rather than philosophy? But this is not unlike the attitude of the conquistadores: "Our philosophy is based on reason, theirs on superstition." The challenge arises when we turn our gazes inward. Which concepts in our own philosophical tradition play a similar role?

When we respond to the challenge of understanding others, Taylor says, it brings about "two connected changes: we will see our peculiarity for the first time, as a formulated fact about us and not simply a taken-for-granted feature of the human condition as such; and at the same time, we perceive the corresponding feature of their life-form undistorted. These two changes are indissolubly linked; you cannot have one without the other."[33] Such a change in perception is not easy to accomplish. Since we are used to seeing things from where we are, shifting our field of vision involves effort and giving up the comfort of the familiar. The simpler path is to try and fit what is different into our preestablished categories, and if this cannot be done, to ignore it.

For comparative philosophers these challenges are especially difficult. The goal is not just to make sense of the other culture's practices, but of its deeper philosophical foundations. But can we understand cultures with different foundations from our own? How do we "shift" that which forms the very basis of how we see the world? And if philosophical foundations are peculiar to their traditions rather than features of the human condition, by what means can different cultural-philosophical traditions engage in meaningful dialogue? We'll explore these questions further in Part II of the book.

The constructive dimension: comparing to make philosophical progress

While the interpretive dimension of comparative philosophy has a range of potential benefits, contemporary representatives of the different cultural-philosophical traditions have worried that since this approach deals primarily with past texts and thinkers, it runs the risk of turning cultural philosophies into artifacts in a museum. As museum pieces these philosophies would be of immense curiosity for appreciating who we are and where we come from, but no longer of any use to us in determining where we are going. To prevent the "mummification" of traditions, we need to consider a second approach to comparative philosophy, one that treats philosophical traditions as living entities that can be sources of inspiration to philosophers working today. Through the mutual exchange of insight, comparative philosophy can help us advance our discussion of contemporary issues.

External criticism

One way in which members of culturally distinct philosophical traditions may interact with one another is by challenging or critiquing each other's basic assumptions. From the beginning, Western philosophy has been concerned with questioning. Yet as some observers have noted, this questioning generally takes place only within certain parameters:

However taken it may be with surpassing itself, Western philosophy never questions itself except from within. However radical it may wish to be, this criticism is always relatively integrated, remaining within the limits of an implicit understanding from which certain positions may emerge. There is always that *on the basis of which* we question ourselves, which, for that very reason, we cannot question.[34]

When we engage in debate with members of our own philosophical tradition, we tend to take certain things for granted. We assume the subject we are arguing about is philosophically important, that the main terms make sense, and that there are particular rules in place that guide how we argue with one another. But progress in philosophy is often made when our foundational beliefs are challenged. Without gaining some distance from our own ways of thinking, the limitations of these beliefs may escape our notice.[35]

This does not mean that meaningful criticism from within is impossible. Socrates served as a gadfly to his fellow Athenians; Nietzsche criticized the Western philosophical tradition while at the same time being an important member of that tradition. Yet in subjecting our tradition to scrutiny from others, we gain the possibility of a more radical approach to philosophy. An intelligent outsider, armed with data and theories we might have ignored or never encountered, can force us to justify our way of life in ways that our own neighbors, steeped as they are in that same way of life, could never do. This outsider will be neutral with regard to the internal debates that take up much of the energy of the tradition's adherents, and can offer a detached perspective on whether the tradition is meeting the challenges of the modern world. Engagement with outsiders can help us preserve the Socratic ideal of philosophy as critique of dogmatism.

Criticism has not just been a feature of Western philosophy. It was the critique of Confucius' teachings by rival schools that led to a revived understanding of these teachings by later adherents such as Mencius and Xunzi. Debate and dialogue were the "nerve center" of the classical Indian philosophical tradition, in which every thinker was required to set forth on their own any possible objections to his point of view.[36] The worry is that today this sense of debate has been lost, and the traditions in question do not have mechanisms in place that allow them to grow and evolve.

Outsiders can subject a system to two different kinds of criticism.[37] On the one hand, they can show that the system has failed to live up to some *external standard*. Even though a soft-drink company is not generally motivated by considerations of health, we can still take it to task for producing unhealthy products. If, however, we criticize the company for not meeting its annual goals in charitable contributions, then we are relying on an *internal standard* of criticism. The weakness of one kind of criticism is the strength of the other. By using an internal standard, it is less likely that we will pose a profound challenge to the system being criticized. What if it is the standard itself that needs to be shifted? However, it is more likely that we will be able to connect with the object of our criticism. If we can give others evidence that they are failing according to their own standards, then they will be more willing to change their behavior.

Because comparative philosophy offers the opportunity to criticize a tradition's philosophical foundations from an external perspective, it has often been allied with philosophical movements that seek to challenge our most entrenched presuppositions. Some feminist philosophers, for instance, have seen a close parallel between their work and the work of comparative philosophers:

> In its most basic form, feminist theorizing begins from the experience of women and considers alternative constructions of traditional ways of seeing, experiencing, cognizing, feeling, and embodying our everyday realities and truths. Just as Asian philosophy has helped expand Westerners' worldviews by presenting reasonable alternatives to metaphysical, epistemological, aesthetic, and ethical assumptions, so too does feminist philosophy challenge the foundations of taken-for-granted theories.[38]

These theorists contend not only that feminist philosophy would benefit from working more closely with the primary philosophical texts from other cultural traditions, but also that comparative philosophers would gain from taking greater account of considerations of gender.

Comparative philosophy has also been used to defend views within a tradition that have been forgotten or marginalized. Some comparativists have faulted contemporary Western ethical theory for viewing life as a "series of isolated moral tests"—an approach which focuses on momentous situations (often involving runaway trolleys, prisoners of war, or kidnapped violinists) that force us to weigh competing ethical principles. This emphasis comes at the expense of the "interstices of life," the moments when we are simply being ourselves in our day-to-day existence.[39] As a remedy, these philosophers look toward Confucian ethics, with its focus on ritual practice and familial relationships. Yet this idea of "philosophy as a way of life," they point out, is also found within ancient Greece. Socrates thinks the most important question of all is how one should live, and Aristotle that the goal of learning ethics is not merely to know what virtue is but to lead a virtuous life. The crisis of contemporary Western ethics is that for all it has to teach us about the nature of knowledge, or language, or historical figures, it has very little to say about how to live.[40] In this regard, it is failing to live up to its historical roots.

Not all cultural theorists have seen cross-cultural criticism as a valid pursuit. Some opponents have argued that since particular beliefs and practices only make sense as part of the larger "cultural wholes" of which they are part, meaningful criticism of these beliefs and practices is impossible. Even if we do not agree with these critics, there is much more to be said about the basis of cross-cultural criticism. We will examine these issues further in subsequent chapters (see especially Chapters 5 and 11).

Problem-solving

A second aspect of the constructive dimension of comparative philosophy involves exploring particular philosophical problems by looking at the resources other traditions have developed to deal with them. Suppose each philosophical tradition has been confined for most of its evolution to a distinct house.[41] The inhabitants of each dwelling have developed tools over time to cope with the particular needs that arise from living there. In today's world, however, one household may borrow tools from another. If a particular household wishes to meet the needs of modern life, it is helpful to have as many tools at one's disposal as possible.

Often those working in this vein want to distinguish their work from the "merely comparative" kind. They begin not by looking for similarities and differences between thinkers and texts from different traditions, but by thinking about living philosophical issues. The goal is to find new resources in other traditions for dealing with the puzzles of personal identity, for instance, or developing virtue-based accounts of ethics. In utilizing these resources, they hope to enrich contemporary philosophy.

The problem-solving approach depends on the idea that different cultural-philosophical traditions face similar problems but develop different ways of dealing with them. As the scholar of Indian philosophy Jay Garfield writes, a central motivation for studying classical Buddhist texts is that "they engage with questions and problems in which we are interested, sharing enough common ground for us to understand what they have to say, and contributing enough that is new that we have some reason to listen to it."[42] It is for this reason that they make such productive conversation partners.

A main challenge of this approach arises from balancing this perception of commonality with the particularities of each tradition's development.[43] If we want to share tools between households, we must think that these tools are "portable." But what if the houses are different enough that the tools required for working in each are unique?[44] In that case, taking a tool out of one home and using it in another will lead to nothing but trouble.

Here is one place where the constructive dimension of comparative philosophy depends on the interpretive one. To assess whether distinctive philosophical-cultural traditions face similar problems, we will need to carefully describe and compare the separate contexts in which they developed. At the same time, the problem-solving approach must give appealing reasons for keeping other households in the picture, rather than just focusing on developing the best tools possible within our own. We will consider these challenges further in our discussion of "global philosophy" (Chapter 11).

Conclusion

Aristotle says that getting at the truth is both easy and difficult. It is easy because everyone manages to find some part of the truth, difficult in that no person attains the whole of it. Since the time of the ancient Greeks, philosophers have aimed for the truth about basic features of human experience: knowledge, happiness, morality, the nature of existence, and the like. To study the great range of philosophers is to get more and more pieces of the puzzle.

Because subjects like these ones are a common human concern, one might wonder why their investigation should be limited to philosophers in one part of the world. Nothing prevents us from taking traditions besides our own as allies in the search for answers to the central philosophical questions, and from considering thinkers like Mencius, Shantideva, and Kwame Gyekye alongside the range of Western thinkers. As Aristotle says, while on our own we contribute very little to the attainment of truth, "by the union of all a considerable amount is amassed."[45]

Despite the many differences between comparative philosophers today, I think most of them would agree with Aristotle's comment about truth. There are things of great philosophical interest in other cultures' philosophical traditions, and that are either ignored by or absent from our own tradition.[46]

3

The Role of Tradition and Culture

We can further refine our understanding of the "comparative" aspect of our subject matter by considering the *scope of comparison*. What is it that comparative philosophers are comparing? Definitions of the field emphasize the study of different *philosophical traditions*, with the added qualification that these traditions have evolved within separate *cultures*:

> Comparative philosophy brings together philosophical traditions that have developed in relative isolation from one another and that are defined quite broadly along cultural and regional lines. . . .[1]
>
> Comparative philosophy can be defined by its attempt to move across the boundaries of otherwise distinct philosophical traditions—especially insofar as these traditions are divided by significant historical or cultural distance. . . .[2]
>
> [C]omparative philosophy . . . aims to understand an alien philosophical tradition (say, Chinese philosophy) embedded within a *disparate* cultural tradition (say, Chinese culture) *from the standpoint of* another philosophical tradition (say, Western philosophy) embedded within its own cultural tradition (say, Western culture).[3]

The joining together of philosophy with tradition and culture raises many questions. What does it mean to be a philosophical tradition? What is the relation of a particular work of philosophy to the culture in which it was composed? How significant are cultural boundaries to philosophical understanding? Is there one thing, philosophy, or many particular cultural philosophies? Which cultural-philosophical traditions should we engage with?

In this chapter we will explore what comparative philosophers have had to say about these questions. We will also introduce some of the puzzles raised by the attempt to do philosophy across culturally distinct traditions, which will be explored in more detail in the next part of the book. Without the attempt to bridge such traditions, there would be none of these puzzles— but there would be no comparative philosophy either.

Philosophy and tradition

The definitions above mention philosophical traditions rather than individual thinkers and texts. Comparative philosophers contend that tradition plays a more significant role in philosophy than is usually thought. It is of central importance not only in understanding past works of philosophy, but in making sense of present philosophical debates.

Why tradition matters

The claim that tradition matters in philosophy is far from obvious. When we reason about philosophical issues, we tend to think of our own views as arrived at independently of whatever things people have endorsed in the past. We may even think that philosophy and tradition are in principle opposed. Philosophy means ceaseless questioning, while tradition implies relying on the authority of the past. Why bother with tradition?

The particularities of tradition are more readily apparent when we look at philosophy from other cultures. The question of whether the state should condone musical performances, for instance, was taken seriously by a number of prominent classical Chinese philosophers. When we read the fifth-century BCE thinker Mozi's lengthy and animated condemnation of state-sponsored music, we may wonder why it was this issue that moved him. Making sense of other cultural-philosophical traditions means taking the time to understand why their members devoted large portions of their time and energy to concerns that seem less central to us.

Yet the peculiarities of other traditions can also be an occasion for self-reflection. There must be issues in our own culture's philosophy that are taken for granted from one generation to the next but appear just as strange to outside observers. As Jay Garfield sums things up, "While we often take ourselves to be asking abstract questions that arise from pure, context-free reflection, this is serious false consciousness.... While this fact may escape us pre-reflectively, it is painfully obvious on even the most cursory self-examination."[4] Studying philosophy from other cultures can lead us to recognize the significance of tradition in our own ways of thinking.

If we look at the issues that make up the chapters of introductory philosophy textbooks, we notice that these issues have a long history in the Western tradition, rather than being invented by the current crop of philosophers. The problem of free will, for example, goes back at least as far as Augustine, who invoked the concept to explain how an all-powerful and perfectly benevolent God could allow evil to occur. The idea of free will depends on certain philosophical presuppositions: that there is a faculty of willing, and a "self" or "soul" that possesses this faculty, and that this self or soul is capable of initiating action independently of the events going on in the world around it. The question of whether or not we are free cannot even be stated in philosophical traditions that do not share these presuppositions. To quote a scholar of Buddhist philosophy, "The problem seems just as weird from the perspective of a Madhyamika as would the problem of explaining the Buddha's omniscience to a Catholic."[5]

If we turn our attention to the means by which these questions are discussed, one finds that they have been developed over long periods of time. The method of philosophical analysis and the question-and-answer style of refutation taught in Western classrooms go all the way back to the ancient Greeks. The essay format that we use for written philosophical engagement has its roots in seventeenth-century Europe. The current generation of philosophers did not invent these methods of philosophical discussion, but rather inherited them. Studying philosophy at the level of tradition can help us become cognizant of the basic premises that established philosophical discourses take for granted.

Yet being part of a philosophical tradition does not mean blindly adhering to whatever is passed down by one's predecessors. Even within the bounds of tradition, individual philosophers can make significant advances. To see this point more clearly, we need to consider the ways in tradition can be philosophically productive.

Tradition as an argument extended through time

Let us turn for a moment to the work of the Scottish-born philosopher Alasdair MacIntyre, who in the 1980s and early 1990s published an important trilogy of works that explored the ways in which tradition shapes philosophical inquiry. While MacIntyre is not known primarily as a comparative philosopher, his views have led to a good deal of discussion about the nature of cross-cultural inquiry.

According to MacIntyre, we can understand an individual human life as a kind of *quest*. Like medieval knights, we are on a journey in search of some good; we learn more about this good—and also, crucially, about ourselves—as the quest unfolds. In undertaking my quest, however, I am never merely an individual. From the beginning I am part of entities older and larger than myself: I was born into a particular family, with particular ethnic affiliations, and I hold citizenship in a certain nation-state. As MacIntyre writes in *After Virtue*, the first book in his trilogy, "What I am ... is in key part what I inherit, a specific past that is present to some degree in my present. I find myself part of a history and that is generally to say, whether I like it or not, whether I recognize it or not, one of the bearers of a *tradition*."[6] The traditions we belong to already contain certain conceptions of the good, which they pass along to help guide us in our journey. (The word tradition itself comes from the Latin *tradere*—"to hand down.") They are *historically extended* and *socially embodied*, extending to communities of individuals through many generations.

This focus on tradition contrasts with the rampant individualism that MacIntyre sees as characteristic of modern Western society. According to the individualist mind-set, you are whatever you want to be; you are encouraged to "be yourself" and to "find your unique purpose in life." Because such messages are everywhere around us, most of us are led to neglect the sociohistorical conditions that help make us who we are. According to MacIntrye, it is a kind of countercultural virtue to know which traditions you belong to.

Our general neglect of tradition is aided by our tendency to think of "traditional" as synonymous with all that is irrational and unevolved. We imagine someone citing tradition when confronted with what makes the most sense from the perspective of the present moment. The point is to cut off any further argument. "Because it's tradition," I say when asked why I want to get a living Christmas tree although it would be cheaper and cleaner to use a plastic one. Traditions are seen as providing stability above all else, offering unchanging sets of principles by which their members can navigate the many difficulties of modern life.

According to MacIntyre, however, this is a serious misunderstanding of what tradition means. Rather than offering something stubborn and constant in the face of disagreement, a tradition is itself "an argument extended through time." This argument takes place both within the tradition among those who profess to be its members, and outside of it through encounters with nonmembers. If you are a member of a certain religious denomination, you might discuss certain teachings of that denomination with your family and friends who are also members; you might also engage in debate with friends or fellow students who belong to other faiths. This does not mean that tradition is all argument since every tradition is made up certain *fundamental agreements* among its members. However, these agreements are not set in stone, but rather "defined and redefined" through internal and external debate.

While comparative philosophers tend to view individual thinkers and texts against the background of their traditions, they emphasize that these traditions are not ancient artifacts to be studied from a distance but living entities. As Lin Ma and Jaap van Brakel write in the first chapter of their work, *Fundamentals of Comparative and Intercultural Philosophy*,

> A tradition is never a homogeneous and static totality, but internally heterogeneous, dynamic, and without sharp boundaries. Hence, a philosophical tradition is a historically heterogeneous entity subject to constant change. It should not be taken as a collection of fixed doctrines and teachings buried in scriptures and classics. Traditions (as well as languages and concepts) are (re)constituted as evolving events in history.[7]

Within a tradition, there may be many different sub-traditions, and within each of these, even further divisions between different schools of thought. For example, the Chinese philosophical tradition includes diverse traditions such as Confucianism, Daoism, Mohism, and Legalism. And just to take Confucianism, it includes Mencian Confucianism, Neo-Confucianism, New Confucianism, each with distinctive understandings of the tradition's basic concepts.

What makes the work of comparative philosophy so fascinating is that it represents a new era in the development of philosophical traditions that have been around for thousands of years. What happens in "Phase II" of our story, as all these different traditions encounter each other in the contemporary world? The view that philosophy and tradition are opposed only arises when we think of traditions as antithetical to reason and progress. Once we rid ourselves of this prejudice, studying philosophical traditions can be invigorating and inspiring.

Working with traditions

In the second book in his trilogy, *Whose Justice? Which Rationality?* MacIntyre develops the idea that standards of reasoning make sense only within the context of a tradition. During the European Enlightenment, various thinkers attempted to establish standards of rationality that would apply universally to all human beings independently of culture and time-period. These standards would replace the role of tradition and authority in people's lives and lead to their intellectual liberation. However, the different Enlightenment thinkers produced competing conceptions of what these standards are, and the dispute between them has only got worse in the time since. Today, according to MacIntyre, we are living out the results of this failed project. Since there are no widely accepted standards of rationality to which we can appeal when we have moral disagreement, what we have is a never-ending struggle among numerous social groups, each with its own notion of what is good.

The *problem of incommensurability* concerns whether it is possible to weigh these competing philosophical traditions against one another, given their diverse conceptions of what matters. We can expect this problem to be especially challenging in the comparative arena, where we attempt to bring together traditions that share relatively little by way of common background. In the next two chapters we shall discuss the different claims about language, justification, and standards of evaluation that motivate the problem of incommensurability.

Another potential problem is that when we focus on traditions as the main element of investigation, we might be less inclined to notice differences between the philosophers who make up these traditions.[8] Our general understanding of what matters to the tradition may take precedence over the unique quest of the individual. The more we see an individual philosopher as bound to a tradition, the less we may appreciate what makes that philosopher worth studying in their own right.

Yet when we look at particular thinkers and texts in isolation from their traditions, we are in danger of *projecting* assumptions from our own cultural and philosophical background onto the texts in question. When we read Buddhist authors, for example, we may mistakenly assume that they share the beliefs related to the "self" and "will" mentioned above. It is only when we comprehend the main questions and concepts that are important to the Buddhist tradition as a whole that we will be able to avoid such misunderstandings. Projection is one of the most pernicious errors that can arise in cross-cultural studies, and we shall consider it at greater length below (Chapter 6).

Nearly all comparisons today are limited to two traditions, rather than three or more.[9] One reason for this limitation is the intricacy to which philosophy gives rise: the closer you get to a great work or important issue, the more complexities you see. If you have ever spent a semester studying one of Plato's early dialogues or reading a few works in contemporary analytic philosophy of mind, then you know that just one area of a philosophy can take years or decades to master. Doing a comparative study of Plato and Confucius, or mind in the analytic and Buddhist traditions, can open a philosopher up to the charge of having failed to master either thinker or tradition. This charge is even more likely for attempts to compare three traditions. Moreover, the methodology involved in comparing three traditions can grow excessively complicated. Would we have to compare tradition A with tradition B, B with C, C with A, and then compare the results of these comparisons with each other? Some pursuits, like baseball or chess, are already complicated enough with two sides.

Philosophy and culture

The philosophical traditions that comparative philosophers bring together are embedded in different cultures. Daoism and Confucianism are products of Chinese culture, Yoga and Vedanta of Indian culture, Aristotelianism and analytic philosophy of Western culture, Sage philosophy of African culture, and so on. A single philosophical tradition can be associated with a number of different cultures. Buddhism, for instance, developed in northern India, but then spread to China, Japan, Korea, Thailand, Vietnam, and other parts of East and Southeast Asia. The cultures in question generally correspond to specific geographic regions or national boundaries. At a very broad level, a cultural designation can be used to refer to all the philosophical traditions that have developed within that culture: *Western* philosophy, *Chinese* philosophy, *African* philosophy, etc. The importance of the cultural aspect in comparative philosophy is reflected in names that are often used in the field, such as *cross-cultural philosophy or intercultural philosophy*.

The introduction of culture into a discussion of philosophy raises more controversy. There are not only difficult theoretical issues concerning cultural relativism, but also real-world concerns about the legacy of Western colonialism and the present global distribution of power. In this section, we will begin our examination of the difficulties raised by extending philosophy across cultural boundaries.

Culture and cultural unity

Definitions of culture abound. According to one prominent description, it is "that complex whole which includes knowledge, belief, art, law, morals, customs, and any other capabilities and habits acquired by man as a member of society."[10] Whether we are talking about ancient Greek culture or contemporary Chinese culture, we are covering a lot of territory—everything that the members of a given society make, do, and think.[11]

Much hinges on whether we conceive of cultures as unified or diverse in nature. According to a view popularized by the anthropologist Ruth Benedict, "A culture, like an individual, is a more or less consistent pattern of thought and action."[12] In line with this view, comparative philosophers often associate distinctive values or other philosophically relevant beliefs with one culture or another:

> [U]nderstanding basic Asian values and ideas is crucial for survival in an interdependent world.[13]
> The Western preference of rest and permanence over becoming and process is well-nigh reversed in Chinese culture.[14]
> Basically, the Igbo and African worldview in general incorporates two essential beliefs.[15]

These characterizations are intended to help us understand the central features of other cultures' ways of thinking and what distinguishes these ways of thinking from our own.

Other scholars have maintained that diversity is the central feature of culture. They approach the study of culture with assumptions like the following in mind:

1 Real cultures are plural, not single.
2 Real cultures contain argument, resistance, and contestation of norms.
3 In real cultures, what most people think is likely to be different from what the most famous artists and intellectuals think.
4 Real cultures have varied domains of thought and activity.
5 Real cultures have a present as well as a past.[16]

The common theme of these points is that we cannot identify a culture with a single feature, whether it be a way of life, point of view, or a particular thinker, text, or time-period. We shouldn't claim, for instance, that the 2,500-year-old philosophy of Confucius defines "Chinese values" as such, when the values found in the current generation of Chinese may differ drastically from Confucian ones (we should be even more skeptical of phrases like "Asian values" or "the African worldview"). Nor should we think that rest or permanence is a "Western preference," when not a few Westerners would find it hard to distinguish Plato from process philosophy.

To emphasize the diversity of cultures, some theorists prefer to distinguish between culture and civilization.[17] The concept of "civilization" presupposes some sort of unifying factor or factors binding together the whole. When we study the development of "Western civilization," we might attempt to trace certain ethical or legal or religious conceptions that run throughout all of it. In talking of Western culture, however, we do not need to presuppose such unity.

Still, don't we need to assert *some* general truths about a culture in order to understand that culture? Isn't it evident that the Confucian tradition has had a massive influence in East Asia, with effects all the way up to the present day? In the past few years, a debate has been brewing among comparative philosophers about the problem of *generalization*: whether broad statements about a culture such as the ones above are a help or hindrance to cross-cultural understanding, and what evidence we might use to support or refute them. We'll discuss this problem as well in the next part of the book (Chapter 7).

How are culture and philosophy related?

In Chapter 1 we considered the issue of the legitimacy of categories like "Chinese philosophy," "Indian Philosophy," etc. on the grounds that philosophy is an inherently Western notion. But there is another reason to look askance at these categories, one which also applies to the idea of "Western philosophy."

The skeptic in this case claims that philosophical reasoning and cultural background are opposed in spirit. Philosophical views must be taken on their own terms, independently of the part of the world they happen to come from. If you and I were having a heated debate about the loop variant of the trolley problem, and suddenly I started to ask you about your cultural background, you would probably wonder why. What does culture have to do with assessing the merits of your view? Similarly, to focus on philosophy from one particular culture or another is to miss the point of philosophy. "Why care about *Chinese* or *Western* philosophy?" the skeptic will ask. "There is just one thing, *philosophy*."[18]

Our response will depend on how we are thinking about the terms in question. We can understand the phrase "Chinese philosophy" as referring to work that happens to have been done in China but is above all an instance of "just philosophy." Or we can take it to mean a distinctively Chinese way of thinking that is opposed in spirit to all others. Perhaps you recognize our friends universalism and particularism here. Is philosophy a single conversation that transcends cultural boundaries, or are there as many different philosophies as there are cultures?

In fact, this question has been the subject of intense debate in non-Western philosophical settings. Some African philosophers have claimed that "philosophy" means two distinct things across Western and African cultures. They argue that since cultures have different ways of relating to reality, "Africans must have a philosophy that is *essentially* different from other philosophies."[19] Similarly, in China we encounter the view that "Chinese tradition is unique, Chinese culture is distinctive and the Chinese way of thinking is incomparable."[20] The particularist position has been used to support claims of China's cultural superiority over the West, with some of its proponents arguing that Chinese philosophical tradition is something that needs to be defended against "contamination" by Westerners.[21]

Many Western philosophy students may find the idea of cultural particularism difficult to understand. One is not expected to be ethnically Greek to understand Greek philosophy or ethnically Danish to understand Kierkegaard; must one be ethnically Chinese to grasp the "Chinese way of thinking"? Many may agree with Wang Guowei (1877–1927), a seminal figure in the introduction of Western philosophy into China, who maintained that "philosophy is true for all time and for everywhere in the world and is not limited to one moment."[22]

The Ghanaian-American philosopher Kwame Anthony Appiah distinguishes between the "folk philosophy" that ordinary people living in a particular region use to comprehend their experiences and the "formal philosophy" done in modern universities. According to Appiah, there are as many folk philosophies as there are cultures, but there is just one formal philosophy. The difference is justification: folk philosophies, if they are defended at all, are done so through appeal to ancestral tradition and cultural heritage, whereas formal philosophy relies on evidence and argumentation.[23] Any person can appeal to these standards, regardless of the accidental circumstances of their cultural birthright.

For the cultural particularist, talk of such standards is often associated with Western hegemony, since it is primarily Western ideas that have spread in the last few centuries to the rest of the world rather than vice versa. Throughout its history cross-cultural philosophy has been afflicted by the problem of *one-sidedness* (Chapter 6), in which philosophical discourse is carried out from within the categories of the more powerful cultural tradition at the expense of the less powerful ones. As a result, "universalism" appears to be a guise for whatever the most dominant philosophy is at the moment. Critics of Appiah have contended that the idea of formal philosophy is parochial in its own fashion, reflecting the values of contemporary Western analytic philosophy and leaving out everything else.

We do not have to pick one side or the other in this debate—not yet, anyway. In doing comparative philosophy (rather than "comparative philosophies") we may be sympathetic to the skeptic's view that "there is just one thing, philosophy." The point of cross-cultural philosophy is not to focus on other cultures' philosophies just because they are from other cultures, but rather to expand the range of ideas that philosophy has at its disposal. Since these cultural traditions are very rarely studied in Western philosophy classrooms and departments, we are currently unable to take advantage of the resources they offer.[24] Grasping these resources in all their fullness and uniqueness means looking at the contexts in which they developed, and that is why the particularities of culture often matter.

How significant a barrier is culture?

The dispute between philosophical universalists and cultural particularists also reflects a difference of opinion regarding what kind of boundary culture sets in our way. Appiah for his part argues that "culture" is an overused term which does not do much work: "Treating international difference ... as an especially profound kind of something called 'cultural difference' is, in my view, a characteristically modern mistake."[25] Much of the bias toward difference, in his view, comes from the field of anthropology, where discoveries of difference make for better press than discoveries of similarity. In reality, however, dialogue across cultures presents no more obstacles than dialogue *within* them.

Some might say the same about philosophical dialogue. Several years ago, I attended a panel at the American Philosophical Association on the difficulties of teaching Chinese philosophy. For a couple of hours, the panelists spoke in great detail about the challenges faced in conveying the full range of this area of philosophy to their students, and the strategies they had worked out to overcome them. At the very end of the session, a hitherto silent audience member spoke up: "Why do you think teaching Chinese philosophy is any more difficult than teaching Heidegger? I'd rather teach Daoism than *Dasein*."

In a recent series of essays, Ralph Weber has criticized comparative philosophers for the assumption that culture is a bearer of philosophical distinctiveness. When we set up a comparison between Nietzsche and Zhuangzi, for example, we are assuming that there is something about these thinkers being embedded in two different cultures that makes them fertile ground for comparison. At the same time, we seem to take it for granted that comparison between Zhuangzi and Confucius does not have the same interest. But as Weber writes, "[P]rima facie, I do not see any reason why philosophical difference may not also or rather be claimed for differences of gender, age, profession, class, or philosophical position, which all cut across so-called cultures."[26]

It's hard to deny, though, that studying philosophy across culturally distinct traditions poses unique and significant challenges. Consider the issue of language. When native English speakers study Greek philosophy, they may learn many connections between the English language and the Greek. All the basic terminology of Western philosophy—ethics, aesthetics, epistemology, metaphysics, logic—is derived from the Greek language. (This is true not just in philosophy, but with many of the prominent words in the arts and sciences: music, physics, biology, psychology, economics, etc.) So, there is already a basis in the English language for understanding many of the central Greek philosophical concepts. Since there is no such connection between English and classical Chinese, explaining Chinese philosophical concepts to native English speakers can be much more difficult than explaining Greek ones.

Besides language, there are other cultural factors that may affect how philosophy developed in Greece or China: ecology, political life, religious orientation, and social customs, to name a few. All these things may become entangled with the philosophy in ways that need to be carefully unraveled. In general, comparative philosophers tend to assume that there are important cultural differences, and that these differences have consequences.[27]

Which traditions to compare?

Since learning a new tradition will require time and effort, it is worth thinking a little in advance about what makes another cultural-philosophical tradition worth engaging. Consider the following candidates for comparative investigation (most of them real):

Chinese vs. Japanese   East Asian vs. Southeast Asian
Chinese vs. Western   European vs. Native American
African vs. European   Western vs. Asian
African vs. Indian   Islamic vs. Western
Earthling vs. Rational Extraterrestrial Continental vs. Analytic

Take note of your intuitions about these candidates. Do some of them, in your view, count as *better* possibilities for comparative engagement than others? Why or why not?

Some possible influences on your ranking may have been the size of the traditions compared, your knowledge of their historical interaction, or your perceptions of cultural difference. Your interests concerning other cultures or cultural philosophies also probably played a significant role. Given the subjectivity of these influences, it is difficult to come up with definitive criteria for determining which traditions to compare. Still, several features of cultural traditions have been significant for comparative philosophers.

Developmental isolation

The first feature, important enough that it is often included in definitions of the subject, is *developmental isolation*: comparative philosophy means engaging traditions which have formed as independently of our own as possible. Such "historically discrete" traditions include those found in the West, Africa, India, and China.[28] The less we have in common with another tradition, the more likely we are to learn something new and interesting from that tradition. Additionally, if we want to determine which ideas transcend cultural boundaries and which do not, we need boundaries that have been more or less impermeable to communication. In this regard, developmental isolation is a kind of constant that allows us to ground the results of comparison. If we can't explain similarities and differences by means of actual encounters between cultures and subsequent acceptance or rejection of these views, what does explain them?

Complete developmental isolation is not a necessary condition for comparative engagement. Often cultural-philosophical traditions that appear to us as distinct have in reality had significant interaction. Throughout the history of African philosophy, for instance, native African philosophers have influenced or been influenced by outside traditions. The Egyptians helped shape ancient Greek philosophy. Augustine, who was born in North Africa to a Roman father and a Berber mother, is a canonical figure in the Western philosophical tradition; he was inspired by Plato and comes up in the work of later philosophers such as Aquinas and Wittgenstein. More recently African thought has been shaped by European missionaries and colonizers.[29] In their introduction to *The Oxford Handbook of World Philosophy*, William Edelglass and Jay L. Garfield point out the ubiquity of such cross-cultural influence:

> Communication between Greek, Persian, and Indian philosophical communities was commonplace. Early European philosophy owes much to Islamic philosophy, as it does to Roman and Greek philosophy, traditions in turn influenced by Persia and India. East Asian philosophy is informed by Buddhism, Confucianism, and other views that spread along the Silk Road; and goods brought from China to the Middle East and Europe were surely accompanied by diverse ideas and cultural practices.[30]

As we can see from these examples, if we required absolute isolation between different cultural traditions as a precondition for comparison, there would not be much left to compare. Edelglass and Garfield contend that "the notion of hermetically sealed traditions in parallel development is largely a historical fiction."[31]

Moral tradition respect

So relative isolation is not enough to tell us which traditions to engage. For one thing, many philosophical traditions might satisfy this qualification, especially when we point out it is not an absolute. How do we choose between them all?

A philosophically richer justification for comparative engagement centers on the notion of *respect* for other traditions. For any dialogue to be productive, we need to have regard for our interlocutor, believing that they can make contributions to the discussion in areas in which we are lacking. Comparative philosophers from diverse backgrounds have cited respect as a basic precondition for the cross-cultural conversation.[32]

However, respect can mean different things. The contemporary philosopher Stephen Darwall distinguishes between two basic kinds. I might respect a particular student just because I think that all people are entitled to a basic level of consideration, and this principle applies especially to one's students. This is an instance of *recognition respect*. Yet I could also respect that student because they strike me as intelligent or courageous or hard working. Such *appraisal respect* is not granted to everyone, but only to those who deserve it. The most developed account of respect in comparative philosophy—the concept of *moral tradition respect* defended by Chad Hansen of the University of Hong Kong—involves this second kind of respect. We do not owe respect to other traditions just for existing; rather, we grant it only to those that strike us as worthy of it.[33]

Hansen cites three criteria for granting respect to another tradition. First, the tradition must be *significantly different* from our own in its approach to ethics. The differences must be deeper than the kinds of disagreements that we find within our own tradition. According to Hansen, the reason Western philosophers have been more interested in comparison with China than with the Middle East is that they sense more of a shared background with the latter than with the former. Engaging another tradition requires seeing it as a genuine alternative, rather than just an alternative expression of features already present within our own.

The second condition is that the tradition must have an "intellectually rich, reflective, hierarchical system of norms."[34] We can imagine an ethical tradition that endures because it serves the needs of a particular society's ruling class; this class forces the rest of society to follow an ancient set of rules that it claims to be unchanging and never attempts to justify. Such a tradition's principles would be philosophically unsophisticated since they have never been challenged or had to evolve. Nor would it be capable of serving as a partner in mutually enriching dialogue since one side merely stating its claims over and over again without providing any reasons for them does not make for good discussion.

Lastly, the other tradition must have produced teachings that strike us as impressive from our present point of view.[35] If a tradition supports practices like slavery and gender inequality, it will probably fail to capture our admiration. Rather, we will recognize in that tradition some primitive and disreputable stage within our own.

As a test case, consider the Buddhist idea that one should practice compassion toward all sentient creatures. Buddhist philosophers deny that there are distinct individuals who experience suffering. Since no suffering belongs to "you" or "me," yet all suffering is bad, we should try to eliminate it wherever we find it. Such an insight into the true nature of the self will lead us to expand the practice of compassion to any person or creature that is suffering.

Buddhist teachings about compassion are significantly different from those found in Western philosophical traditions, and they are also rooted in higher-order claims about the nature of reality and the self. Yet Western ethical systems suppose that there are individual human beings who make choices, feel pleasure and pain, or have basic rights. Given that these traditions disagree with one another at a fundamental level, how could Buddhist ethics strike Western philosophers as impressive from their present point of view?[36]

It is this last criterion that Hansen's critics have seen as most problematic. What does it mean to require that the other tradition produces conclusions that "strike us as impressive"? Impressive in what sense? Do these conclusions need to be *compatible* with our current perspective? Must we accept the premises on which they are based? Also, who is the *us* in question? Some philosophers have turned to other traditions as the result of intense dissatisfaction with the perspectives found in their own.[37]

We can also find some problems with the idea of moral tradition respect as a whole. It could lead to a kind of cultural chauvinism: this culture deserves our respect for its philosophical richness, but that one does not. There may be some cultural traditions we initially judge to be unworthy of our respect, which in fact offer plenty we can learn from. Even in traditions that do not strike us as impressive or reflective on the whole, there may be individual thinkers that we can learn something from. While surely respect has some role to play in choosing the cultural traditions we engage, these considerations suggest that the precise formulation of moral tradition respect is still in progress.

Traditions within one's own culture

So far, we have been discussing the question of which traditions to engage from other cultures. But suppose we already have chosen to study, say, the Buddhist ethical tradition. Within contemporary Western philosophy, there are a wide range of resources available for engagement with Buddhist thought. Which of these Western traditions should we select for our comparison?

Of course, our selection on our own side as well will be influenced by our philosophical interests, previous training, and so on. Nonetheless, some comparative philosophers have maintained that it is the non-mainstream traditions within Western philosophy that serve as the best point of departure for engagement with other cultural traditions. In Chinese-Western comparative philosophy, the most prominent defenders of this approach have been David L. Hall and Roger T. Ames, who use resources like American pragmatism and process philosophy to engage with classical Chinese sources.

As mentioned earlier in this chapter, one danger of comparative philosophy, especially when undertaken by members of the dominant tradition, is that we impose our own views on other traditions, reading them in our own image. Using a tradition like process philosophy, which challenges many of the dominant assumptions of the Western philosophical canon, may help us resist this tendency. If we find that Chinese philosophy has more in common with process philosophy than it does with the mainstream of the Western tradition, then we realize more readily that our tradition is just one available philosophical path among others. In this way, as Robert Smid writes, "the presence of alternative traditions allows one to recognize the contingency of the dominant philosophic tradition and enables one to prevent the dominant tradition from becoming the default standard for all philosophy."[38]

Picking two items to compare may seem like the easiest part of comparative philosophy—the part we take for granted before the real work of comparison begins. Yet merely in choosing which philosophies to compare, we have already made certain commitments regarding how philosophical traditions around the world have developed, which traditions from other cultures are worthy of comparative engagement, and how we think about the dominant assumptions embedded within our own cultural tradition. The most important decisions in comparative philosophy happen right at the beginning!

Conclusion

In this chapter, we have considered some of the reasons comparative philosophers think culture and tradition matter in philosophy. A recurring question in this book concerns what comparative philosophy is supposed to ultimately accomplish with respect to culturally distinct philosophical traditions. Are culture and tradition a means or an end?

For the universalist, cross-cultural philosophy is a ladder that we can kick away once we are done using it.[39] The more progress is made in comparative philosophy, the more the particularities associated with different cultural traditions will fade away. Yet the particularist will worry about this result, not only because of allegiance to an ancient tradition that is now in danger of "contamination," but out of the conviction that difference is worth preserving. If we were the researchers studying Planet Phi, we would make sure to set up our next version of the experiment so that when Phase II begins, Phase I would continue on in a parallel simulation, each tribe being allowed to develop in its own manner independently of all the rest. Then at the end of the experiment we could compare philosophies from both simulations to see which was better off.

Part II

The Problems of Comparative Philosophy

4

Linguistic Incommensurability

Perhaps the most perplexing problem in comparative philosophy is that there are no neutral means for describing and evaluating culturally distinct philosophical traditions. The philosophical vocabularies and standards we possess are always internal to one tradition or another and have deep roots in the culture in which a tradition develops. Without shared vocabulary or standards, the different cultural-philosophical traditions are thought to be *incommensurable*—literally "incapable of being measured together." Attempts to compare these traditions will result in misunderstanding and disagreement.

Incommensurability is a fundamental problem in comparative philosophy. In this chapter we will consider the issue of *linguistic incommensurability*: Do speakers of different languages have incomparable ways of perceiving reality? How much of a barrier is language difference in comparative philosophy? But first, a little discussion of the term and how it has come to be used in cross-cultural philosophy.

Background on the term

The term "incommensurable" has a complex history. It has been used in areas of philosophy outside of the comparative kind, as well as in areas of study outside of philosophy. The story of incommensurability begins in fifth-century Greece, with a school founded by the philosopher Pythagoras (570–490 BCE). Pythagorean mathematicians believed that for any two units of length there was a smaller third unit that could be used to subdivide both; but then one of the members of this school, Hippasus of Metapontum, discovered he could refute this belief by showing that the diagonal of a square is incommensurable with its side.[1] According to one story, the Pythagoreans were so angry with Hippasus for publicizing his discovery that they kicked him out of their community and considered him to be dead (another has it that while at sea he was thrown overboard and drowned). This would not be the last time that the concept caused trouble.

Incommensurability and cultural anthropology

In the twentieth century, the anthropologist Ruth Benedict applied the notion of incommensurability to issues of culture.[2] In her influential book *Patterns of Culture* (1934), she pointed to the endless diversity that can be found in different societies, maintaining that things we might suppose to be self-evident to everyone in the world are not at all so. As an example, she asks us to consider attitudes toward killing:

> We might suppose that in the matter of taking life all peoples would agree in condemnation. On the contrary, in the matter of homicide, it may be held that one is blameless if diplomatic relations have been severed between neighbouring countries, or that one kills by custom his first two children, or that a husband has right of life and death over his wife, or that it is the duty of the child to kill his parents before they are old. It may be that those are killed who steal a fowl, or who cut their upper teeth first, or who are born on a Wednesday.[3]

These different customs and attitudes are not random; rather, each can be understood within the entire context of the culture of which it is part. Each culture, according to Benedict, is an integrated whole with its own characteristic purposes: "All the miscellaneous behaviour directed toward getting a living, mating, warring, and worshipping the gods, is made over into consistent patterns in accordance with unconscious canons of choice that develop with the culture."[4] Cultural difference is not primarily a matter of different traits being present in different societies, but rather arises from the fact that each society is oriented in a unique direction. Even traits that strike us as similar from one society to another will have quite distinctive places in the overall configurations of those societies.

When we hear of some of the above-mentioned practices related to homicide, our first reaction is to condemn them. This reaction, however, is problematic precisely because those practices fit perfectly well into the overall orientations of the cultures in which they are manifested. Since as outsiders we have no way of grasping these orientations, we are not in a position to pass judgment on societies other than our own. The ends and means of one society, as Benedict writes, "cannot be judged in terms of another society, because essentially they are incommensurable."[5]

Kuhn's structure of scientific revolutions

The philosophical debate surrounding incommensurability begins with Thomas Kuhn's 1962 book *The Structure of Scientific Revolutions*, one of the most broadly influential works of philosophy of the twentieth century.

The inspiration for *Structure* first came to Kuhn when he was a student reading Aristotle's *Physics*. Looking for possible connections between Aristotle's view of motion and Newtonian mechanics, he found himself disappointed. Despite his best efforts to understand the text, Aristotle appeared to be an incompetent scientist. In particular, he seemed to misunderstand the nature of motion in fundamental ways. How is it possible that such a thinker's physics had formed the dominant worldview for two millennia?

Perplexed, Kuhn continued to study the *Physics*. Then one day, looking out the window above his desk, he had an epiphany:

> Suddenly the fragments in my head sorted themselves out in a new way, and fell into place together. My jaw dropped, for all at once Aristotle seemed a very good physicist indeed, but of a sort I'd never dreamed possible. Now I could understand why he had said what he'd said, and what his authority had been. Statements that had previously seemed egregious mistakes, now seemed at worst near misses within a powerful and generally successful tradition.[6]

Kuhn realized that Aristotle was working with a much broader definition of motion, one that incorporated not only an object moving from one place to another, but also change in general: things growing and decaying, or altering in quality from hot to cold, or light to dark, or wet to dry. He also grasped that it was such qualities that Aristotle considered to be fundamentally real, rather than the underlying matter which takes them on—the reverse of Newtonian physics. Given these assumptions, other less central ideas in Aristotle's *Physics* suddenly began to fall into place.

His experience in reading the *Physics* left Kuhn with an insight into the concepts that would form the basis of a radical new idea of science. Fifteen years later, he would publish his seminal work.

According to the view defended in *The Structure of Scientific Revolutions*, definitive works of science like the *Physics* or Newton's *Principia* spawn *paradigms* that direct the research of generations of scientists thereafter. A paradigm is like a judicial decision that is accepted as part of common law; it provides guidance for future decisions rather than itself being an object of investigation. The science that carries out the work of a dominant paradigm is what Kuhn refers to as *normal science*. During periods of normal science, the consensus among researchers is that we generally understand the world around us. Progress occurs incrementally through specialized investigations, and current research is based on a solid foundation of past research summed up in textbooks.

At some point, however, phenomena appear that cannot be explained by the current paradigm. These anomalies are ignored at first; as they accumulate, various modifications are made to the paradigm to make sense of them. Yet these attempts fail, throwing proponents of the dominant paradigm into disarray. What is needed is not modification of the old, but rather "a new set of commitments, a new basis for the practice of science."[7] The process in which a new paradigm replaces the old one is what Kuhn calls a *scientific revolution*. Such revolutions "are the tradition-shattering complements to the tradition-bound activity of normal science."[8]

Kuhn argues that the prerevolutionary and postrevolutionary paradigms are *incommensurable* in three respects. The first is that they have different norms regarding what questions and problems science is supposed to concern itself with. It is these basic foundations that need to be shifted in order to make sense of the new phenomena.

Secondly, while the new paradigm may employ some of the vocabulary of the old one, it uses the terms in new and different ways. Einstein's general theory of relativity depended on a new conception of space, a conception on which Newton's physics would not have worked. Those who challenged Einstein's new theory based on Newtonian ideas were not necessarily in the wrong, but simply working within an older paradigm. "To make the transition to Einstein's universe," Kuhn writes, "the whole conceptual web whose strands are space, time, matter, force, and so on, had to be shifted and laid down again on nature whole."[9] To someone not immersed in the entire apparatus of the new paradigm, its language will appear incoherent.

This brings us to the third—and according to Kuhn, the most important—sense in which different paradigms are incommensurable. Followers of competing paradigms "practice their trades in different worlds"; they "see different things when they look from the same point in the same direction."[10] Pre-Copernican scientists who thought the earth did not move inhabited a different universe; so different, in fact, that it was not until after Copernicus' death that his heliocentric model of the universe won any followers. Because paradigms are so different, a scientist who switches from one paradigm to another has had a sort of "conversion" which "can only be made on faith."[11] Kuhn likens this experience to the kind of shift in which I can now see a duck in the drawing where before I could only see a rabbit—a shift which happens "all at once . . . or not at all."[12] What is required for the new paradigm to be adopted is not so much rational persuasion, then, but that the proponents of the old paradigm eventually begin to die off.

Incommensurability and comparative philosophy

Kuhn's conception of incommensurability seems ripe for application to items like ethical and metaphysical worldviews. Think of the last time you debated someone with different religious views. Weren't your differences in fact much wider than the particular issue being argued? The Christian worldview, for instance, presupposes a vocabulary, including terms like "sin," "evil," and "faith," that only makes sense if one accepts the entirety of that worldview. People from diverse religious backgrounds also have different ideas about what counts as having support for one's view, how we should judge a particular ethical claim, or what the ideal society looks like. Is it any surprise that such debates often end with each party thinking they are wholly in the right, and the other in the wrong?

The discussion becomes all the more difficult when such worldviews are set within diverse cultural frameworks. Roughly in line with the three types of incommensurability between different paradigms Kuhn outlined in *Structure*, there are three different senses in which philosophies from different cultural traditions are sometimes said to be incommensurable:

1 *Linguistic incommensurability*: philosophical traditions from different cultures depend on distinctive languages that cannot be translated into one another.

2 *Foundational incommensurability*: the foundations that traditions use to make sense of the world around them are so different from one another that members of these traditions cannot understand one another.

3 *Evaluative incommensurability*: there are no rational grounds for deciding whether a view from one tradition is superior to a view from another.

Proponents of incommensurability may defend one version but not another. For instance, Benedict seems to suppose that we can understand other cultures, but what we cannot do is evaluate them. When we encounter someone using the term "incommensurable," we should pay close attention to which kind they are talking about. Let us discuss each of the three in turn, beginning with linguistic incommensurability.

The linguistic relativity thesis

There is reason to think that the language issue will be even more of a problem with culturally distinct philosophical traditions than it is with prerevolutionary and postrevolutionary scientific paradigms. Since these philosophical traditions have developed in relative isolation from one another, we can expect there to be little in the way of overlapping vocabulary. How serious a problem is this for comparing across cultures?

Sapir-Whorf and philosophy

Some philosophers have thought that linguistic diversity does not pose any special problem for understanding others. The many languages are simply different means of describing and reflecting upon the world all of us inhabit. While a speaker of another language uses different marks and sounds to refer to things, the things referred to are at least the same. Once we have translated the speaker's marks and sounds into our own, we will grasp what they are talking about.

The American linguists Edward Sapir (1884–1939) and Benjamin Lee Whorf (1897–1941) sought to overthrow this view. They contended that *language determines thought* rather than being merely a vehicle for expressing it. The effects of my language on how I think are outside of my control since I acquired the speech habits of my society very early in life. What is more, since languages divide up the world in unique ways, one's view of reality is relative to one's language. "No two languages," Sapir wrote, "are ever sufficiently similar to be considered as representing the same social reality. The worlds in which different societies live are distinct worlds, not merely the same world with different labels attached."[13] To translate the sounds and marks that others make, we will not be able to simply replace their labels with our labels. We don't even know what it is that they are labeling.

The wider the difference in language, the more distinct the worlds. The most basic division that exists today is between languages of different *families*. Languages such as Sanskrit, Hindi, English, Greek, Latin, French, and German are members of the Indo-European family, all having developed from a common ancestor, or *protolanguage*, spoken over 5,000 years ago. Other groupings include the Sino-Tibetan (including Mandarin, Cantonese, Thai, Burmese), the Afro-Asiatic (Arabic, Hebrew, Oromo, Hausa), and the Niger-Congo (Swahili, Yoruba, Igbo). Since comparative philosophers often bring together texts written in languages from different families, they must be prepared to deal with questions about the relationship between language and thought.

The possibility of the linguistic determination of philosophy along familial lines was recognized as early as Nietzsche. "Where there is affinity of languages," he wrote, "it cannot fail ... that everything is prepared at the outset for a similar development and sequence of philosophical systems; just as the way seems barred against certain other possibilities of world-interpretation."[14] Believing that the various resemblances between Greek, German, and Indian philosophy could be explained by virtue of their common ancestry, Nietzsche predicted that when we examined philosophies written in languages from other families, we would find very different ways of looking at the world.

The language of being

A favorite case study concerns what I came to think of as an undergraduate as the deepest of all philosophical issues: the question of the nature of "being." This question has been a staple of so many of the best-known Western philosophers, including Parmenides, Plato, Aristotle, Berkeley, Descartes, Heidegger, and Sartre, that one might expect it to be present in every developed philosophical tradition. Heidegger for one contends that it

Table 4.1. Classical Chinese equivalents of English verb "to be"

Function of "to be"	English example	Classical Chinese term
Existence	"There is a man."	*you*有; negative *wu* 無
Copula linking nouns or a noun and an adjective	"He is a man." "He is tall."	*ye* 也, negative *fei* 非 . . . *ye* 也
Location	"He is in Paris."	*zai* 在
Identity	"He is Charles."	*ji* 即
Roles	"He is a soldier."	*wei* 為
Truth	"It is so."	*ran* 然

is both the broadest question, in that it covers more reality than any other, and the deepest, in that it seeks the ultimate ground of all there is.

Chinese philosophy is an interesting test case, since it is a developed philosophical tradition that falls outside the Indo-European family.[15] The first thing we notice when we compare English and other Indo-European languages with classical Chinese is that the latter uses many different terms to capture the different senses of our verb "to be."[16]

You and *wu* are sometimes translated as "being" and "non-being" (unlike English verbs, classical Chinese verbs are uninflected; they do not change their number or tense, and also lack participial forms). For instance, a passage in Chapter 2 of the *Daodejing* is sometimes rendered as "Being (*you*) and non-being (*wu*) give birth to one another." But the two terms are not quite the same as their English counterparts. While in Indo-European languages we can say that some *x* exists in its own right, in classical Chinese one treats the thing that exists from the point of view of the larger entity that contains it: "in the world there is/there is not *x*."[17]

This linguistic feature may be connected to more general ways in which Chinese philosophers perceived the world. Some observers have argued that since the term *you* encourages a focus on concrete things contained within the world, Chinese philosophers were never led to treat abstract entities the way Plato treated "Beauty," "Goodness," and the like, as if they were realities in themselves, more fundamental than their particular instances in the material world.[18] Instead of focusing on the most general features of reality—the being of beings—Chinese philosophers tended to look at the appropriate arrangement of the things immediately around us. As one pair of scholars sums it up:

> The Chinese language disposes those who employ the notions of *you* and *wu* to concern themselves with the presence or absence of concrete particular

things and the effect of having or not having them at hand.... One must assume that the practical, concrete disposition of Chinese thinkers is both cause and consequence of this characteristic feature of linguistic usage.[19]

As you can see, these scholars are careful to avoid the conclusion that Chinese thinkers were *determined* by their language. Yet they maintain that, being present from the beginning, distinctive linguistic features helped to pull Chinese thought in a different direction from its Western counterpart.

Assessing linguistic relativity

Many of the specific claims regarding how language influences cognition have not been studied in enough detail to draw conclusions about the linguistic relativity thesis. Where these claims have been tested, they have often failed. More recent research has shown, for instance, that ways of naming colors do not vary across different languages as much as the proponent of linguistic relativity would predict.[20]

In philosophy, there is reason to be wary of blanket statements concerning the effect of language on thought. Philosophers are far from being passive subjects of the languages which they speak and write. Early Confucian thinkers sought to change the language of the day to promote their social teachings. Plato and Aristotle pointed to the inadequacies of the Greek language in their attempts to make sense of the nature of being.[21] Philosophers are often the first to try and sort out the meanings of important but ambiguous terms in ordinary language, often inventing new terminology when current usage is lacking.

Regardless of whether or not language determines thought, the vocabulary of our own tradition has a significant effect on how we understand works of philosophy from other cultures. Comparative philosophers pay close attention to differences in language between the traditions they are studying.

Understanding other languages

Besides looking at particular cases, we can also approach the linguistic relativity issue by considering the basic principles involved in interpreting others. How is it possible that we can grasp the meaning of someone who speaks a language that is different from our own? Is it always possible?

Davidson's challenge to the incommensurability thesis

Consider a case in which just one word is different. Suppose you and your friend are walking along the seashore one evening and a yacht is sailing by. "Look at that handsome yawl," they exclaims. You are a bit surprised by this, since you happen to know for a fact that it is a ketch (both types of yacht have two masts and three or four sails, but the after-mast on a yawl is smaller). How could your friend think otherwise?

One possibility is that your friend has a way of viewing the harbor in front of you that is completely different from your own. Yet you know that their eyesight is as reliable as yours, that they are looking at the yacht from roughly the same spot as you, that they are not intoxicated, and so on. Given these facts, how can you make sense of what they have just said?

The twentieth-century American philosopher Donald Davidson used this example in his essay "On the Very Idea of a Conceptual Scheme" to challenge the coherence of the notion that there are incommensurable points of view, or "conceptual schemes," by which different cultures, languages, or scientific paradigms organize reality. The view of interpretation that Davidson lays out in this paper has served as a focal point of discussion among comparative philosophers.

Davidson points out near the beginning of his essay that authors who think that different conceptual schemes are incommensurable seem to find themselves perfectly capable of describing the differences between these schemes. Kuhn can explain what is distinctive about Aristotle's theory of motion in relation to postrevolutionary physics, and Whorf is able to convey in English what he takes to be the insurmountable differences between this language and Native American ones. Yet if these schemes were truly incommensurable, would such explanations be possible? As Davidson puts it, "Different points of view make sense, but only if there is a common coordinate system on which to plot them; yet the existence of a common system belies the claim of dramatic incomparability."[22] In the rest of his essay, he develops this into a general theory of how we are able to successfully understand those who speak other languages.

Suppose, he says, we grant Sapir and Whorf's assumption that languages express different conceptual schemes. In that case, translation between languages becomes a kind of test of the incommensurability of conceptual schemes. If we cannot translate one language into another, then we can conclude that the associated conceptual schemes are irreducibly different.

Cases like the one with the yacht allow us to understand how the process of translation works. The first step is to see the connection between language and belief. When your friend says to you "Look at that handsome yawl," they depict themselves as believing that it is in fact a yawl (a handsome one); it's because they believe it that they say it. For your part, if you want to understand what they say, you must understand something about their beliefs, but you understand their beliefs in turn by understanding what they say.

So, the question is where to begin the process of understanding: with your friend's beliefs or their words? Given that the meaning of the particular word is precisely what is so confusing—it is, as it were, in another language—the only solution is to start from your friend's beliefs. According to Davidson, you must begin from the assumption that these beliefs are like your own. In doing so, you will comprehend that your friend simply uses the word "yawl" in a different way than you do.

When we interpret others in a way that maximizes agreement between us and them, rather than in a way that assumes they are irrational or incomprehensible, we are employing what Davidson calls the *principle of charity*. In applying this principle, we ask what it would make sense for us to believe if we were in a position similar to the other person's. Davidson contends that if we want to understand others, this principle is a necessity rather than an option. Without first having some measure of agreement, we would not even be able to recognize the fact that we disagree. As he puts it in another of his writings,

> [W]idespread agreement is the only possible background against which disputes and mistakes can be interpreted. Making sense of the utterances and behavior of others, even their most aberrant behavior, requires us to find a great deal of reason and truth in them. To see too much unreason on the part of others is simply to undermine our ability to understand what it is they are so unreasonable about.[23]

Think for a moment about what would happen if you assume your friend has a different way of forming beliefs than you do. You would have no clue why they said "yawl" rather than "ketch"; from your point of view, their words have come out of some incomprehensible thought-process. In that case, you would not really know at all whether your friend uses the word differently from you. You would have no clue about anything they meant. The only way you can make sense of the different words you and your friend use for the passing vessel is to assume that their process of forming a belief about what kind of yacht is in front of you works much the same way as your own.

Since we always need a common ground to say in what respects two views are different, we can never judge that the views are truly incommensurable. The "very idea" of incommensurable conceptual schemes—whether based on language, culture, explanatory paradigms, or anything else—is an incoherent one.

MacIntyre's defense of partial intranslatibility

Alasdair MacIntyre has criticized Davidson's account of translation for being too removed from the concrete historical and social circumstances in which the process of understanding takes place. Languages are always used by particular communities living at particular times. As a consequence, they cannot help but reflect the particular beliefs of those communities. It is these communally shared beliefs that may be untranslatable.

MacIntyre tells the story of what is today the second largest city in Northern Ireland.[24] While Catholics used the name "Doire Columcille" to emphasize that place's continuity with the sixth-century CE Saint Columba, Protestants called their seventeenth-century settlement on the same location "Londonderry" so as to capture their own historical roots in England. Since these groups have been in conflict with one another, using one name rather than the other means identifying oneself with one group while at the same time denying that the other's name is valid.

Other examples abound. Consider "Noble Sanctuary" and "Temple Mount," the English translations of the names used by Muslims and Jews, respectively, for a contested place of worship in Jerusalem. The location is home to one of the oldest mosques in the world, commemorating the place where the prophet Muhammad is said to have ascended into heaven, while at the same time it is the single holiest place in the Jewish religion, thought to be the site of two ancient temples. Jewish activists have been increasingly demanding that they be allowed to pray there, yet these demands have been strongly resisted by the other side, with some even saying that this will lead to a third Palestinian Intifada. At a recent hearing in the Israeli parliament, when one member said that Jews should have the right to pray on the "Temple Mount," an Arab Israeli member reportedly responded that "There is no such thing as the Temple Mount! It does not exist. It is not there."[25] Here the different names do seem to refer to distinct realities. Think as well of the differing beliefs among groups of Americans who use the names "Christmas" or "Holidays," or "Civil War" or "War of Northern Aggression."

In such cases, as MacIntyre puts it, language is used in such a way that "to share in its use is to presuppose one cosmology rather than another, one relationship of local law and custom to cosmic order rather than another, one justification of particular relationships of individual to community and of both to land and to landscape rather than another."[26] (J.R.R. Tolkien for one seems to have appreciated the idea that we can only make sense of a community after we have understood the particularities of its language. When he was creating all the different creatures that populated the *Lord of the Rings* series, it was their languages he invented first.)

We see the significance of these linguistically embedded presuppositions when we try to translate the name used by one group into the language of its rival. For the rival group to understand the name in its full context, it will have to accept the beliefs accepted by the first community. But if this is so, we will not really be translating the name into the language of the rival community, which presupposes a commitment to *its own* set of beliefs. Nor will it work to translate the name into the language of a third group with no attachment to the place in question, since the language of this group will also suppose commitment to a set of beliefs different from that of the first group. There is simply no way to understand the term independently of the belief-sets associated with each group.

According to MacIntyre, the idea that nothing is untranslatable is a quintessentially modern one. This notion arises from the fact that languages like twenty-first-century English are transnational in character, involving little of the commitment to shared beliefs that would have distinguished past communities of language users from one another. When we read important philosophical texts from other time-periods in translation, it is likely that we miss a great deal of the beliefs of the communities for which these texts were originally composed.

MacIntyre compares the way we read texts from past cultures with the way we look at art. When you visit a museum in a major city, you see all sorts of objects—paintings, sculptures, illuminated manuscripts, decorative items, and tapestries—laid out for your gaze. But you do not experience these items in the ways that they were experienced by members of the communities which produced them: some of them were used in rituals associated with competition, some as objects of worship, some as burial shrouds that reflect a particular conception of death, and so on. When past cultural artifacts are brought together into a twenty-first-century context, the particular beliefs that motivated their creation are lost on most observers.

If we want to understand the meaning of the words used by members of another community, we must become as fluent in their language as we are in our own: "one has, so to speak, to become a child all over again and learn this language … as a second first language."[27] Only upon mastering the new language will we begin to understand the whole set of beliefs inscribed therein. MacIntyre compares the process to that of an anthropologist who goes to live in an alien society and gradually takes on its whole way of life.

Even at this stage, however, the "bilingual" person may recognize that certain words from the other language cannot be translated into their own because they do not share the underlying beliefs that these words express. If that is the case, there will always be a part of the community in question that remains inaccessible.

Two recent views in comparative philosophy

Two recent works on the foundations of comparative philosophy show the increasingly sophisticated discussions of linguistic incommensurability that one may encounter these days.

In his book *Cross-Tradition Engagement in Philosophy: A Constructive-Engagement Account* (2020), Bo Mou develops Davidson's idea of the *underlying agreement* that must already be in place to make sense of different perspectives. In Mou's view, even when people disagree, they "still talk about and point to *the same object* on which they would agree."[28]

First, consider that someone can talk about a single object in different ways. For example, if I say that "Barrack Obama was the President of the United States," I am referring to Obama the person as a whole, while at the same time pointing to his specific role in the past as president. Even though I am talking about Obama in two different ways, I understand that it is the same person. Without this recognition, which Mou calls the *same-object-whole-recognizing* norm, I would not be able to grasp what I am talking about when I mention different aspects of Obama or use the name from one moment to the next.

Mou argues that the *same-object-whole-recognizing* norm is "pre-theoretic" in that it reflects our everyday ways of thinking and talking about things rather than being the result of sustained philosophical inquiry. It not only helps us understand what we ourselves are talking about, but also allows meaningful communication with others to take place. When someone describes an object in a very different way than we ourselves would describe it, we still are able to recognize the thing they are talking about. In Mou's understanding, the norm applies to physical objects in the natural world around us, and even the natural world itself. It also holds when we are discussing more abstract objects like texts or philosophical issues.

In our comparisons between culturally distinct philosophical traditions, we may think that members of these traditions are talking about fundamentally different realities. However, given the norm just mentioned, Mou contends that that this may be only an appearance. "[I]n many cases," he writes,

> those seemingly different objects of study turn out to be distinct aspects or layers of a larger object of study; those seemingly different "unique" issues on their own in different traditions turn out to point to distinct aspects, layers, or dimensions of a larger or more general issue that can be, or actually is, jointly concerned . . . in philosophical inquiry, especially from a higher and broader philosophical vantage point.[29]

In cases where we perceive apparently incommensurable approaches in the philosophies we are studying, the solution is to look at things with a broader vision. It could turn out that members of different traditions are simply talking about different aspects of the same philosophical issue. Even for issues that appear "different, remote, or irrelevant" when comparing one tradition and another, the comparativist can treat them as talking about different aspects of the same world.[30]

A competing account of incommensurability is given by Lin Ma and Jaap van Brakel in their work *Fundamentals of Comparative and Intercultural Philosophy* (2016). On their view, we do not need to appeal to a single shared world for meaningful cross-cultural communication to take place. Members of different cultures use different conceptual schemes for organizing and making sense or their environment, challenging the idea that we are all talking about the "same" world. As Ma and van Brakel point out, "There is no context and conceptual scheme independent answer to the question in what sense two people are seeing the same (thing(s))."[31]

Successful communication is possible because members of the cultures in question "will exploit whatever common ground they can find" in their interactions with one another.[32] When members of different cultures encounter one another for the first time, they may see some similarities in the ways that their cultures respond to their shared environment. For understanding to take place, participants in cross-cultural dialogue must begin from these perceived *family resemblances* (Chapter 1), using them as a means of further engagement. However, members of each tradition may perceive different points of resemblance and describe them in different ways. And as they become more familiar with each other's languages, they will realize that there are immeasurable differences in their respective pictures of the world.

The main challenge to cross-cultural communication, according to Ma and van Brakel, arises not from linguistic incommensurability but rather from "center-periphery forces"—the pull that the dominant political group in a region exerts on those in the minority. In the era of globalization, the dominant group requires standardization of language in order to quicken economic growth, make education more centralized and controllable, and enable colonial power.[33] This standardization seeps into academic disciplines, including philosophy, so that today, as Ma and van Brakel write, "no philosopher in Africa or China (or Europe or America, for that matter) is free to conduct philosophical reflection completely independent of European conceptual schemes."[34] Understanding concepts from other traditions will not only mean finding the appropriate model of interpretation, but it also will involve resisting the homogenizing tendency of the dominant philosophical discourse—a project that we will return to in Chapter 6.

Further issues for comparative philosophers

Here are three additional issues that have received attention from those working in cross-cultural philosophy.

The role of particular terms

First, how much do particular terms matter in comparing philosophies written in distinct languages? If we lack a precise word in our language to translate a term from an ancient Chinese or Indian philosophical text, does it mean that we cannot fully understand the term? If the authors of those texts do not have words that correspond to modern philosophical terminology, are we wrong to use such terminology to interpret the texts?

The last question in particular has been the subject of controversy. Some comparativists have argued that when contemporary Westerners read a text like the *Analects*, it is foolish for them to ask what Confucius' view of democracy or human rights might be. As the Confucian scholar Henry Rosemont, Jr., has written, "the only way it can be maintained that a particular concept was held by an author is to find a term expressing that concept in his text. Thus, we cannot say that so-and-so had a 'theory of *X*,' or that he 'espoused *X* principles,' if there is no *X* in the lexicon of the language in which the author wrote."[35] If there is no corresponding term for "rights," then Confucius did not have a concept of rights. And if he did not have the concept, then of course it makes no sense to compare "Confucius' view of rights" with our own.

Yet a number of others have challenged the "no term, no concept" principle. To begin, it is unclear what is required for one term to have another that corresponds to it. In the case of Chinese texts, does the term in question have to be a single Chinese character, or can it be composed of multiple characters? Can there be more than one such term? Does it have to correspond to the English term every time it is used?[36] There are also plenty of counterexamples to the principle. Do you have the term "aglet" in your lexicon? If not, could someone then argue that you do not have the concept of the plastic tip at the end of your shoelace?[37] Similarly, the *Analects* does not have a single term that corresponds to "self-cultivation," but it is clear that it has important things to say on the issue.[38]

These criticisms do not mean that particular terms are unimportant in comparative philosophy. In fact, anyone who wants a basic understanding of a work of philosophy written in a different language must master its distinctive vocabulary. In the case of the *Analects*, this means being familiar with important Chinese terms such as *ren* 仁, *li* 禮, and *yi* 義. However, we cannot tell how different the worldview of the *Analects* is from our own merely on the basis of these terms.

Questioning the principle of charity

Davidson's principle of charity has also been an issue of debate. If it is true that language and belief are interrelated, then we will need to assume something about other speakers' beliefs in order to understand their speech. But is Davidson right that we need to assume "widespread agreement" between their beliefs and ours?

The principle of charity may lead us "to make too quick sense of the stranger."[39] If someone says something that I do not immediately grasp, and I react by imagining what I would believe if I were in that person's shoes, I run the risk of misunderstanding that person, who is, in fact, not I. Understanding the other, as we saw in Chapter 2, is difficult precisely because it involves revision of our own ways of thinking about things. The principle of charity does not appear to leave room for expansion of our own horizons. It seems to defeat the purpose of engaging with other traditions, which is to learn something new.[40]

For this reason, some have argued that the principle of charity needs to be supplemented by a further principle: the *principle of humanity*.[41] The latter says that we understand a speaker of another language not by imputing to them beliefs that we hold to be true, but rather ones that would be *reasonable* for them to hold given their own background. If we shared the other person's entire constellation of beliefs, desires, and other mental states as informed by the culture of which they are a member, what would it make sense for us to believe? Such an understanding must employ our own background as an analogy for the other person's; a condition of successful translation is that "the imputed pattern of beliefs, desires, and the world, be as similar to our own as possible."[42] Yet it allows us to make sense of the different contexts in which speech takes place.

Others have contended that even the principle of humanity needs to be qualified further in order to accommodate cultural difference. Since understanding is always understanding *for us*, we do need to use ourselves as models to some degree for making sense of other cultures. Nonetheless, in comprehending others, we must be prepared for a diversity of cultural responses to the conditions that make up human life, forming patterns of beliefs and desires that differ from our own. "[T]he resulting picture," as one comparativist writes, "when all the pieces are put together, may expand our conception of the variety to be found in humanity."[43]

Incommensurable or incommensurate?

MacIntyre too has come in for his share of criticism. If an outsider who takes the time to master the language and culture of a particular community can understand the set of commitments associated with names like "Temple Mount" or "Doire Columcille," why can't other members of this outsider's community be led to some degree of understanding as well? Why think that the other community's beliefs will always remain inaccessible, given the potential role of "bilinguals" in translation?[44] When MacIntyre says that the way some term is used within one community is "incommensurable" with the way it is used in another, it sounds as if this is something that will always be the case. But supposing two communities committed themselves to overcoming the differences in belief that would otherwise lead to failure to comprehend one another, it seems possible that their languages could evolve over time to accommodate these differences.

Some critics of MacIntyre have preferred to use the term *incommensurate* rather than *incommensurable*.[45] Terms that are incommensurate now may be made commensurate through committed dialogue. Comparative philosophers have a role to play both in planning and carrying out such dialogue.

Conclusion

Even if we do not accept radical incommensurability, the recognition that another tradition may be in some respects incommensurate with our own can help us to become better comparative philosophers. The idea of untranslatability can free us from thinking that we understand a term from another cultural tradition just because we think we understand its English translation. The noted twentieth-century Sinologist A.C. Graham compared terms that seem to us to mean the same thing to apparently equal lines. "With a further focusing of the microscope," he wrote, "a difference will appear."[46] While we might never fully understand how culturally distant traditions use a particular term, we can at least learn to listen more carefully to what these traditions have to say.

5

Foundational and Evaluative Incommensurability

One day in a large cosmopolitan city a murder is committed. The police chief and judge know that it was a member of a certain ethnic group who carried out the crime, but they do not know *who*. On similar occasions in the past many of the city's residents have engaged in antiethnic rioting, and the police chief and judge have reason to believe that if they don't act quickly the same response is almost certain. Members of the ethnic group in question will be hurt and killed, and property will be damaged. To prevent these things from happening, they decide to arrest, convict, and imprison Mr. Smith, a member of the minority group who is innocent of the murder. With Smith in jail, no rioting occurs.

Researchers presented this hypothetical case, known as the "Magistrate and the Mob," to groups of European Americans and Chinese, asking them whether the police chief and judge were justified in what they did to Mr. Smith.[1] In comparing answers, they found two interesting results. First, the European Americans were more likely to think that the leaders were in the wrong and should be punished. Secondly, the Chinese respondents were more likely to blame the rioters rather than the police chief and judge for Mr. Smith's fate. Since it is often taken for granted by Western ethicists that the case represents an insurmountable objection to utilitarian-style reasoning, the answers from the Chinese side come as a surprise.

Even if translation between different cultural-philosophical traditions is successful, we still face the problem of incommensurability at the *foundational* and *evaluative* levels. With regard to foundational incommensurability, some observers have thought that the above responses correspond to deeper cultural differences. Since Western societies tend to be more individualist in outlook, Americans of European descent view the accused person's rights as the most important consideration; because East Asian societies are more oriented toward collectivism, the Chinese respondents favor the interests of the group over the individual. The respondents appear to inhabit two distinct cultural worlds, seeing (as Kuhn would say) "different things when they look from the same point in the same direction." With such different foundations for making sense of reality, how can members of the one group understand what it is like to view the world through the eyes of those of the other?

At the evaluative level, there is the issue of how to weigh these views against one another. There appears to be no neutral ground on which we could determine which response to the "Magistrate" case is the right one. Rather, there is only *our way* of responding and *their way*. But in that case, how do we make any further progress? Does comparative philosophy end when it comes up against these cultural divisions? Let us consider the problems of foundational and evaluative incommensurability in turn.

Foundational incommensurability

The British philosopher R.G. Collingwood proposed that to figure out what a person's foundational beliefs are, we should ask them a series of "But why do you think that?" questions. A patient and their pathologist are discussing a symptom associated with a certain disease. "What causes this symptom?" the patient asks. When the doctor tells them, the patient asks how the doctor knows. "Because there is such-and-such body of research which supports that this is the cause." "But why," the patient continues, "do you assume that it has a cause in the first place?" "Because everything has a cause," says the doctor. When asked the basis of this belief, however, they begin to grow irritable—a sure sign that we have reached the level of "absolute presupposition." If they tried to give an answer, Collingwood writes, they would be forced to say something like, "That is a thing we take for granted in my job. We don't question it. We don't try to verify it. It isn't a thing anybody has discovered, like microbes or the circulation of the blood. It is a thing we just take for granted."[2]

A philosophical tradition's absolute presuppositions are the starting points from which its members make sense of the world, organizing their collective philosophical output into a coherent whole. The problem arises when we try to understand a tradition with different presuppositions than our own. A statement that makes perfect sense according to the presuppositions of that tradition may appear incomprehensible to those outside of it. These presuppositions are often hidden far beneath the surface, below the conscious awareness even of those who share in them. Even if we could get at them, we would have to get around the fact that we too have our foundational beliefs which shape our understanding. What if there is no shared foundation, no common point of reference from which we can make sense of others?

Understanding a "primitive" society

A primary way in which the Zande people of Central Africa regulate their conduct and make sense of the world around them is through witchcraft. According to one early study, witchcraft

> plays its part in every activity of Zande life; in agricultural, fishing, and hunting pursuits; in domestic life of homesteads as well as in communal life of district and court; it is an important theme of mental life in which it forms the background of a vast panorama of oracles and magic; its influence is plainly stamped on law and morals, etiquette and religion; it is prominent in technology and language; there is no niche or corner of Zande culture into which it does not twist itself.[3]

From the view of a scientifically literate person, this looks like a mistake. Scientific explanations are in harmony with the objective facts; explanations that refer to witches and the like are not. The difficulty lies in understanding the widespread appeal of these beliefs to the Azande. How can beliefs that are obviously false to us be so engrained in their way of life?

The philosopher of social science Peter Winch gives an influential answer to this question in his 1964 essay "Understanding a Primitive Society." The crucial first step, according to Winch, is to realize that modern Westerners do not have an available category for comprehending Zande witchcraft. In our mind-set, the term witchcraft tends to be associated with certain practices that are considered perversions of orthodox religion; the concept of a "black mass," for instance, only makes sense given the notion of a proper Christian one. However, this idea of witchcraft will not help us understand the Zande version, since in the latter case witchcraft is, as it were, the orthodox view. Nor are our categories of science and nonscience a good fit for understanding Zande practices, since these practices are not meant to reflect a systematic method of understanding nature. Since by imposing Western categories on the Zande worldview we will only end up in misunderstanding, we should instead try to think of ways in which our categories can be expanded to fit their worldview.

Winch argues that the key to understanding Zande witchcraft is to see how the Azande are dependent on a successful harvest, and how their magic rituals give them a chance to contemplate this dependency. In particular, they "express an attitude toward contingencies . . . which involves recognition that one's life is subject to contingencies, rather than an attempt to control these."[4] We can find some parallel to this attitude in our own culture if we look hard enough. Winch notes that in the Judeo-Christian tradition prayers such as "If it be Thy will" can serve to free a person from dependence on the objects of their prayers. In the case of the Azande, these rituals help to achieve a kind of "attunement" toward the natural world, an attitude which contrasts with the modern scientific view of nature simply as something to be controlled.[5]

While Winch's explanation is a fascinating one, later contributors to the debate have argued that it hinders rather than helps our understanding of Zande practices. They maintain that the Azande's use of witchcraft does resemble science in certain respects. One particular ritual involves questioning an oracle by feeding a small amount of poison to a chicken; whether the chicken lives or dies determines whether the answer is "yes" or "no." Such behavior seems best construed as attempting to determine what the facts are about a particular case, or to make predictions about the future. But if this interpretation is correct, then the Azande are simply in error. Perhaps we can understand this error to some extent based on our experiences with superstition in segments of our own society, but we can never comprehend it as a total belief system.[6]

How we understand a culturally distant society depends on which of our own concepts or practices we take as an analogy. We will have to defend the interpretive accuracy of the categories we use against other plausible alternatives. In some cases, we may think the best interpretation is that we do not understand the other society at all.

Argumentation and Chinese philosophy

Are there fundamentally different modes of philosophical reasoning? Some textbook definitions of philosophy (see for instance the last definition in Ch. 12, exercise 1.1 below) highlight the use of arguments. In a typical philosophy paper, you are expected to clearly state your position, provide good arguments for it, and anticipate possible objections and respond to them. If you ask your professors why philosophy is done this way, they may tell you about Socrates, or about how philosophy teaches critical thinking, or about the difference between philosophy and religious belief.

When we turn to the Chinese philosophical classics, however, we notice that clearly stated arguments and counterarguments are not a central feature of these texts. For the most part the authors' views are simply asserted, often with what seems like intentional ambiguity. Consider these two takes on a similar issue from the *Daodejing* and *Analects*, respectively:

1. The more clear the laws and edicts, the more thieves and robbers.
   And so sages say,
   "I do nothing and the people transform themselves;
   I prefer stillness and the people correct and regulate themselves;
   I engage in no activity and the people prosper on their own;
   I am without desires and the people simplify their own lives."[7]

2. Ji Kangzi was concerned about the prevalence of robbers in Lu and asked Confucius about how to deal with this problem.
   Confucius said, "If you could just get rid of your own excessive desires, the people would not steal even if you rewarded them for it."[8]

Each of these passages discusses the problem of how to prevent theft, with the solution listing some steps a ruler might take to eliminate such behavior in his subjects. No additional explanation is given: no attempt to say why this is the ideal solution, to show how it fits in to a theory of crime-prevention, or to put forth objections to competing views.[9] The passages suggest a less abstract and more practical orientation on the part of classical Chinese thinkers. As the influential scholar A.C. Graham once wrote, "the crucial question for [classical Chinese thinkers] is not the Western philosopher's 'What is the truth?' but 'Where is the Way?', the way to order the state and conduct personal life."[10]

One possibility is that there are fundamentally different modes of philosophizing in classical Chinese and ancient Greek philosophy. Some scholars of Chinese philosophy have argued that the classical Chinese texts are informed by "correlative thinking," which contrasts strongly with the type of rational and logical argumentation that came to define the Western tradition. As explained by David L. Hall and Roger T. Ames, correlative thinking is spontaneous and informal and meant to suggest emergent possibilities for ordering the particular elements that are present in a given situation.[11] In the case of the above examples from the *Analects* and *Daodejing*, rather than applying a general ethical principle to help us understand the wrongness of theft, the suggestion seems to be instead of how to restore a harmonious balance between the ruler and the people.

Other scholars argue, however, that the Chinese masters did have arguments for their views, and that we can understand them by attempting to reconstruct these arguments. Even with texts in Western philosophy, understanding the structure of the author's arguments—making sense of key terms, identifying unstated assumptions, and clarifying the argument's chain of reasoning—can be a challenge. As Bryan W. Van Norden writes, "Scholars already working on Chinese thought should not be quick to dismiss the argumentative quality of these texts merely because the arguments are sometimes difficult to interpret."[12] He contends that people in every culture make arguments as a means of resolving their disagreements, and distinguish between those that are persuasive and those that are not persuasive in the expectation that they can reach intersubjective agreement.

A third approach is to think of philosophical reasoning as a family resemblance concept.[13] The above passages might meet some features of philosophical reasoning—such as justifying a certain mode of statecraft or thinking about how to solve practical problems within a society—while other features—such as clearly defined terms and logically ordered arguments—are not as striking. The process of understanding these features begins by finding the relevant point of comparison within our own tradition. As with the above case of Zande society, whether there are fundamental differences between culturally distinct philosophical traditions is a matter of dispute. Some comparativists have pointed out that ancient Greek ethics also has a practical motivation, seeing the ultimate goal of studying ethics not as learning to argue one's views, but rather to become a good person. In that case, the more important difference may not be that between Chinese and Western ethics, but rather between contemporary ethics and ancient ethics.[14]

Assessing the case for foundational incommensurability

One explanation for the divergent responses to the Magistrate and Mob example mentioned at the beginning of this chapter is that there are fundamental differences between Chinese and European-American cultures. These differences, the proponent of foundational incommensurability will say, pose a barrier to cross-cultural understanding. As an example, we can point to philosophers in the English-speaking world who have taken it for granted that the right answer is that what the police chief and judge did was wrong. The great twentieth-century moral thinker Elizabeth Anscombe claimed that it wasn't legitimate even to debate the issue: "[I]f someone really thinks, *in advance*, that it is open to question whether such an action as procuring the judicial execution of the innocent should be quite excluded from consideration—I do not want to argue with him; he shows a corrupt mind."[15]

For the proponent of foundational incommensurability, this response is understandable. If certain presuppositions really are fundamental to the way we see things, why would we entertain conflicting views? An ethical tradition based on rights and individual freedoms is antithetical to one based on the collective good of society. For someone steeped in the former tradition to make sense of the latter one, they would have to unlearn the values that have been a part of their education since the very beginning.

Yet even if we suppose that the responses to the Magistrate and Mob example indicate some deep difference between the two groups of respondents, this state of affairs would support the need for comparative philosophy, rather than undermining its possibility. Comparative philosophy is just as useful when it teaches us about significant differences between cultures as when it tells us about underlying similarities. If we want to understand why Chinese respondents tended to answer the way they did, it helps to know something about the central philosophical texts in the Chinese tradition, and to have thought about their points of contact with Western ethics. The value of comparative philosophy is not just in knowing other cultures' texts, however, but in training us how to respond to foundational differences. Awareness of different standards of justification can serve as a check on foisting our philosophical prejudices on other traditions.

As with linguistic incommensurability, it is difficult to know whether our failure to understand another cultural tradition's absolute presuppositions is a permanent state of affairs, or rather something that can be overcome by finding the right point of comparison in our own tradition. Cases of apparently incommensurable foundations show the need for more comparative philosophy, rather than less.

Evaluative incommensurability

Yet in cases of genuine disagreement, what can we do to resolve the matter? Once we have understood that their reasons are not our reasons, and that the differences run deep enough that neither side is likely to change its position, debating things further seems pointless. The classical Chinese philosopher Zhuangzi pointed out the difficulty of trying to attain a neutral point of view in such cases:

> Shall we get someone who agrees with you to decide? But if he already agrees with you, how can he decide fairly? Shall we get someone who agrees with me? But if he already agrees with me, how can he decide? Shall we get someone who disagrees with both of us? But if he already disagrees with both of us, how can he decide? Shall we get someone who agrees with both of us? But if he already agrees with both of us, how can he decide?[16]

If you have ever been involved in an argument with someone who shares little of your point of view about the morality of abortion, the role of religion in politics, or some other matter of controversy, perhaps you can appreciate this line of reasoning. It is not just that little gets resolved in such arguments, but that they seem incapable of resolution.

The problem is especially pressing in cases of cross-cultural disagreement. If Americans disagree with one another about the abortion issue, there is at least a shared political process to which they can appeal. However, if members of independently developed cultural traditions disagree about the proper balance between individual rights and the security of the community, what common ground can they draw upon to resolve their dispute?

Support for evaluative commensurability

In some cases, the problem of evaluative incommensurability may arise because the traditions in question don't understand one another. If we cannot translate key terms from another tradition into our own, there is no way of knowing whether that tradition's views are better or worse than ours. The same goes if we cannot understand the absolute presuppositions that inform that tradition's view of reality. In cases of linguistic and foundational incommensurability, there is no way of keeping score between us and them, because we do not know what their rules of scorekeeping are.

A stronger case for evaluative incommensurability arises, however, when we do understand the other tradition, at least enough to know that its way of keeping score is very different from our own.[17] As MacIntyre puts it in an essay on Confucian and Aristotelian ethics, comparison of the two traditions leads to the recognition that "each system has its own standard and measures of interpretation, explanation, and justification internal to itself. . . . [T]here are indeed no shared standards and measures, external to both systems and neutral between them, to which appeal might be made to adjudicate between their rival claims."[18] Even after all the work of translation and comparative interpretation has been accomplished, the only progress that has been made is "from mutual incomprehension to inevitable rejection."[19] But this rejection is on shaky ground. If at bottom the two traditions are committed to different philosophical ideals, which themselves admit of no further justification, then how can one of them claim to be better than the other? Once members of a philosophical tradition recognize that the case for their tradition's superiority rests on a circular argument, they may see no reason to continue to subscribe to that tradition.[20]

Even in cases where we have some independent grounds for saying our own tradition is better, the problem of evaluative incommensurability may still arise. Suppose, for instance, that we think our own scientific worldview is preferable to Zande witchcraft because it gives us a more accurate understanding of the world around us. We may still recognize that in some respects the Zande way of life is better than our own: more connected with the natural world, more present in the moment, and free from many of the burdens of life in modern Western societies. This insight may lead us to the conviction that there is more than one way to live a good human life, and that between these ways no decision can be made.[21]

The relativist response to cultural difference

The idea that there are deep and irresolvable differences across cultures is part of a broader debate regarding moral relativism. Note the role this idea plays in the following relativist argument:

If we had acquired our moral views in the way we acquire scientific views, namely, by means of a rational fact-finding procedure, then we could criticize other cultures when their morality differs from ours. . . . But we do *not* acquire our moral views by discovering objective moral facts. (This becomes obvious when we realize that moral principles differ from culture to culture, for this state of affairs would not exist if there were a realm of objective moral facts *everyone* can discern—as everyone can discern that the sky is blue.) Moral principles are acquired, not by any *rational* process, but by the *causal* process of "enculturative conditioning," that is, they are impressed upon us in subtle ways by the culture in which we are raised. We do not, therefore, have any grounds—any good *reasons*—for holding the moral views that we do hold. And that being so, it is a mistake to think that our moral views are both (a) *known* by us to be true and (b) apply to people of other cultures who don't share our moral views.[22]

The whole argument rests on the premise stated within the parentheses: that moral principles differ from culture to culture. It is because they differ, the relativist claims, that we can be sure that morality is a matter of enculturation, that we do not have any good reasons for holding the views we do, and that we cannot know these views to be true.

In the Magistrate and Mob case, as we have seen, many philosophers have thought it an absolute truth that an innocent person should not be falsely imprisoned to bring about a greater good. If the relativist is right, this conviction does not result from the facts of the case, but rather from the accidental circumstances of one's birth. If you happened to be born in China, you would probably have a different view, and you would be just as convinced that this view was true.

On the relativist view, our moral views are only applicable within the cultural context in which they were formed. While statements such as "the world is flat" are true regardless of whatever anyone happens to think, statements about morality are "culturally contingent. . . . [T]here is no way of assessing their truth or falsity apart from people's beliefs. . . ."[23] If members of the Aztec culture believe that the gods require human sacrifice, then for them it is so. As one proponent of relativism writes,

> Imagine the priestess called upon to explain the consequences of a failure to sacrifice the requisite virgins in the requisite manner. She might well say, "Society will fall apart. Our women and our land will become barren because our men will become impotent as lovers and ineffective as cultivators." *And she will be right.* Believing themselves to be impotent in the hammock and ineffective in the field, the men will be unable to perform in either context. The birth rate will decline, and the harvest will fail. Society *will* fall apart. Believing is seeing: beliefs bring about the very conditions that will make these beliefs come true.[24]

A belief or practice that seems objectionable to outsiders, as we saw Ruth Benedict arguing in the last chapter, must be understood as part of the "cultural whole" to which it belongs. When we criticize such a belief or practice, our mistake is to strip it from its context and see it only within our own cultural framework. There is simply no independent way of evaluating the belief or practice apart from its efficacy in a particular culture. In demanding that the Aztecs give up the practice of human sacrifice, the author of the above passage contends, we are asking them to cease to be Aztecs.

Criticizing a practice in another culture that strikes us as objectionable may be the first step in forcing our own values on that culture. We identify the practice with the culture as a whole and use this association as a mark of its inferiority. One Western author recounts how in his early education, the main thing he was taught about Indian culture was the Hindu custom of *sati*, in which a wife is supposed to fling herself onto the funeral pyre of her recently deceased husband. The custom is memorably described in Jules Verne's novel *Around the World in Eighty Days* (later turned into a popular movie). At one point in the story, the hero Phileas Fogg and his French servant Passepartout stumble upon a band of priests devoted to the death-god Kali who are about to burn a young widow alive. She turns out to be an Indian princess named Aouda, English-educated with skin as "fair as a European" (in the film adaptation, she is played by the American actress Shirley MacLaine). Fogg and Passepartout risk precious time in their journey to make a daring rescue of Aouda from the clutches of the priests; she eventually marries Fogg out of love and gratitude. As the author, now a prominent political scientist, later realized, "[T]he focus on this practice was not an accident. It served to identify the British with civilization and the Indians with barbarism and thus to legitimate British colonialism."[25] This is not to say that *sati* isn't an abominable practice, but only that its place in Western representations of Indian culture is problematic.

We pay homage to the power of the relativist argument any time we excuse behavior we would otherwise consider immoral on the grounds of a person's cultural background. Wouldn't you react differently to a polygamist who grew up in West Africa than to one who was raised next door to you in Des Moines? "Well, it's a different culture." But if we really believed it was an absolute moral truth that "a person should be monogamous"—as sure as "the sky is blue"—it seems we should react the same way in both cases.

Assessing the relativist response

Often the relativist appears to overstate the differences between cultures in order to make their case. Though we know the Aztecs practiced human sacrifice, there is debate about how extensive the practice was. Would their society really have "fallen apart" without it? In identifying human sacrifice with the Aztec "cultural whole," we end up with a very one-sided representation of this society. Who counts as representative of a culture's morality? What is the "average" view of practices like abortion or euthanasia in our own society? As the philosopher Michele Moody-Adams writes, "[I]t is profoundly difficult to construct a reliable description of the moral practices of an entire *culture*—a description of the sort that could license judgments contrasting one culture's basic moral beliefs with those of other."[26] To see the entire Aztec culture as oriented toward human sacrifice is also to ignore the role this practice played in keeping the lower classes of Aztec society in submission. Is human sacrifice a matter of incomparable cultural difference, or rather an instantly recognizable feature of how power was managed in early human societies?

In any case, the mere presence of different moral principles from one culture to the next does not show that morality is culturally relative.[27] Suppose that members of the one culture are able to persuade members of the other to change their ways. In that event we might think that morality is still a matter of objective moral facts, just ones that are harder to discern than the fact that the sky is blue. Cross-cultural conversation would have an important role to play in uncovering such facts. The relativist conclusion follows only when the disagreement is *fundamental*, persisting even after debate between fully informed and fully rational interlocutors.

Even with disagreements that appear to be fundamental, we can often find additional factors that "explain away" or "defuse" the disagreement.[28] This may be done by showing that the disagreement in question is superficial rather than genuine. The beliefs on one side could be adopted for reasons other than because they are deeply held moral convictions.

My wife and I both grew up in different cities in the American Midwest. When we first moved to our current home, a small town ninety minutes away from New York City, we discovered that the social interactions there were very different to those we experienced growing up. While in the places we grew up it wouldn't be unusual to say hello to a stranger on the street, in our new town virtually no one says hello. The lack of regard for others appeared to us to grow the further east we went; on the street in downtown

Newark or a subway in Manhattan, even making eye contact with a stranger seemed to be a breach of etiquette.

For the first year or two in our new home, I took this to be a matter of different norms concerning sociability. "People sure were friendlier back home, weren't they?" But eventually we arrived other explanations. In the big city, one encounters too many different people in the course of a given day to be able to greet everyone. And while the populations in our hometowns were more or less stable, where we live now there is greater turnover as waves of newcomers move westward from the nearby metropolitan areas in search of cheaper housing. The different ways of treating strangers are not the result of genuine disagreement about how to interact with one's fellow human beings, but of contingent features of the two environments.

We can look for similar explanations of the apparent disagreement in the case of the Magistrate and the Mob. The scholar of Chinese philosophy Shirong Luo points out that the issue may be simpler than the one given by the experimenters:

> There is an obvious flaw in the design of the survey—given that racial riots are exceedingly rare in China, the Chinese respondents were given a scenario that seemed to them outlandish. The perniciousness of racial riots in the imagination of the Chinese subjects might have loomed much larger than in the minds of their American counterparts because of the "fear of the unknown," which might better explain why the Chinese responders were more likely to blame the rioters rather than the police chief and the judge.[29]

If this is the case, then it is a mistake to assume that the different responses are attributable to deep cultural differences.

We will not know which philosophical disagreements are fundamental until we make a careful examination of the basic texts of the traditions in question and allow for dialogue between their living adherents. An important task of comparative philosophy is to assess which cross-cultural disagreements are fundamental, or if any of them are.

The relativist position has value insofar as it draws our attention to the deeper philosophical foundations of beliefs and practices that we might find objectionable. Though we may not ever agree with the way members of a different culture approach a given ethical issue, we can still gain from considering the underlying values that motivate their response. A natural inclination in such encounters is to leave our own moral principles untouched, keeping them as fixed standards for measuring everything else. Such one-sided evaluation is just as much a threat to genuine cross-cultural dialogue as incommensurability, and we will say more about it shortly.

While as comparativists we must be cognizant of different cultural standards, this does not mean giving up our role as philosophers who make evaluative judgments. Philosophical progress means scrutinizing others' views and opening our own views up to scrutiny. To engage with problems that affect people all over the world, we must be prepared to navigate between the many opposing cultural perspectives that are present, saying which parts of a given cultural perspective help or hinder their solution. Talk of "cultural differences" often provides a self-serving defense to tyrants. It is not only condescending to think that members of certain cultures are not capable of reasoned discussion with outsiders; it can also mean allowing oppressive practices to persist. Martha Nussbaum puts this point well:

> It is bad to use one's own way of life as a standard to which the other is expected to measure up, as if there were no way other than one's own of living a reasonable human life, but it is at least as bad to refuse all application of standards, as if one were dealing with an alien form of life that one could not expect to come up to standards that one happens to think terribly important oneself.[30]

In cutting off the possibility of constructive dialogue between people with different standards, the relativist asks us to give up too much.

Other responses to disagreement

Relativism is not the only response to cultural disagreement. At the opposite end of the spectrum, we could reject the other tradition in its entirety. Even after long consideration, we might maintain that a tradition that does not afford a fundamental place to individual rights does not have anything to offer. Since we think that rights are not just for those in certain societies, but for all human beings, we want to see them integrated into the moral and legal framework of other cultures. This desire is especially strong if we see the persecution of less powerful constituencies within those cultures.

Nonetheless, the criticism can go both ways. Members of other cultures may argue that our society's emphasis on individual rights comes at a price: each person is concerned mainly with the rights society owes them, and less so with the duties they owe to society. Insisting on a rights-based morality may also prevent us from exploring alternative grounds for respecting others. It could be that rights-based moralities are compatible with community-oriented ones.[31]

MacIntyre argues that even in the absence of any neutral standards there are still ways that one tradition can be shown to be superior to another.[32] It could happen that one of the traditions fails according to its own standards, and its rival is able to explain why that tradition failed at the time it did. He uses Kuhn's example of Aristotelian and Newtonian physics. Even though these systems have incommensurable standards, it eventually became clear that the latter system was more productive, comprehensive, and internally coherent.

Yet some comparativists have criticized MacIntyre's account for making encounters between traditions into an "all-or-nothing" contest in which one defeats the other. As one author writes in response, "it is an extremely narrow conception of comparative philosophy that the goal of it is to determine, between the parties being compared, which side is the winner."[33] Why engage another tradition in the first place if this were the goal?

As it happens, there are other responses to cross-cultural disagreement besides those of the relativist and winner-take-all. We will introduce three of them briefly here, exploring them in more detail in Part III of the book.

Some comparative philosophers have argued that respect for another tradition leads to the possibility of *synthesis*. We may see the value of certain features of a community-oriented morality, such as the Confucian notion that children have an obligation to take care of their parents, while at the same time recognizing these features are in tension with the premium that Western societies place on individual freedom. As a result, we may envision some sort of ethical theory which has room for both.

Synthesis faces an uphill battle. Critics have argued that there is little historical evidence that different moral traditions can achieve synthesis; the great religious traditions, despite centuries of interaction, show little signs of converging with one another.[34] We will look more at this approach in Chapter 8.

A second alternative maintains that there are multiple goods that can reasonably be put at the center of human life, and these goods are irreducible to one another. This is *pluralism* rather than relativism, since it accepts that more than one way of life is good, yet rejects the idea that all ways of life are equal. If there is more than one version of the good life, then we will have to learn to tolerate the competing versions found in other cultures. Perhaps we should not only acknowledge these different goods but strive to understand and appreciate what is valuable about each. We will discuss some potential strengths and weaknesses of this view in Chapter 9.

A third response concedes that there are fundamental disagreements between cultures but attempts to establish agreement on certain norms of conduct. There may be other grounds for condemning the abuse of minority groups besides human rights.[35] Persecution of certain groups could be wrong because we believe in the equal educability of all human beings; because we think it shows a lack of compassion on the part of the persecutor; or because it hinders members of those groups from contributing to the common good. We should not try to argue further about these different foundations, but rather work to achieve *consensus* on the norm that persecution of certain groups is wrong. For more discussion, see Chapter 10.

Conclusion

If we are prepared to see other cultures' philosophies as working from different absolute presuppositions than our own, then we are not only less likely to misunderstand them, but also more liable to gain something new ourselves. As Winch writes, "What we may learn by studying other cultures are not merely possibilities of different ways of doing things, other techniques. More importantly we may learn different possibilities of making sense of human life."[36] Relativism, as we have seen, is only one possible response among others to our encounter with these different possibilities. Even if we think that the divergent ethical approaches present in two different cultures due to the influence of incommensurable cultural-philosophical standards, the available models of comparative philosophy leave us with plenty of work to be done.

6

One-Sidedness

The Borg are a highly adaptable species of cybernetic organisms on *Star Trek* whose primary mission is to absorb other forms of life into their own collective hive mind. By injecting nanoprobes into their victims, they are able to take over their bodies and gain control of their thoughts and actions. In one episode, they rewrite the control system of a Starfleet ship to make it compatible with their own; the ship then becomes a zombie that they can control from a distance. "We are the Borg," they say upon encountering new prey. "Lower your shields and surrender your ships. We will add your biological and technological distinctiveness to our own. Your culture will adapt to service us. *Resistance is futile.*"

An ever-present problem in comparative philosophy is that, wittingly or not, we assimilate other cultural traditions into our own familiar ways of thinking. One-sided comparison is bad enough when carried out by individuals; as a widespread practice, it can wreak havoc of Borgian proportions. The dominant philosophical worldview turns into "a sort of omnivorous monster, one that swallows up all other cultures . . . destroying all possibility of cultural difference."[1] Comparative philosophy becomes a devious means of pushing one way of thinking onto the rest of the world.

Whereas the problem of incommensurability occurs in the absence of tradition-neutral language or standards that allow meaningful dialogue to take place, the problem of one-sidedness arises when one party in the conversation forces its language and standards onto the other. If we want comparative philosophy to teach us anything new, we need to reflect on this problem as well, learning to recognize it and mitigate its effects in our comparisons.

The meaning of one-sidedness

One-sidedness has taken different forms in the history of comparative philosophy. In the eighteenth and nineteenth centuries, many European philosophers who encountered non-Western thinkers and texts ended up *projecting* their own fixations onto them, assuming that these thinkers and texts had the same concerns as they did. Though the same thing may easily happen today, projection is now generally recognized as an interpretive vice. Yet there still exists the problem of the *asymmetry* of comparative philosophy: when we look at the discipline as a whole, Western philosophical categories dominate much of the discourse, to the exclusion of other cultural traditions.

Projection

The projection error occurs when, in ignorance of the meaning or motivation of philosophy from another culture, we understand it solely in categories already familiar to us.[2] Instead of shifting our horizon to meet the horizon of the other, we remain exactly where we are, absorbing the other into our fixed way of seeing things. We do not let our interlocutors speak for themselves as equal partners in dialogue, but rather do all the talking for them.

The tendency to project is most apparent in early Western encounters with other cultures' philosophies. Classic Confucian texts were first translated into Latin in 1687 and were read by many eighteenth-century European intellectuals. The moral and social wisdom these texts contained was interpreted in different and sometimes opposed ways. For the Jesuit missionaries who traveled to China, this wisdom was a sign that the Chinese had an implicit knowledge of God based on natural reason, indicating they were capable of conversion to Christianity.[3] *Philosophes* such as Voltaire, on the other hand, took the texts' teachings as proof that morality can be built on an entirely rational foundation. In the discussion of Confucius in his *Philosophical Dictionary*, we do not see Confucius so much as we do Voltaire's own criticisms of the religion of his day and age: "Confucius had no interest in falsehood: he did not pretend to be a prophet; he claimed no inspiration; he taught no new religion; he used no delusions."[4]

In the nineteenth century, European intellectuals turned their attention to Indian philosophy. A forerunner of this interest was the great German philosopher Arthur Schopenhauer, an enthusiastic appreciator of the ancient Hindu *Upanishads*. In the preface to the first edition of *The World as Will and Representation*, Schopenhauer claimed that possession of knowledge of Indian philosophy was the main advantage of the nineteenth century over the one that had preceded it. Those readers who had "already received and been receptive to the consecration of the ancient Indian wisdom," he maintained, would be in the best position to understand his own philosophy.[5]

Though Schopenhauer's relationship to Indian philosophy was a complex one, his use of Indian texts often shows the interpretive immobility characteristic of projection. The historical record suggests that the German thinker had already worked out his own philosophy well in advance of reading the ancient texts. He famously claimed that while his main ideas could not be found in the *Upanishads*, the entirety of the *Upanishads* could be deduced from his ideas.

The comparisons of Indian and Western modes of thought in *The World as Will* often bring out points of similarity that buttress Schopenhauer's own philosophy. These points tend to be asserted rather than supported with relevant contextual detail. To establish the ubiquity of the phenomenon he calls "negation of the will to life," for instance, Schopenhauer considers the experiences of the Christian saint and the Indian one. "The two," he writes, "have *exactly the same* strivings and inner lives, despite such fundamentally different dogmas, customs, and environments."[6] He also claims that their teachings are "the same," emphasizing the vanity of earthly pleasure and the priority of spiritual perfection to external works. The similarities showed convincing evidence of the negation of the will to life: "So many points of agreement in spite of such different times and peoples is a factual proof that what is expressed here is not some craze or eccentricity, as optimistic platitudes would have it, but rather an essential side of human nature that rarely comes forward only because of its excellence."[7]

Schopenhauer's use of the *Upanishads* exemplified a more general tendency. "Throughout the nineteenth century," as Andrew Tuck writes in a historical study of Western interest in Indian philosophy, "European scholars consistently grafted their own intellectual concerns and discursive practices onto an India that was virtually of their own creation and treated Indian texts as exotic expressions of their own presuppositions and philosophies."[8] Tuck traces this trend into the twentieth century, showing the extent to which the dominant views during each successive period of Western philosophy were used as standards to interpret and evaluate classical Indian thinkers and texts. When idealism was the dominant school in Germany and Britain, Western interpreters disputed the extent to which different Indian schools of philosophy were idealistic. When analytic philosophy became ascendant, scholars turned their attention away from metaphysics and toward issues of language and logic in Indian texts. When Wittgenstein's philosophy was in fashion, they claimed that his views had been anticipated by Indian philosophers several millennia before.

Asymmetry

One-sidedness remains a major issue in comparative philosophy today. The scholar of early Chinese philosophy Kwong-loi Shun has drawn attention to the *asymmetry* which has characterized recent Chinese-Western comparisons:

> while we see frequent deployment of Western philosophical frameworks in the study of Chinese thought, we rarely encounter the reverse phenomenon, namely, the deployment of Chinese philosophical frameworks in the study of Western thought.... This asymmetrical tendency in the study of comparative ethics is puzzling, and further investigation is needed to understand its possible grounding.[9]

Whereas projection is an individual interpretive vice, asymmetry refers to a collective phenomenon. When a few Western philosophers ask whether Buddhism is a consequentialist philosophy, this does not by itself make the dialogue skewed. Suppose, however, that nearly all comparative philosophers use Western categories to describe and evaluate non-Western thought. Even if each of these philosophers strives to avoid projection in their own work, the conversation as a whole is being dictated by one side.

Surprisingly, the predominant use of Western categories is not limited to Western philosophers but applies also to comparisons written in the Chinese language. Nor is the bias toward Western categories confined to Chinese-Western comparisons, as philosophers working in the Indian and African traditions have called attention to the same issue.[10] This state of affairs is all the more perplexing when we consider that today's comparative philosophers have plenty of historical examples of the dangers of one-sided comparison, and tend to be more reflective than their predecessors about their methods and aims.

One possible explanation for the situation is that Western philosophical categories are broad and systematic, whereas philosophical concepts drawn from other cultures are more parochial.[11] Traditions like Confucianism are difficult to discuss apart from their attachments to particular cultural practices. Confucius claimed to be transmitting the ways of ancient Chinese sage-kings, and his philosophy eventually developed into a state-sanctioned ideology. Today there is a debate about whether the Confucian tradition can be applied to societies outside of East Asia. There is much less argument, on the other hand, about whether Aristotle's virtue ethics is relevant to non-Mediterranean societies. So it seems more natural to ask whether Confucius is an Aristotelian virtue ethicist than it does to consider whether Aristotle possesses a Confucian ethics. The Western category is more universal.

We can find plenty of counterexamples to Western philosophical universality, however. Concepts like "ritual" and "love of learning" on the Confucian side have broad applicability, whereas ones like "sensus divinitatis" or "eidetic reduction" are difficult to understand apart from the basic assumptions of the Western traditions in which they developed. One instance of asymmetry Shun mentions is the tendency to refer to the classical Chinese philosopher Mozi as a utilitarian. Mozi was a critic of the lavish spending and constant warmongering of the rulers of his day who developed his own distinctive vision of human society based on the ideal of "universal love" (jian'ai 兼愛). While we need not be Westerners to understand the idea of the greatest good for the greatest number, we do not have to be Chinese either to see the appeal of Mozi's teachings. In that case, why doesn't anyone ask whether John Stuart Mill is a Mohist?

Comparative philosophy and power

Edward Said offers an influential analysis of Western representations of non-Westerners in terms of power relations in his 1978 book *Orientalism*. As inspiration for this work, Said cited the disconnect between his own experiences as a Palestinian and the distortions of Arabic culture he perceived in Western art, literature, and scholarship. He came to refer to the entire system of Western representation of the Middle East as "orientalism," characterizing it as "a Western style for dominating, restructuring, and having authority," or "a kind of Western projection onto and will to govern the Orient."[12] Later authors have extended this analysis to European representations of other non-Western cultures.

Said claims that scholars who study other cultures cannot be detached from their membership in a particular class, society, and set of beliefs. Academic studies which aim to give us pure and objective knowledge of these cultures necessarily reflect the broader political environment in which they were produced. Orientalism, he writes, is

> a *distribution* of geopolitical awareness into aesthetic, scholarly, economic, sociological, historical, and philological texts; it is an *elaboration* not only of a basic geographic distinction (the world is made up of two unequal halves, Orient and Occident) but also of a whole series of "interests" *which*, by such means as scholarly discovery, philological reconstruction, psychological analysis, landscape and sociological description, it not only creates but also maintains; it *is* . . . a certain *will* or *intention* to understand, in some cases to control, manipulate, even to incorporate, what is a manifestly different (or alternative and novel) world; it is, above all, a discourse that is . . . produced and exists in uneven exchange with various kinds of power.[13]

Scholarship in comparative philosophy may be seen as subject to the same conditions. The United States is currently the world's largest economic and military power. It has some of the most prestigious universities in the world, which possess massive financial endowments and are able to attract competitive academics and students from many other countries. The philosophy departments at these universities are also relatively well funded and attract the same sorts of candidates. Philosophy produced in these departments eventually spreads to many others, both in the United States and the world at large. Work in cross-cultural philosophy cannot be described in isolation from these broader political circumstances. Given the underlying power structures that support contemporary philosophical practice, it should be no surprise that philosophy from wealthy and powerful nations has come to dominate the rest.

To some, this explanation may appear too crude to account for all the sorts of philosophies that have been influential. Plato and Aristotle form a substantial part of the Western curriculum, yet it has been a long time since Greek economic and military power wielded the sort of influence the modern-day United States does. We cannot explain this solely in terms of their connection to Western culture, since other philosophers—like Boethius, Suarez, or Schlegel—may have had a similar connection but are not considered as important.[14] The comparative study of non-Western cultures has also served as a tool of criticism of Western modes of thought.[15] Given these facts, it does not make sense to explain philosophical influence solely in terms of military and economic power.

Yet it seems even more misguided for the comparativist to ignore these concerns. As Monika Kirloskar-Steinbach and Leah Kalmanson write in the conclusion to their recent *A Practical Guide to World Philosophies: Selves, Worlds, and Ways of Knowing* (2021), "Wherever we are located today, our standard conceptions of philosophy still, it seems, reflect the exercise of [colonial] power."[16] An Anglo-European center, which retains the title of "philosophy," is orbited by numerous cultural traditions on the periphery, stuck with the labels of "Chinese philosophy," "Indian Philosophy," "African Philosophy," and others. In 2014, Kirloskar-Steinbach co-founded the *Journal of World Philosophies*, with the mission of promoting philosophical work that was not subservient to the dominant conception of Anglo-European philosophy.

With economic and military power increasingly shifting away from the West, it appears inevitable that there will be greater influence on the part of non-Western traditions. As the logician Graham Priest wrote at the beginning of the current century:

> China and India between them account for nearly half of the world's population. And China, at least, has the potential to develop very fast economically. Once the economies of these countries are fully capitalized, they will swamp the rest of the world, in the way that the US has in the second half of the twentieth century.
>
> So what will play a major role in philosophy in the twenty-first century? My guess: Asian philosophy.[17]

Within the next decade, some analysts predict that China will overtake the U.S. as the world's largest economy. Once this occurs, it may be only a matter of time before the asymmetry runs in the other direction.[18]

The harm of one-sidedness

Understanding any philosophy involves some degree of putting our own interests and aims into that philosophy. We always come to a text with prior assumptions about the nature of philosophy, religion, morality, and so on that shape our reading, focusing on the parts of it that seem most relevant to us, while ignoring others. The same principle holds for selection of texts. Philosophers read Aristotle's *Ethics* more than his biological works; religiously oriented philosophers read Aquinas more than others do. If our interests didn't shape our reading patterns, our time would be spent much less efficiently. Why should it be surprising that comparative philosophers begin with what is familiar to them?

Nor is using categories from our own tradition to interpret others necessarily a bad thing. As we saw in Chapter 2, conceptual translation is an important goal of comparative philosophy. If a philosophy from one culture can be put into the concepts of another, it shows that philosophy has some appeal beyond its original setting.[19] If Mozi can be understood as a utilitarian, and one who can speak to twenty-first-century Western philosophers, then there is something profound about Mozi.

The trouble arises when we use *only* external categories to interpret another culture's philosophy. Consider the experience of Kwasi Wiredu, who began learning philosophy as an undergraduate at a university in his native Ghana around the time of the country's independence from Britain. Since during that period African philosophy was taught in anthropology and religion departments, his philosophy courses consisted entirely of Western subject matter. Scholarship on African thought was written in French, German, and English, rather than African languages, and employed conceptual frameworks of European origin. Categories like secular and religious, natural and supernatural, spiritual and physical were the norm.

Not only did these European scholars misunderstand African thought and culture, but many African philosophers themselves began to believe in the misunderstandings:

> When African thought was approached with intellectual categories such as the ones just mentioned some quite lopsided results ensued.... Some of the findings of this sort of study of African thought that were, and still are, assiduously disseminated are that Africans see the world as being full of spiritual entities, that Africans are religious in all things, not even separating the secular from the religious, that African thought is, through and through, mystical, and so on. Some African philosophers have followed this way of talking of African thought quite cheerfully. One reason may be that in their academic training they may themselves have come to internalize such accounts of African thought so thoroughly that they have become part of the furniture of their minds.[20]

This story illustrates how the categories we use to understand a culture's philosophy can take hold so deeply that we do not even realize that they are outside impositions. These categories can be transmitted through our philosophical education, the very thing that is supposed to teach us to think critically and reflectively. According to Wiredu, those who accept outside categories to understand themselves have become *intellectually colonized*.

Here is a case—and perhaps there are others—where cross-cultural philosophy seems to have done more harm than good. Our understanding of African thought, Wiredu argues, would be better off without the categories of another culture. What is needed to understand African thought is not more interaction with outsiders, but rather a process of *de-colonization*.

When we rely solely on our own philosophical structures to interpret and evaluate a non-Western philosophy, we end up focusing only on the elements that fit within these structures. The result will be a deformed image of the other body of thought. Even when we filter the target philosophy through classifications like ethics, epistemology, metaphysics, etc., we may end up recreating that philosophy as a "phantom body" which exists only in our own minds. The other tradition will be considered strong in those aspects that match up with our own categories, but weak or irrelevant in those that do not.[21] The core of the tradition may be altogether missing.

One-sidedness is also bad for the dominant tradition. Imagine one of the students in your philosophy seminar is a lifelong devotee of a certain political or religious ideology; no matter what the topic at hand, they choose to interpret it in terms of that ideology. Not only would this be incredibly annoying to everyone else in the class, but you might feel a bit sorry for the student as well. Part of the pleasure and the interest of studying philosophy is that we may discover and explore previously unimagined ways of thinking. Even if comparison starts with what is already familiar to us, it should allow us in the end to go beyond ourselves.

When comparative philosophers only uncover in other cultures' texts what they knew beforehand, they deprive contemporary discussions of the full wealth of resources at hand. As Shun writes at the conclusion of his essay, "Chinese ethical traditions themselves have rich insights into the ethical experiences of human beings that are conveyed through concepts distinctive of these traditions. Viewing Chinese thought from the perspective of Western philosophical conceptions will not do full justice to these insights."[22] Ultimately, one-sided comparisons are bad for philosophy itself.

Avoiding one-sidedness

Regardless of whether much of past comparative philosophy has been one-sided, the question is how to avoid the effects of one-sidedness in our present comparisons. In getting to this goal, mere rhetoric about "genuine dialogue" or "openness to new ideas" is not going to be enough. Instead, we must employ specific methods that counteract our tendency to rest on what is already familiar. While each of the following strategies has its limitations, all of them force us to be less complacent in our reading of non-Western texts.

Contextualization

Interpretive projection and ignorance of context are mutually reinforcing. Since closer scrutiny of the other tradition usually shows that the projected categories do not map so easily onto it, the one-sided interpreter often ignores relevant historical and contextual details. If, on the other hand, we know nothing about the larger cultural and philosophical tradition that a particular text is part of, we will have little alternative but to impose our own background on that text. We will end up cherry-picking one or two quotes that seem to line up with what we already know, then conclude that we understand what the text is saying.

The most basic way to avoid superficial comparison is by gaining a thorough understanding of the philosophical setting in which a text was composed. What issue or issues is the text's author responding to, and why were those issues considered important during the period? What are the accepted methods for responding to these issues? What are the key terms in the debate, and how have these terms been used prior to the text's composition? Being a good interlocutor means trying to comprehend where the other party in the dialogue is coming from. Without the context, we won't understand the text.[23]

Philip J. Ivanhoe, a scholar of Chinese philosophy at Georgetown University, refers to this process as *reconstructing historical meaning*.

> [I]n order to understand the writings of a traditional Chinese thinker, I need to project myself empathetically into his point of view. Guided by what I find in the text and what I know about the surrounding culture, I imaginatively reconstruct the philosophical views of someone from the past. In the course of this process, I not only understand the propositions recorded in the text before me but also come to see and appreciate, to some degree, why someone might hold the particular views that I discover.[24]

The more we can project ourselves *into* the intellectual and cultural surroundings of a thinker, the less we will be projecting our own surroundings *onto* that thinker. Attaining this understanding of context is not a simple task. We will need to study not just the main texts written by the philosophers in question, but also the texts that influenced them, the cultural forces that shaped their interests, and the languages in which they wrote. Given the amount of work involved, it is much easier to make superficial pronouncements about similarities and differences.

Seeing how a classic text is understood within its own tradition can serve as a further check on projecting our assumptions onto it. Many of the great non-Western texts have spawned centuries of commentaries by later writers who were trying to unpack their meaning. When we read these secondary sources, we notice that the concepts and debates the commentators bring to bear on the texts in question are very different from the ones we do. We glimpse how their interests shift over time and realize the limited nature of our own reading of the text. A good commentator can be a valuable partner in our discussion, challenging our biases and encouraging us to deeper engagement with the philosophy in question. Several recently published editions of classical Chinese texts include selections from later commentators.

To be sure, it is possible to exaggerate the significance of a given text's historical and cultural background. Paying too much attention to context can lead us to miss out on important connections between philosophers who practiced their craft in different times and places. There is a trade-off between looking at the uniqueness of an individual thinker's context in our efforts to reconstruct historical meaning and focusing on the similarities necessary to get our comparison off the ground.[25] Still, contextualization is the single most important thing we can do to avoid projecting our own interests onto non-Western thinkers.

Differentiation

A second and related strategy is to consider how the general assumptions of the cultural tradition in which the text was written differ from our own. The most influential advocate of this approach in Chinese-Western comparison has been the duo of scholars named David L. Hall and Roger T. Ames. In their view, Chinese and Western cultures took different paths and critical moments, to the point that the art, politics, religion, and morality of each culture are quite distinct. However, because Western scholars are heirs to the European Enlightenment assumption of the universality of human reason, they have failed to notice these differences and distorted Chinese thought with foreign categories. To understand Chinese thought as it is, we must get rid of the concepts and theories that have become predominant in the Western philosophical tradition—"the useless lumber blocking the path to China."[26]

According to Hall and Ames, the translation of non-Western concepts into Western languages is a main source of projection. For example, translators of classical Chinese texts often use the word "Heaven" to render the character *tian* 天. The danger in this translation is that we will substitute our own culture's conception of "Heaven" whenever we read that word in our texts. If we have reason to believe that key terms do not have exact matches in English or other Western languages, then the best policy is to leave those terms untranslated, so that we are forced to understand them in their own right rather than settling for our own substitute. The original terms could then enter our philosophical lexicon, enriching the concepts we have at our disposal. In their translation of the *Analects*, Hall and Ames leave the term *tian* as it is rather than settling for an English equivalent.

Yet when we think Chinese philosophy is so different from the Western kind that any concepts, methods, or values associated with the latter cannot be applied to the former, it seems that we are still taking Western philosophy as our basic point of reference. Categories are as significant for what they exclude as for what they include. If we say that whatever *tian* may be, it is not at all like the Christian concept of "Heaven," aren't we still using the Western concept as our standard for measuring the Chinese one?

Nor do we always understand a thinker's point of view in the fullest sense possible by placing them within the particularities of context or culture. Historical and cultural distance can sometimes help us understand things in a way that proximity cannot.[27] Comparing thinkers from disparate settings will necessarily involve looking beyond these settings to find common ground.

Yet if Hall and Ames are correct in their opinion that there are vast differences in outlook between China and the West, then it is hard to see how the similarities we discover will be anything other than superficial. We will take a look at the evidence for broad cultural differences in the next chapter.

Bridge concepts

A third strategy is to try to set up the conversation in neutral terms, using a vocabulary that is independent of either tradition. Aaron Stalnaker of Indiana University has defended the use of "bridge concepts": general terms—such as "person," "virtue," or "human nature"—that are used to guide and ground our discussion of culturally distinct philosophies without projecting a foreign vocabulary onto one of them. These terms would allow us a neutral framework for the conversation to take place.

Picking bridge concepts is something of an art. Stalnaker argues that a concept like "person" is better than one such as "self," since in using the latter term, it is hard to avoid projecting a distinction between self and others that may not be applicable to the other tradition. Terms like "subject" or "agent" are also laden with modern connotations. Since the main risk of bringing culturally diverse philosophies into a shared framework is "to obscure or confuse differences," when we pick our bridge concepts "we should strive to take nothing for granted that may be at issue between the two, and in general to be as spare as possible."[28]

Do bridge concepts solve the problem of one-sidedness? Skeptics have pointed out that in picking terms like "virtue" or "human nature" to frame our comparison, we may already be importing a host of connotations from Western philosophy. Could the corresponding terms in Chinese, *de* 德 and *renxing* 人性, respectively, be used as bridge concepts? Wouldn't it feel as if we were already incorporating some specific content into our discussion?[29] If so, it may be wishful thinking to suppose that the English-language terms are neutral.

This criticism may hold the concepts in question to an unreasonable standard, however. The goal is to be "as spare as possible," not to attain complete neutrality. What is more, as we have to start the bridge from our side, general terms drawn from the Chinese language may be of little help to us in initiating the comparison.

Family resemblance, again

Don't forget about family resemblance! In Chapter 1, we discussed the idea that we might avoid projecting a narrow notion of philosophy onto other traditions by treating "philosophy" as a family resemblance concept. We assume that there is no single feature that makes a given practice philosophy, but rather various overlapping sets of features that are found in different traditions. These "family resemblances" form a basis for comparison without making philosophy into just one thing.

Lin Ma and Jaap van Brakel argue in their recent book on the foundations of cross-cultural philosophy we should assume that *all* the concepts involved in interpretation are family resemblance concepts. When we study concepts from another cultural tradition, we need to avoid thinking that these concepts have fixed meanings and obvious translations into English.[30] We should also look at our own concepts as vague and open-ended with respect to their definitions and how we might use them.[31] When we compare our concepts and theirs, the goal is not to determine whether they are "the same" or "different," but instead to look for features of the concepts that overlap.

For example, when we take our concept of "emotion" and compare it with the classical Chinese concept of *qing* 情, we should not assume that "emotion" is a human universal and *qing* is merely the corresponding Chinese label for this concept.[32] Even within Western philosophy, the concept of "emotion" does not mean just one thing, but rather has a range of features that have shifted over time or according to the philosopher in question. When we study classical texts in which the character *qing* appears, we find that it too has numerous meanings. When we compare "emotion" and *qing*, we extend certain features of the one concept to include certain features of the other. Ma and van Brakel argue that the family resemblance approach is a central means for avoiding distortion in comparative philosophy.

Dual and reverse interpretation

So far we have been assuming that interpreter is on one side looking at the other, but suppose they are equally at home in both cultures. In that case, they will not be forced to use one or the other as the standard against which to judge the other, but rather will be able to move back and forth between the two. Such *dual interpretation* could result in a more balanced picture of the philosophies being compared.

Jiyuan Yu, best known for his comparative studies of Aristotle and Confucius, has defended this approach. The whole notion of "one-sidedness," he argues, is incoherent. Since in every tradition there is controversy about how to interpret key thinkers and texts in that tradition's history, it is not as if there is one settled understanding of Aristotle by which we might understand a thinker like Confucius, or vice versa. Instead of using one as a preestablished framework for understanding the other, we should employ them as "mirrors" for each other. Doing so can help us to make sense of both philosophers.[33]

Consider Aristotle's claim in the *Nicomachean Ethics* that virtue is a mean between two extremes: courage is a mean between the excessive fear of the coward and the deficient fear of the rash person, temperance between feeling too much pleasure and too little, and so on. Though most philosophy students are familiar with this idea, it is surprisingly difficult to explain what Aristotle is getting at. He says the mean is not the exact middle, and that it is "relative to us"; his discussion of courage also leads us to believe that this virtue is not really a mean at all, but rather a matter of feeling the right amount of fear in the given situation. Because of these ambiguities, some contemporary philosophers have claimed that the mean is the weakest part of Aristotle's ethics. Yet since it is the central part, it is hard to get rid of it.

As it happens, Confucius also claims that virtue is a mean. In the *Analects* he speaks (at least in one translation!) of "Acquiring Virtue by applying the mean," and the "Doctrine of the Mean" (*Zhongyong* 中庸) is a central text in the Confucian tradition. As with Aristotle, however, contemporary interpreters of the Confucian mean have found the idea to be lacking in substance.

Comparing the two thinkers allows us to ask questions of each thinker that would otherwise elude us. Aristotle could have approached the mean the way Confucius did, but he did not—why not? A feature of one account that we have never noticed before may strike us afresh when we see it present in the other. For instance, Yu notices that both Aristotle and Confucius use the metaphor of an archer hitting a target in describing their respective conceptions of virtue. This common theme gives him a crucial clue for reconstructing each thinker's view.

Some may claim that introducing Confucius into the discussion needlessly complicates the issue of interpreting Aristotle, since now we have two difficult thinkers to explain rather than one. Others have contended that the method has a tendency to slide into one-sidedness, pointing out that comparisons of Confucius and Aristotle often seem to result in the conclusion that something is lacking in the Chinese thinker. Still, its proponents argue that the approach has not only led to novel insights about each thinker, but also generated interest in approaching the subject of virtue ethics from a Chinese-Western perspective. For thinkers who have been read for centuries within their own traditions, the "mirror" approach can open up new territory.

A more radical cure for one-sidedness is a kind of "reverse interpretation" in which we intentionally employ categories from the less dominant tradition to understand the more dominant one. Jay Garfield uses the Cittamātra school of Indian philosophy to interpret Western varieties of idealism such as those found in Berkeley, Kant, and Schopenhauer. He argues that each of the three thinkers can be viewed as a particular stage of idealism as envisioned by the fourth-century CE Buddhist philosopher Vasubandhu.

Perhaps because it requires an already extensive knowledge of the target tradition, comparative philosophers on the Western side have employed reverse interpretation very rarely. Yet as Garfield reminds us, one condition of genuine conversation between philosophical traditions is "taking seriously one's own tradition not as a lens through which to view another's, but also as specimen under one's colleague's lens."[34] If it sounds strange to us to hear canonical Western thinkers classified according to whether they view phenomena in terms of *parikalpita-svabhāva*, *paratantra-svabhāva*, or *paranispanna-svabhāva*, it is only because we have become used to thinking of Western categories as preeminent. For your next assignment, try explaining Plato's theory of *yin* and *yang*![35]

Beyond "East-West" comparisons

A final way of avoiding comparisons that privilege Western philosophy is to leave Western philosophy out of the comparison. What about comparisons between Chinese and Indian philosophy, or thinkers and texts from Asia and Africa or Latin America? Dialogue between different traditions in the global South and East can help counter the unequal concentration of cultural, economic, and military power in Western countries.[36]

Comparing two non-Western traditions also helps us see ways in which philosophy may be expanded beyond the Western tradition. Studying African and Chinese philosophy together, for example, may show the fundamental importance of community in human life, in contrast to contemporary Western ethical systems that focus on individual rights. As Daniel A. Bell and Thaddeus Metz ask in a study comparing Chinese Confucianism with the African value of Ubuntu, "What if it turned out that two major non-Western traditions, together comprised of more than two billion people, have more in common than either has with the liberal tradition? What if it turned out that many more people in the world actually adhere to such 'non-Western' values?"[37] Such a comparison might not only lead us to underappreciated ideas and arguments, but also new approaches to philosophical dialogue.[38]

In a recent exploration of Sino-African comparisons, Paul Dottin notes that while there has been a remarkable growth in political and economic interaction between China and Africa, philosophical comparisons between the two regions have maintained a fairly small presence in comparative philosophy. While scholars have discussed topics such as "personhood" and "community," there are still many additional philosophical topics to be explored as well as a number of different traditions in China and Africa that merit engagement. Like Bell and Metz, Dottin thinks comparison between the two regions may show that Chinese and African philosophy may have more in common with each other than either has with Western philosophy.[39]

While comparative philosophers have always tried to be at the forefront of cross-cultural exchanges of ideas, East-South and South-South comparisons remain largely unexplored. As one scholar writes, "The radicalization of comparative philosophy requires dispensing with de facto conceptualizations of this subfield as consisting of 'philosophy: East meets West.' ... There are a plethora of cultures, philosophical schools, and wisdom traditions throughout the global South awaiting comparison and investigation."[40] If we are serious about moving beyond the one-sidedness that has continued to plague cross-cultural philosophy, we should embrace these comparisons.

Some reflection

Projection is often the result of arrogance or indifference. The other culture's philosophy is used merely as a means to advance one's own philosophical agenda, without any regard for anything new and different it might contribute. A problem with conversation in general is that some people want to do all the talking and none of the listening.

Still, the projection error can affect even well-intentioned students of other cultural traditions. Our own presuppositions about philosophy can be so engrained that we unwittingly transfer them onto others. In doing so, we may be lulled into the belief that we have actually understood other cultures' philosophies, when in fact we have just remade them in our own image. Because the projection error is so insidious, as a final exercise it's worth reviewing some main areas in which it may occur.[41]

Classifications. What are the main ways we divide up other cultures' philosophies? Comparative philosophers tend to use predominantly Western categories like epistemology, ethics, metaphysics, logic, aesthetics, philosophy of mind, etc., to characterize non-Western thought (not to mention, as we saw in Chapter 1, the category of "philosophy" itself). The same goes for competing theories within these categories, so that we end up discussing whether Buddhist ethics is best classified as deontological or consequentialist, or whether the Chinese view of mind is best understood as dualist or materialist. While the use of the terms themselves is not necessarily problematic, if we are too inflexible in our understanding of what they mean, we may be guilty of the projection error.

Concepts. Another mode of projection involves unconsciously imposing one's concepts on others. When this happens, we will not be comparing two culturally distinct philosophies, but rather our own culture's views with a projection of those very same views. This is especially worrisome when we read texts from other cultures in translation. As Hall and Ames write, "To settle upon an English equivalent for each major concept and then pursue the analysis through the equivalent rather than the original term is unquestionably the most problematic methodological pitfall of Western interpreters of Chinese philosophy.?[42]

We need to constantly remind ourselves that the translation we are reading is a kind of image that has been set up by the translator. Schopenhauer himself was working with a nineteenth-century Latin translation of an incomplete seventeenth-century Persian translation of the *Upanishads*, originally written in Sanskrit in the first millennium BCE—an image of a partial image. Don't mistake the translation for the real thing.

Methods. It's also tempting to transfer our preferred methods of philosophy onto other texts. For philosophy students in Western classrooms, the paradigm example of a philosopher is Socrates: someone who does philosophy by subjecting his interlocutors' beliefs as well as his own to careful examination. We may transpose this image of philosophy onto other cultures, considering non-Western texts that do not proceed by Socratic *elenchus* to be less philosophical. But as we saw in the last chapter, there may be other means of judging whether a philosophy is successful.

Ways of reading. We may even project our ways of reading a work of philosophy onto works from other cultures. The traditional Chinese way of engaging with the Confucian Four Books was through a long process of memorization and recitation. Students began at the age of seven and continued a basic course of study for the next eight years. Then they would proceed through an increasingly difficult series of examinations that tested their knowledge of these texts and the associated commentaries.[43] Think of how differently students in many Western classrooms read these texts today, usually over the course of a single college semester, once the whole way through if they have the time, discussing their philosophical merits as they go. We should not assume that great works of philosophy are always read this way.

Ways of writing. Our ways of writing philosophy also contain certain presuppositions that we can unthinkingly transfer onto the target tradition. Today the dominant written form is the academic essay, a vehicle for expressing one's original ideas about a text backed up by appropriate evidence. The essay is largely a European invention, first developed by sixteenth- and seventeenth-century philosophers such as Montaigne, Erasmus, and Bacon. The form it replaced, the *commentary*, is much more ancient and varied in its origins, with vast traditions surrounding prominent texts in China, India, and other parts of the world (including Europe). Classical commentators had different assumptions than our own, believing that the texts in question contained comprehensive knowledge of the world around them, and that their main task was to unpack and apply this knowledge.[44] The academic essay is a unique way of interacting with a text that embodies a whole set of modern assumptions.

Purpose. Are we studying philosophy from another tradition for the same purpose that members of that tradition would have pursued it? Perhaps we are looking for knowledge of different cultural worldviews, or alternative ways of thinking about some important contemporary philosophical issue, whereas the member of that tradition may pursue philosophy for the sake of self-cultivation or spiritual enlightenment or political progress. It is always worth considering how this difference in purpose affects our understanding of the text we are reading. Are we missing the things that would have mattered most to the original students of the philosophy in question?[45]

This list is just a start. If it is true that our own absolute presuppositions are often invisible to us, then there are probably forms of projection that we have yet to recognize as such. What are they? (If you come up with anything significant, let me know and I'll add it to the next edition of this book.)

Conclusion

In one memorable episode of *Star Trek*, the Borg attack a Starfleet ship. As the ship's technology begins to go haywire due to Borg hackers, a crew member curses the fact that the Borg are so adaptable. Another finds time to respond with a bit of wisdom: "The Borg adapt their environment to suit their needs. True adaptability involves changing oneself to suit their environment."

Mastering comparative philosophy will mean moving from Borg-style adaptability to the genuine kind. While none of the above strategies will serve as a total cure, we can at least see the kind of balancing act a solution must engage in. It must offer some initial basis for recognizing enough similarity between ourselves and others to get the comparison off the ground, yet at the same time give us some means for engaging with what is new and different. Properly done comparison should take us from one place to another, building a bridge or fusing horizons or whatever the appropriate metaphor may be. The problem of one-sidedness is not an argument for the abandonment of comparative philosophy, but rather for doing it in the right sort of way.

7

Generalization

Many comparisons include broad characterizations of the culture and philosophical tradition in which a work was produced. These general statements provide a background against which we can make more refined statements about the work in question, helping us to see the "big picture" beyond all the details, and serving as a kind of barrier against our tendency to force our own assumptions about philosophy onto the text.[1] Since the projection error is so pervasive, it is dangerous to proceed without first taking stock of basic differences between our ways of thinking and theirs.

Yet generalizations about other cultures and their philosophical traditions can also be a source of misunderstanding. As one scholar writes, "Perhaps the greatest obstacle to descriptive adequacy, whether in teaching or in life, is the desire to summarize the essence of a culture in a pithy way."[2] Comparison *between* previously isolated cultures and philosophical traditions necessarily involves some leveling out of differences *within* those cultures and traditions. When we rely on generalizations, we miss out on a culture's internal complexity; we also may end up simplifying our own culture as an imagined contrast to it. Some authors have argued that we should resist generalizations in comparative philosophy, or even that the aim of comparison is to challenge generalizations wherever we find them.

Are generalizations a help or hindrance in comparative philosophy? Can we generalize at all about things as sophisticated and diverse as cultures and culturally bound philosophies? What evidence makes a generalization accurate or inaccurate? Since generalizations abound not just in comparative philosophy, but in broader areas of discourse that inform our understanding of culture, we need to be prepared to assess them when we come across them. In this chapter, we will look at several of the main generalizations that show up in cross-cultural comparisons, as well as consider the issue of generalization in its own right. We will also examine the role of evidence from the social sciences in the comparing of culturally distinct philosophical traditions.

Cultural essentialism

To begin, it is useful to consider the extreme case of holistic representations of culture. *Cultural essentialism* is the belief that some quality is possessed by every member of a culture, is unique to that culture, and that it exists independently of its particular instances.[3] If a person is Chinese, the essentialist believes that there is some eternal and unchanging feature, "Chinese-ness," which necessarily attaches to that person and distinguishes them by nature from other human beings.

Essentialist rhetoric often features prominently in wider political discussions of cultural conflict in the contemporary world. Training in comparative methodology can help us to recognize such discourse and look at it with a critical eye. Because cultural generalizations can easily slide into essentialist views of ourselves and others when they become entrenched in the public imagination, defenders of the role of generalization in comparative philosophy want to carefully distinguish between the two practices.

The problem of essentialism

A thing's essence is "what it is to be" that thing. One of the first usages of the concept occurs in Plato's *Euthyphro*, which details a meeting outside the Athenian court of law between Socrates, who is there to answer charges of impiety and corrupting the youth, and the title-character, who is prosecuting his father for the death of one of his servants. Their conversation quickly turns to the issue of piety, with Euthyphro claiming that what is pious is precisely what he is now doing, namely, taking his own father to task for his wrongdoing. Socrates is not interested in examples of piety, however, but in what the thing itself is:

> I did not bid you tell me one or two of the many pious actions but that form itself which makes all the pious actions pious.... Tell me then what this form itself is, so that I may look upon it, and using it as a model, say that any action of yours or another's that is of that kind is pious, and if it is not, that it is not.[4]

As Socrates conceives it, the form or essence of piety is something to be explained independently of its instances, a standard to which we can look to judge whether someone has acted piously in a particular case. In subsequent dialogues like the *Phaedo* and *Republic*, Plato held that a thing's essence exists apart from the physical world, eternal and unchanging.

Now suppose the subject of the *Euthyphro* were not piety or one of the virtues, but instead some cultural feature, like "Chinese-ness" or "African-ness" or "Western-ness." Socrates asks Euthyphro not to point out one or two examples of a Chinese person, but rather to tell him what the form of Chinese is, above and beyond any of its instances. Well, what is it to be Chinese?

Some prominent figures have claimed that there are defining features of such cultural groupings. In a widely read 1994 interview with the magazine *Foreign Affairs*, Lee Kuan Yew, the former prime minister of Singapore, claimed that East Asian societies are distinguished by the values of self-cultivation and family. As Lee said, "We have a whole people immersed in these beliefs.... It is the basic concept of our civilization. Governments will come, governments will go, but this endures."[5] Like one of Plato's Forms, these cultural values appear to hover above the ever-changing visible world.

A main problem with attributing essences to items like cultures is that doing so neglects the diversity present within any society. Just as Socrates invokes the form of piety as a standard by which to measure particular cases, cultural essences can be used to exclude members of a society who do not fit the given definition. If a person has little regard for the values Lee mentions, do they not count as fully East Asian? Essentialism also marks off the culture in question from the rest of humanity: Chinese-ness as opposed to all that is non-Chinese, East Asian as distinguished from non-East Asian. Think of Rudyard Kipling's well-known couplet: "East is East, and West is West, and never the twain shall meet." Are "East" and "West" really like Even and Odd? Are the values of family and self-cultivation unique to East Asian societies?

Essentialism in regard to non-Western cultures often reflects the legacy of colonialism. Rajeev Bhargava reminds us that it is often the case that when one group encounters another, it "sees them only as an undifferentiated mass, through a crude stereotype, as if they are all the same, each merely instantiating the broad features shared equally by all."[6] This focus on group identity rather than individuality becomes a means by which colonial powers strip indigenous cultures of self-determination.

Cultures are not fixed and unchanging entities, but transient human constructions. As one critic puts it, "Essentialist pictures of culture represent 'cultures' as if they were natural givens, entities that existed neatly distinct and separate in the world, entirely independent of our projects of distinguishing them."[7] Cultural essentialism is a close relative of essentialism with respect to race or gender, where categories such as "black" and "white," "masculine" and "feminine" are treated as part of the structure of the universe.

Essentialist views of culture are often hidden in the language we use to refer to different groups. The historian of cross-cultural philosophy J.J. Clarke warns that "Crucial terms such as 'East', 'Orient', and 'West' become devices for reducing endless complexities and diversities into manageable and falsifying unities."[8] Virtually none of the important figures in the history of philosophy have thought of themselves as "Eastern" philosophers or "Western" philosophers. Though phrases like "Eastern philosophy," "the Western imagination," or "the Chinese mind" are still employed today, they are usually constructs on the part of scholars standing at a distance.

A case study: the clash of civilizations

When cultures are treated as entities in their own right, unattached to a particular time and place, the tendency is to see them as locked in eternal struggle, battling one another for cosmic dominance. The stark picture of global reality that results is best exemplified in "The Clash of Civilizations?", an influential essay published in 1993 by the American political scientist Samuel P. Huntington (it was later turned into a book, which dropped the question mark from the title).

Huntington argues that we are entering a new era of world history, in which the important dividing lines between groups of human beings will be based not on nationality, politics, or economics, but rather on culture. The largest units of cultural grouping are civilizations, with the Western, Confucian, Japanese, Islamic, Hindu, Slavic, Latin American, and African being the most prominent examples. Huntington's most important claim is about the boundaries between these groups:

[D]ifferences among civilizations are not only real; they are basic. Civilizations are differentiated from each other by history, language, culture, tradition and, most important, religion.... These differences are the product of centuries. They will not soon disappear. They are far more fundamental than differences among political ideologies and political regimes.[9]

Past conflicts have occurred primarily within civilizations. In the West, power struggles between princes gave way to those among nation-states, and the latter to those between competing political ideologies. But the conflicts of the future, Huntington predicts, will occur "along the cultural fault lines separating these civilizations from one another." Since Western values—liberty, equality, human rights, and separation of Church and State—are fundamentally distinct from those which hold sway in non-Western civilizations, the primary struggle will be between "the West and the rest."

After the 9/11 terrorist attacks on the United States, it became fashionable to speak about the clash as one between the West and Islam in particular. In a conflict which Huntington claims goes as far back as 1,300 years, the West is taken to represent freedom and progress while Islam is depicted as embodying authoritarianism and social inequality. Those who questioned this picture were often accused of a misplaced political correctness or of being complicit in the oppression that takes place in certain Muslim societies.

Nonetheless, one may challenge the "Clash of Civilizations" thesis on a purely descriptive level. Opponents of the thesis point out that it treats civilizations which encompass billions of people as if they were monolithic entities, portrays recently emerging features of certain societies as products of transcendent ancient roots, and considers principles important for human life in general as confined to isolated regions of the globe.[10] When we are unsympathetic to members of another culture, we tend to reduce them to a discrete set of characteristics. Any unjust practices in the other society strike us as reflective of all its members, whereas similar practices in our own society seem to us to be merely accidental.[11]

These points are perhaps less likely to make their way into the public imagination. Nonetheless, critique of essentialism can be a valuable critical tool for deflating narratives of "us vs. them." Just as philosophy in general can train us to recognize the false dichotomies and straw man arguments that often inform political discourse, comparative philosophy can nurture in us a healthy skepticism of the rhetoric of cultural opposition. The ability to recognize the trappings of essentialist discourse is today an important skill.

The generalizations debate

General statements about a culture are weaker than essentialist ones. The claim that "Generally speaking, Chinese culture has a special place for familial relationships" is not intended to be true of every Chinese person, or to imply that no other culture holds the family in high regard. Comparativists who engage in such claims are motivated by the desire to understand other cultures and engage them in dialogue, rather than to perpetuate the idea that we are in conflict with them.[12] Essentialism aside, isn't there a place for informed and responsible generalizations in comparative philosophy?

Given how quickly they can take hold among scholars and the wider public alike, it is important that we weigh the arguments for and against the use of cultural generalizations carefully. Since prominent comparative philosophers have disagreed on this subject, we will begin by looking at the arguments on either side.

The case for generalizations

If you pick up one of the many books aimed at training today's global business leaders, you will find statements like the following:

American business-people focus on business targets and goals rather than personal relationships with their counterparts, whereas Chinese business-people will want to develop a personal relationship before they develop a business relationship.[13]

Indian employees are easily trained and very attentive. Indian culture is very hierarchical with the group playing a very strong role.[14]

In Middle Eastern countries, business revolves around their religion—Islam. Islam affects their culture, how women are perceived in business, what the proper clothing is for business, and many other business rules.[15]

These cultural generalizations are meant to help readers avoid mistakes and miscommunications that hinder cross-cultural interaction. Since such errors most often occur when we assume that our own beliefs and practices are universal, an obvious remedy is to grasp those respects in which another culture's basic orientation differs from ours.

While staying at a hostel in Kyoto, Thomas Kasulis found himself entangled in a dispute between a Japanese man and an American couple caused by the behavior of the couple's eighteenth-month-old child. Seeing the child transfixed by his wristwatch, the man had taken it off his wrist to let her play with it; but the child suddenly flung it at the wall, breaking it into pieces. The man expected the parents to apologize on behalf of the child and perhaps offer to pay for the watch. The parents, however, blamed the man for not telling their daughter to stop when she was swinging the watch. Should well-raised children, he retorted, need to be told not to throw watches against walls? By the time Kasulis arrived, everyone was upset.

Hearing what had happened, he tried to explain to each side the different child-rearing customs in Japan and America. Japanese mothers tend to carry their children along with them on their backs. Consequently, these children experience firsthand how their mothers respond to lots of different situations and learn to imitate them. American children in turn are usually left to explore the world freely on their own until someone tells them "no!"

Despite his efforts, each party in the conversation continued to believe that the other was in the wrong. What struck Kasulis, who later became a scholar of comparative studies at Ohio State University, was that each side was missing the bigger picture behind the other side's behavior, failing to see how the different reactions fit into broader cultural values such as personal responsibility and obedience to rules on the one hand, situational responsiveness and intuitive learning on the other. As he writes at the beginning of his book *Intimacy or Integrity: Philosophy and Cultural Difference*, "This recognition led me to the unsettling conclusion that if I were, for example, to teach my American students about Japanese culture, I somehow had to compare *all* of American and *all* of Japanese culture."[16]

Without a holistic appreciation of another culture, we cannot begin to organize our experience of that culture. In isolation from the larger picture, the smaller details lose their meaning, appearing to us as senseless. Generalizations about our own culture can also help us to take stock of the assumptions we bring to our encounters with others. If I know that leaving one's children to freely explore their environments is a tendency particular to American parenting, then I will be more careful about judging other cultures in this light.

A similar argument can be extended to philosophical interactions. Generalizations about the culture and tradition in which a work of philosophy originated remind us that we are on unfamiliar ground—that we should tread cautiously, and not force our presuppositions on the text. Without a picture of the culture at large, we will end up in the same position as a traveling businessperson who, assuming everyone is like themselves, inflicts one transgression after another upon their hosts.

David Hall and Roger Ames have been instrumental in drawing comparative philosophers' attention to the necessity of taking stock of cultural assumptions. As discussed in the last chapter, they contend that the basic premises of the Chinese and Western philosophical traditions run counter to one another. At the outset of their influential book on the *Analects*, they write that "[t]he primary defect of the majority of Confucius' interpreters ... has been the failure to search out and articulate those distinctive presuppositions which have dominated the Chinese tradition."[17] Whereas Western philosophers tend to focus on substances (that is, individual things) and attributes (properties of individual things), Chinese philosophers see events and processes as primary. The emphasis on events rather than things in Chinese philosophy entails a different vision of the cosmos, in which reality is ordered through the "creation of novel patterns" rather than by means of a fixed order of being imposed by a transcendent God.[18] Only when we understand these presuppositions, Hall and Ames maintain, will we be capable of grasping Confucius' teachings.

To be sure, the presuppositions are not explicitly contained in Confucius' text. But neither were the presuppositions of American child-rearing immediately evident in the behavior of the parents and child in Kasulis' story—this absence is what made the behavior so prone to misinterpretation on the part of an outside observer. But in either case, the background assumptions can be uncovered through a careful and thorough examination of the surrounding cultural tradition. Without the guidance of a general understanding of the target culture or philosophical tradition, we will end up imposing our own conceptual framework upon the details we observe.[19]

Against generalizations

The most prominent objection to the use of generalizations in comparative philosophy is that cultural entities such as "China" or "the West" are simply too complex and diverse for meaningful generalizations to be drawn. Thinking of just the population of students at my relatively small American university, mostly eighteen to twenty-two-year-olds who grew up within a few hours of the Pocono Mountains, I notice significant dissimilarities between students from New Jersey and those from Pennsylvania, those from cities such as Philadelphia or Newark and those who grew up in rural areas, those whose parents attended universities and those who are first-generation college students. If someone were to ask me about the basic values and assumptions of the students at my university, I would say that it depends on which ones we are talking about.

The larger the scope of the generalization, the more compelling the objection from internal diversity. As the historian Paul Goldin writes, "If there is one valid generalization about China, it is that China defies generalization. Chinese civilization is simply too huge, too diverse, and too old for neat maxims."[20] Another critic challenges the existence of "Asian values":

> Asia is a huge and exceptionally diverse landmass, encompassing much of the world's population. It hosts a number of religions, such as Islam, Hinduism, Buddhism, Confucianism, Taoism, Christianity, and Judaism, as well as a myriad of races, ethnicities, customs, and languages. The assumption that Asia has its own cultural essence fundamentally different from that of the West is, to say the least, dubious.[21]

We could easily say the same thing about other regions of the world. Africa is roughly equal in size to the continental United States, Europe, India, and China combined. In Nigeria alone, there are more than 250 ethnic groups and over 500 indigenous languages. For every generalization about such cultural groupings, there will be countless counterexamples.

We can expect just as much, and possibly more, diversity among the philosophers within a given culture. "Western philosophy" contains countless philosophical systems, many of them extraordinarily intricate—think of Spinoza's *Ethics* or Wittgenstein's *Tractatus*. These systems disagree with one another about even the fundamentals; if one philosopher takes some premise for granted, you can be sure that there are others who vigorously dispute that premise. Aristotle thought the Principle of Non-Contradiction is fundamental, but contemporary logicians such as Graham Priest have challenged this principle. Descartes argued that "I am, I exist" is the most certain thing of all, whereas later thinkers like Hume and Nietzsche criticized him for smuggling in the notion of a unitary "I." While some prominent Western metaphysicians have divided the world into substances and their attributes, others have seen processes as the primary ingredients of reality.

When everything is open to dispute, it is difficult to mark off the "distinctive presuppositions" of the Western tradition. In trying to force these thinkers and texts into a single cultural or philosophical framework, we may miss out on what made their claims unique and powerful at the time they were written.[22] An administrative assistant at my graduate department used to say that getting a bunch of philosophers to agree on anything was "like herding cats."

While claiming to prevent us from projecting our own presuppositions onto another culture or philosophical tradition, generalizations often seem to involve their own kind of projection. If some feature is thought to be definitive of Western philosophy, the other culture's philosophy is seen as possessing the opposite feature. This "projection in reverse" is just as bad as the usual kind. As Goldin puts it:

> What is wrong with declaring...that China has no capitalism, or monotheism, or epic poetry, or science, or human rights, or democracy, or creation *ex nihilo* is not just that most of these phenomena *can* be found, in their own way, in Chinese sources; rather, what is most wrong is that this mode of inquiry prevents China from being anything more than a pallid reflection of the West.[23]

When we dislike certain features of our own culture—its rampant individualism, its antagonism toward the natural world, its lack of spirituality—we are prone to see other cultures' worldviews as happy inversions of our own. If the predominant philosophy strikes us as overly theoretical and argumentative, then we may view philosophy in other parts of the world as more down-to-earth and intuitive. In that case, we will understand Chinese or Indian or African philosophy not on its own terms, but rather as a "myth of the Other, a symbol of difference, the imaginary foil to whatever the West is supposed to be."[24]

It is not enough to avoid cultural generalizations, the opponents argue; rather, we must try to dismantle them if we are to make any progress in our understanding of other cultures. Clichés about distant philosophies are barriers to real communication, and need to be dismantled before such communication can take place.[25]

Weighing the debate

Some philosophers have thought that successful interpretation relies on a "hermeneutic circle," in which we understand an object by understanding the greater whole of which it is part, and we understand the greater whole in light of its component parts. Reading a particular paragraph of a philosophy book requires an understanding of what the whole book is saying, but we cannot understand what the whole book is saying apart from any of its paragraphs. Progress in understanding depends on a reciprocal relationship between the whole and the part; the more we understand this paragraph, the more we will understand the whole book, and vice versa.

In the same way, broad statements about background presuppositions can help frame our initial understanding of philosophical texts from other cultures. But the more we read of the text, the more things we might notice which challenge the picture with which we started, causing us to refine it. We advance as we move back and forth between a general view of a culture's philosophy and a close reading of the texts that comprise it. Understood this way, there may be hope that the conflict about generalizations is not as stark as it appears.

The descriptive value of a generalization may also depend on our proximity to the target culture. For someone completely unfamiliar with another society, the general picture may be the necessary point of entry. Yet the same picture would seem inadequate for the person who is immersed in its beliefs and practices.

Nonetheless, the critics argue that generalizations about cultural differences tend to be self-fulfilling. If we start from the idea that these differences are present, we will tend to end with this idea after we have examined the textual evidence. What we need is some consideration of the conditions under which a particular generalization should be revised or abandoned.

Generalizations and evidence

While generalizations are fairly common in comparative philosophy, there has not been much extended discussion of what counts as evidence for or against such statements. In this section, we will look at two distinct kinds of evidence that might be used to support generalizations about different cultures' philosophies, as well as how this evidence has been used in particular cases.

Evidence from philosophical texts

One of the most frequently encountered generalizations is that Eastern philosophers look at things in a more harmonious manner than their Western counterparts. As *The Complete Idiot's Guide to Eastern Philosophy* explains it, "In general, Eastern philosophy is holistic, looking at reality as a unified oneness in a constant state of flux. The purpose of its teaching is to promote harmony within the unified whole."[26] This characterization has seeped into popular culture, appearing everywhere from a *Time* magazine cover story to Star Wars discussion threads. Western philosophers in turn are said to be obsessed with positing dualities and divisions between things. The holism/dualism generalization has many incarnations, used to explain not only differences in metaphysics but also in practical matters relating to the environment, medical treatment, and political and economic systems.

One means of assessing such generalizations is to look at the philosophical texts produced within the cultures in question. We can make a case for our general understanding of a cultural tradition in the same way as we would for any of these texts on its own. We think about how well the particular things we have read fit into our interpretation of the whole, considering whether this interpretation is more coherent, comprehensive, and compelling than its alternatives. The "case" we put together is much like one that might be offered in a court of law.[27] Given the available textual evidence, what is the most convincing interpretation we can offer?

With items as large as cultures, however, there will always be counterexamples to whatever account we can give. How should we treat these instances? Hall and Ames maintain that while it is important to be attuned to the internal complexity of a culture, we should not become "lost in the details":

> As important as such details are when performing analyses of this or that aspect of a society or culture, comparativists will be prevented from making sense of a culture if they do not diligently avoid the Fallacy of the Counterexample. After all, generalizations concerning cultural importances are often vindicated, not falsified, by resort to counterexamples precisely to the extent that such examples suggest the relative absence of a particular belief or doctrine.[28]

As mentioned earlier, generalizations are weaker than universal statements. "All Americans are ignorant of the world around them" is easier to refute than "In general, Americans are ignorant of the world around them." Whereas a single counterexample would be enough to falsify the first statement, the "in general" qualifier in the second one already concedes that there are counterexamples.[29]

Yet the danger of downplaying the significance of counterexamples is that any exceptions to the cultural norm will get ignored at the expense of the rule. A prominent version of the holism/dualism generalization contrasts the spirituality and mysticism found in Indian culture with the reason-based approaches that dominate Western intellectual life. But this portrait excludes important elements of Indian heritage, such as the development of mathematics, invention of games like chess, or interest in statecraft. It also glosses over important exceptions within philosophy, such as the atheism of schools like the Carvaka, or the Buddha's agnosticism.[30] The trouble with the generalization is not what it includes—Indian philosophy and culture does possess plenty of what we might characterize as "mysticism"—but what it leaves out.

Without attention to contrary evidence, the generalizations may quickly become detached from concrete reality. In Chinese-Western comparisons, a widespread version of the "Eastern harmony/Western duality" generalization contends that while Western philosophers treat mind and body as radically distinct, Chinese philosophers conceive of their relationship in a more unified way:

> In the Western tradition the body usually figures in philosophy in terms of its dualistic opposition to the mind or the soul, as matter set against spirit. The Chinese, in contrast, accepted that the mind was part of the body.[31]
>
> [T]he correlative relationship between the psychical and the somatic militated against the emergence of a mind/body problem [in the classical Chinese tradition]. It was not that the Chinese thinkers were able to "reconcile" this dichotomy; rather, it did not arise.[32]
>
> How do we compare athletics or physical self-cultivation between a tradition [i.e. the classical Chinese one] that is monistic in the sense that body, mind, and spirit form a continuum with an aggressively dualistic tradition [the ancient Greek one] that posits a complete separation between mind and body?[33]

Though these authors may disagree about the extent to which the ancient Chinese saw the mind/body relationship as a philosophical issue, they all think the Chinese conception of this relationship forms a strong contrast to the Western one.

Recent work by Edward Slingerland, professor of philosophy at the University of British Columbia, has challenged this common presentation of mind and body in Chinese philosophy.[34] Mind/body holism, as Slingerland notes, contradicts central aspects of the ancient Chinese worldview. There is strong evidence that the ancient Chinese believed that the immaterial spirits of their ancestors were present after death, consciously interacting with the world around them, a belief which suggests the idea that a person's identity is independent of the body. Some passages in classical Chinese texts suggest that when we see a creature's body after death, something fundamental is missing. Others contrast the *xin* 心, a term often translated as "heart/mind," with the body (*xing* 形). The *xin* is said to possess many of the features Western philosophers associate with the mind, such as thinking, intending, willing, and ruling over the body.

Slingerland noticed that those who accept the holistic interpretation tended to downplay or ignore these passages, pointing to others that confirmed their own view. To test which interpretation was correct, he decided to adopt some techniques from the natural sciences. First, he and several graduate students, themselves unaware of his purposes, collected 1,321 passages from online databases of early Chinese texts which contained the term *xin*. Based on a random sample of sixty of these passages, twenty-nine different categories were developed to classify how *xin* was being used. Finally, the research team randomly selected 620 passages and, working independently of one another, sorted them into the twenty-nine categories. These techniques of random sampling and independent coding were meant to counteract the problem of confirmation bias, where we emphasize only those passages that support our previously established interpretation. What they discovered was that passages contrasting *xin* and the body were fairly common, and that they increased over time. This pattern suggests that the ancient Chinese eventually converged on a dualistic view of mind and body.

This research has important implications for the generalizations debate. As Slingerland writes in a paper presenting his findings, evidence has "typically been gathered and presented in a highly biased and unsystematic manner. Scholars arguing for mind-body holism in early China, for instance, will cherry pick a dozen or so passages from among hundreds or thousands on the topic to defend their claim."[35] When we encounter a generalization, we need to look not merely at the textual evidence offered in favor of it, but also how this evidence has been collected and assessed, and whether steps have been taken to counteract researcher bias. Methodology matters.

Evidence from the social sciences

Another means of assessing cultural-philosophical generalizations is to go out into the world and find out what various members of a culture believe. A pioneer of this approach was the cross-cultural psychologist Geert Hofstede, who in the early 1970s obtained access to a database containing 116,000 questionnaires capturing the differing outlooks IBM employees in more than fifty countries.[36] From the collected data, Hofstede derived four dimensions of cultural difference: *power distance*, that is, the extent to which a society accepts hierarchy; *uncertainty avoidance*, or the degree to which it allows for ambiguity and difference of opinion; *individualism vs. collectivism*, the value the society places on the support of groups; and finally, *masculinity vs. femininity*, the preference for values associated with one gender or the other. What he discovered was that employees from the United States, Great Britain, and Australia scored extremely high in individualism, whereas those from East and West Africa, Hong Kong, Taiwan, and many countries in Central and South America scored very low. Results from the other categories also differed significantly along geographical boundaries.

More recently, Richard Nisbett's book, *The Geography of Thought: How Asians and Westerners Think Differently . . . and Why*, relies on experimental evidence to support claims of cultural difference. In one study, he and a colleague named Taka Masuda showed animated underwater scenes to groups of students at Kyoto University and the University of Michigan.[37] In each of the scenes, they placed one or two "focal" fish that were larger, quicker, and more brightly colored than the others. After the students had viewed each vignette for two brief periods of twenty seconds each, they were asked to describe what they had seen. What Masuda and Nisbett found was that the American students were three times as likely to start their descriptions by referring to the focal fish, whereas the Japanese ones tended to begin with a reference to the whole environment. The Japanese also made 60 percent more references to elements in the background of the scenes, such as rocks, plants, and bubbles. When the experimenters later showed the students still pictures from the scenes, with some of the objects placed in new backgrounds, the Japanese students were much more likely to make mistakes in recalling which objects they had seen in the animated vignettes. Switching the backgrounds made no difference to the American students.

Nisbett draws on this and other social scientific evidence to argue for his own version of the holist/dualism distinction between East Asians (including Chinese, Japanese, and Koreans) and Westerners (people of European culture):

[M]odern Asians, like the ancient Chinese, view the world in holistic terms: They see a great deal of the field, especially background events; they are skilled in observing relationships between events; they regard the world as complex and highly changeable and its components as interrelated; they see events as moving in cycles between extremes; and they feel that control over events requires coordination with others. Modern Westerners, like the ancient Greeks, see the world in analytic, atomistic terms; they see objects as discrete and separate from their environments; they see events as moving in a linear fashion when they move at all; and they feel themselves to be personally in control of events even when they are not.[38]

He connects these ways of viewing reality with distinctive social systems. Most Westerners believe that each individual is unique, and that life is about expressing oneself and achieving one's goals. They favor equality in their relationships and want the same rules to apply to everyone. Asians, on the other hand, are less concerned with individuality and personal success, and more with pursuing well-ordered relationships and the goals of the group. They are more accepting of social hierarchy, and believe that rules should be adjusted on a case-by-case basis.[39]

Since we lack the space to pursue all the generalizations mentioned in the preceding paragraph, let us focus on the individualist/collectivist dimension. Many comparative philosophers have seen individualism as a distinctive feature of Western thought, most readily apparent in the modern period. In the epistemological framework established by Descartes' *Meditations*, I know most fundamentally that I exist as a thinking being; since I only have access to my own thoughts, I cannot even be certain that other minds exist. In Kant's moral and political philosophy, a human being is defined most fundamentally by autonomy, the ability to determine the course of one's life through the use of one's own reason. For Locke, individual rights to life, liberty, and property are the basis of legitimate government.

Yet some dissenters have maintained that the Western individualism/non-Western collectivism thesis does not hold up to scrutiny. One worry is that these categories project a running debate in Western philosophy onto the rest of the world. As Kwame Anthony Appiah writes, "[W]hat has been dramatized in terms of Us and Them, the West and the Rest, really plays out familiar conflicts between liberals and communitarians, between 'atomistic' and 'holistic' conceptions of society, conflicts that are *internal* to the West."[40] Others argue that the generalization ignores prominent Western philosophers who have embraced the collectivist position.[41]

Evidence from the social sciences confirms that individualism and collectivism vary from culture to culture. A 2002 meta-analysis of dozens of different studies on the subject by researchers at the University of Michigan found that Americans scored higher in individualism and lower in collectivism than East Asians, South Asians, Africans, Middle Easterners, and Europeans; and that they scored lower in collectivism but no differently in individualism than Latin and South Americans.[42] Within the East Asian category the results were diverse: Americans were more individualist but no less collectivist than Japanese or Koreans, but in comparison to people from mainland China they were much more individualist and less collectivist. The most significant differences were evident when Americans were contrasted with Africans and Middle Easterners. Even so, several factors complicate the use of evidence from the social sciences to support this and other cultural-philosophical generalizations.

Issues to consider

One fallacy of generalization is drawing conclusions about a whole population on the basis of a nonrepresentative subset of that population. If we have only read one or two texts in the Buddhist tradition, our conclusions shouldn't refer to Indian or Asian philosophy as such. With regard to the mind and body in China and the West, Slingerland notes how easily things "slide into cultural caricature: the actually rather odd position defended by Descartes is what 'Western' thought always has been about, which means that, since the Chinese are not Cartesians, they must be somehow radically different."[43]

In the case of evidence from the social sciences, we should likewise consider whether the scope of the generalization is supported by the evidence. Because of differences between the various groups of East Asians included in their study, as well as those between Americans and Europeans, the authors of the Michigan meta-analysis warn against making generalizations regarding "East Asian collectivism" or "Western individualism." The anthropologist Sherry Ortner criticizes Nisbett's *Geography of Thought* on precisely these grounds. Noting that Nisbett's thesis about differences between Asians and Westerners does not always hold up when broken down by specific nationalities, she refers to it as "a relentless attempt to cram everything into the Asian/Western dichotomy." As she writes,

> Nisbett seems to think this is a minor issue. At the beginning of the book he "apologizes" to those readers who might be "upset" to see "billions of people labeled with the single term 'East Asian' and treated as if they are identical." But it is not a matter of being upset. It is a matter of wondering whether the differences within these absurdly large categories aren't at least as large and important as the differences between them. It is in fact a question about the scientific validity of the enterprise.[44]

Other critics have focused on Nisbett's use of "Western" and "East Asian" as categories extending all the way back to ancient Greece and ancient China.[45] While Nisbett often qualifies his use of these terms, one suspects it is the general opposition between East Asia and the West rather than these qualifications that will stick in reader's minds.

We must also consider how the main terms in the generalization are used. The term "individualism" has been used to refer to a number of different philosophical positions in Western philosophy.[46] It can denote a metaphysical view that individual things are fundamentally real, an epistemological view that firsthand experience is the source of knowledge, a moral view that emphasizes self-interest (or another that emphasizes self-reliance, or another that emphasizes autonomy), or the political view that individual rights are fundamental. If someone says that Western philosophy is "individualistic," which of these views do they mean?

The authors of the Michigan study point out that social scientists also have different ways of defining what counts as individualism and collectivism. They disagree, for instance, about whether concern for family relationships is a sign of collectivism. What if I care about my immediate family and no one else? On some measures, such as how much a person values belonging to groups or seeking advice from others, American subjects come across as relatively collectivist. On others, such as one's duty to assist other members of a group, Americans score very low in collectivism. Clarity about the terms is essential.

Finally, we should ask about the connection between the two domains of evidence, that is, the philosophical-textual and the social-scientific. Comparative philosophers working on their own are at most qualified to make general claims about culturally bound philosophical traditions: African philosophy, Chinese philosophy, Western metaphysics, etc. To connect the general patterns found in a philosophy with those in its host culture, they must employ resources from the social sciences.[47] This interaction can go in both directions; Nisbett, for instance, relies on the work of comparative philosophers to support his claims of psychological differences between Asians and Westerners.

Such an approach depends on the assumption that there is an intimate connection between a philosophy and its host culture. This assumption may arise from the belief that philosophers such as Confucius and Aristotle have had profound effects on the cultures that claim them, or from the belief that the ideas of these philosophers survived because they reflected their respective societies.[48] But the views of philosophers do not always match the views of society at large. Many well-known philosophers in the West have been critics of dominant cultural norms: Socrates took his fellow Athenians to task for disregarding the cultivation of virtue, just as Peter Singer challenges Western attitudes toward animal rights, third-world poverty, and the sanctity of human life. What philosophers believe can also be very different from what the majority of their fellow citizens believe. In America, most philosophers are atheists, whereas the general population is overwhelmingly theist. Members of the American Philosophical Association overwhelmingly approved a resolution condemning the 2003 invasion of Iraq, whereas most of the general population supported it. Even if there were values that are representative of "Western philosophy," they would not necessarily represent "Western" values. In our search for a holistic representation of a culturally bound philosophy, we need to be cautious in how we link the relevant evidence in the social sciences to that found in philosophical texts.

Using generalizations responsibly

In spite of some scholars' resistance to the use of *any* generalizations, it is likely that at least some sort of holistic interpretation will be inevitable in our study of cultural traditions. As Steven Burik, Robert Smid, and Ralph Weber write in the epilogue to their recent edited collection *Comparative Philosophy and Method* (2022), "One cannot compare without generalizations; one cannot even translate or interpret without generalizations, and claiming to do so only obscures those generalizations."[49] So keeping that in mind, we end this chapter with a list of guidelines about the responsible use of generalization in comparative philosophy.

1. Any generalizations we use should be open to revision as we learn more about the culture or philosophical tradition in question
Openness to revision is a key feature that distinguishes the responsible use of generalization from cultural essentialism. Generalizations, as Joshua Mason writes, are "not eternal essences, and should change or be dropped if new evidence challenges them."[50] We should always be on the lookout for evidence that challenges the received view about a culture or philosophical tradition.

2. Generalizations used in comparative philosophy should be checked against the evidence from other disciplines
Chenyang Li writes that in identifying patterns within a particular culture, comparative philosophers "need to go beyond pure philosophical reflection. We need to go interdisciplinary. Anthropologists, historians, sociologists, and cultural psychologists, for example, present their studies on the basis of empirical research. Is our philosophical reasoning congruent with the large pattern of empirical studies?"[51] If it does not match the evidence from other disciplines, then we will need to rethink either our understanding of the philosophy in question, or its connection to the culture from which it emerged.

3. Generalizations about a culture or philosophical tradition should not mean that we ignore views that go against the overall trend

While some views in Western philosophy may be more influential than others, thinkers and texts that go against the overall trend may be just as philosophically rewarding to study (and potentially more rewarding, if we think of philosophy as concerned with challenging received wisdom). When we study philosophy from China, for instance, there is a danger that we focus on ideas taken to represent the cultural mainstream and ignore everything else. As Alexus McLeod and Joshua Brown point out in a recent book, "There are a host of neglected concepts in early Chinese thought that have received insufficient attention due to persistent views that they 'don't exist' or are otherwise unimportant in early Chinese thought."[52]

4. In working with generalizations, one should be wary of the ways in which past and present power asymmetries may shape the categories we use to understand other cultures

Generalizations may also contribute to furthering a history of epistemic injustice in representations of non-Western cultures. As Douglas Berger tells us, many attempts at cultural generalizations are "at least intellectual, if not political, descendants of early Orientalist scholarship that came to exert influence on Western philosophers from the seventeenth-twentieth centuries, and this scholarship often sought to identify points of fundamental cultural difference between 'the West and the rest' that in either subtle or overt ways elevated the former over the latter."[53]

5. The broader the philosophical or cultural entity being generalized, the more likely there will be significant exceptions

And if there are significant exceptions, the generalization is not that useful. Statements about "Eastern philosophy" or "Asian culture" are likely to meet with skepticism from scholars who study specific areas of these vast categories. Mason reminds us that even relatively small traditions or time-periods can be a challenge to generalize: "Really narrow targets are also risky if there is not much source material and we rely on just a few examples. I think it is the same attitude of caution all the time."[54]

Conclusion

The problem of generalization in comparative philosophy involves a wide range of issues, including how we think about culture, interpret particular philosophical texts, and see the relation of one to another. The debate about the usefulness of broad statements of cultural-philosophical difference is ongoing.

For newcomers to comparative philosophy, making sweeping generalizations is often more attractive than engaging in close readings of a text. The generalizations give us something quick and easy, and of apparently unlimited application, to hold on to. It's worth emphasizing that the bulk of comparative philosophy consists of making detailed comparisons of particular passages or issues from different traditions. For those comparativists who do engage in generalizations, it is usually as the result of exhaustively detailed study.

Part III

Approaches to Comparison

8

Universalism

In this section of the book, we will discuss four distinct approaches to comparative philosophy: universalism, pluralism, consensus, and global philosophy. While these are not the only possible points of departure for the study of culturally distinct philosophical traditions, they illustrate some of the basic frameworks in which comparative work may take place. Each of these approaches has been pursued with various aims and methods.

"Universalism" has several different meanings. It can refer to the idea that there is a constant human nature, or the view that we can reach universally applicable conclusions through the use of reason. In philosophy today, the term most often means *moral universalism*: the notion that there are moral principles that apply to everyone. Proponents of human rights, for instance, maintain all individuals are entitled to these rights, regardless of culture, race, gender, sexual orientation, or economic status.

Those who take a universalist approach to comparative philosophy are likewise interested in principles that transcend the particularities of culture and the rest. Comparative universalists do not take it for granted, however, that we are already in possession of such principles, or that we can discern them *a priori*. Rather, they seek to uncover them through engagement with other cultural-philosophical traditions. The motivation is not the desire to defend our own philosophical convictions about what these principles are, but rather a curiosity about their existence and nature. As one philosopher explains it, his interest in cross-cultural comparison arose from the belief "that either there was or wasn't wisdom about the human condition, and that studying different, and if possible unrelated traditions, would reveal which it was, and if there was any, what it was."[1]

The search for cross-cultural philosophical universals can take two general forms, which correspond to the interpretive and constructive dimensions of comparison introduced in Chapter 2. First, it can mean searching for commonalities in past works of philosophy from different cultural traditions. The point of studying these works and their larger traditions alongside one another is to arrive at a "kind of periodic table of the elements of philosophy."[2] It can also involve attempts to combine elements from different traditions into new philosophies that would transcend the limitations of those bound to a single culture.

The universalist approach to comparative philosophy faces both methodological obstacles and substantive objections. Before discussing these questions, however, we must say more about the meaning of universalism in comparative philosophy.

Varieties of universalism

Since the term "universalism" is usually associated with a view that gained prominence in the European Enlightenment and has since received criticism from many quarters, we will begin by distinguishing comparative universalism from this more prominent predecessor. After that, we will explore the two general forms of universalism in comparative philosophy.

Comparative universalism vs. enlightenment universalism

Universalism about human nature, reason, and morality reached its height in the European Enlightenment of the seventeenth and eighteenth centuries. In his essay "What is Enlightenment?" Kant contends that every man is capable of achieving liberation from the bonds of tradition and authority through the exercise of his own reason. Political documents like the French *Declaration of the Rights of Man* and the American *Declaration of Independence* state that principles of equality and liberty apply to all.

These principles were largely derived from rational reflection on the part of philosophers. In his ethical writings, Kant maintained that studying actual human behavior can at most tell us what people do; it can never tell us what they *ought* to do. Since any genuine morality must be binding for all rational beings, moral principles must be derived in an *a priori* fashion, rather than being based on empirical observation.

While the central tenets of Enlightenment universalism remain guiding ideals for many moral and political philosophers today, others have seen them as parochial, ignorant of cultural difference, and prone to imposition by force on the rest of the world. The death of universalism has been proclaimed in some quarters; as one author writes, "The dismantling of the universal is widely considered one of the founding gestures of twentieth-century thought."[3]

The critics claim that Enlightenment universalism is nothing more than the particular values of seventeenth- and eighteenth-century European intellectuals masquerading as transcendent truths. It is "Western universalism," a contradiction in terms. One obvious limitation lies in Enlightenment conceptions of race and gender: the principles of liberty and equality were not extended to all, but only to a certain few. Simply making the principles more inclusive is seen by the critics as inadequate. Some feminist philosophers have contended, for instance, that the ideals themselves are constructed on a masculine model that bases morality on abstract principles rather than the development of caring relationships with those closest to us.

Neglect of cultural diversity is another charge against the Enlightenment view. The contemporary English political philosopher John Gray maintains that according to the philosophical anthropology of the time, "Distinctive cultural identities, along with their constitutive histories, were like streams, whose destiny was to flow irresistibly into the great ocean of universal humanity."[4] Non-European societies were seen as civilized to the degree that they approximated Europe. When Enlightenment intellectuals did engage with the thought of other cultures, the tendency was to project their own debates and inclinations onto these cultures. As illustrated by the reception of Chinese philosophy in the eighteenth century and Indian philosophy in the nineteenth (discussed in Chapter 6), other cultures' philosophical traditions were quickly assimilated into the debates of the time.

Opponents of Enlightenment universalism have also pointed out that the belief that one's moral principles apply to all rational creatures goes hand in hand with the desire to inflict them on everyone else. As evidence, they can point to past attempts by representatives of European culture to force their practices onto other societies. Even today, the competing universalisms of different cultures lead to a "clash of civilizations" picture of global reality.[5]

Comparative universalism rejects the method of Enlightenment universalism while retaining its goal. As one prominent comparativist puts it, "There is nothing wrong with seeking universalist values. . . . Rather does the wrongness lie in the belief that we—or any single culture—are already fully in possession of those values, and therefore feel justified . . . in foisting them on everyone else."[6] The problem with the Enlightenment method of establishing universals was that it assumed, prior to any investigation, that the rational reflections of philosophers from different parts of the world would result in the same conclusions. The universality of human experience is not something we can take for granted.

The purpose of comparative philosophy, on this approach, is precisely "to move toward a more genuine universalism."[7] To attain this goal, we must go out and engage philosophical traditions from other parts of the world, looking at their central texts to see if their foundational values are compatible with our own, and talking to their living adherents to find how these values can be adapted to the modern world. As Zhao Dunhua of Peking University writes, "universalism is not something ready at hand, but a matter of reconstruction, a potentiality to be realized, and a consequence of collaborative dialogues."[8]

Because comparative philosophers work closely with more than one culturally bound tradition, they are more likely than others to recognize the extent to which our values and concepts are shaped by the context of cultural and tradition, appearing to us as universal only because of long use. As a result, they may be in a better position to avoid mistaking the values of their own tradition for universal ones, or thinking that other people's philosophical traditions are things that can simply be cast aside.

In undertaking the dialogues mentioned by Zhao, comparative universalists also have more sophisticated methodological tools at their disposal than did their Enlightenment predecessors. Problems like "incommensurability" and "projection" were unknown to seventeenth- and eighteenth-century European intellectuals, much less any strategies to avoid them. This is not to say that comparative universalism is free from error—we will look at some of its potential limitations in a moment—but only that there is reason to believe it can avoid some of the failures of previous attempts at establishing universal values.

Comparative universalists may draw on Aristotle rather than Kant for their methodological basis. According to the Greek thinker, whenever we approach a particular problem, we must begin by setting forth the most prominent views on that problem, both those found among the majority and among the wise. After seeing what conflicts arise from considering these views alongside one another, we should try to *preserve* the truth of as many of them as possible. On this model, philosophy is not about defending the view that we have reasoned on our own as true against its competitors in a winner-take-all combat, but instead about reconciling the many truths that have been handed down over long periods of time within the different philosophical traditions.[9]

Historical universalism

One form of comparative universalism is historical in nature, attempting to uncover enduring themes in past works of philosophy from different cultures. What common values do we find in these works? Are there shared responses to the central philosophical questions?

The German philosopher Karl Jaspers' notion of the "Axial Age," set forth in his 1953 book *The Origin and Goal of History*, is probably the most dramatic example of the historical approach. Jaspers argues that the period between 800 and 200 BCE, which saw the rise of the great philosophies of the Western, Chinese, and Indian traditions, was the pivotal moment in world history:

> In this age were born the fundamental categories within which we still think today, and the beginnings of the world religions, by which human beings still live, were created. The step into universality was taken in every sense.
>
> As a result of this process, hitherto unconsciously accepted ideas, customs and conditions were subjected to examination, questioned and liquidated. Everything was swept into the vortex. In so far as the traditional substance still possessed vitality and reality, its manifestations were clarified and thereby transmuted.
>
> The *Mythical Age*, with its tranquillity and self-evidence, was at an end.... Religion was rendered ethical, and the majesty of the deity thereby increased ....
>
> For the first time *philosophers* appeared. Human beings dared to rely on themselves as individuals. Hermits and wandering thinkers in China, ascetics in India, philosophers in Greece and prophets in Israel all belong together, however much they may differ from each other in their beliefs, the contents of their thought and their inner dispositions. Man proved capable of contrasting himself inwardly with the entire universe. He discovered within himself the origin from which to raise himself above his own self and the world.[10]

In developing this narrative, Jaspers hoped to overcome the limitations of previous accounts of the shape of human history. While the belief that the birth of Christ is the turning point in world history may be appealing to Christians, the focus on the concurrent philosophical revolutions in Greece, China, and India allows for a more encompassing vision of humanity's past. This common philosophical heritage can serve as the foundation of a universal ethic. "To visualize the facts of the Axial Age," Jaspers writes, "is to gain possession of something *common to all mankind*, beyond all differences of creed."[11]

Recent versions of comparative-historical universalism have depended on a more careful examination of the content, rather than the general spirit, of the world-philosophical traditions. But they retain Jasper's focus on deriving themes of universal significance from culturally bound texts.

One example is found in the German Sinologist Heiner Roetz's *Confucian Ethics of the Axial Age*. The book begins by criticizing differentialist accounts of Chinese philosophy for going too far in emphasizing its roots in traditional Chinese culture. The implication of these accounts is that modern Western values are not applicable to contemporary China, which possesses a distinctive way of life rooted in its ancient past. As Roetz argues, however, "Ideas of human dignity, equality, and autonomy were developed in China no less than in the Occident."[12] Classic Chinese thinkers were in fact opponents of the inherited tradition who attempted to establish values that would counteract the narrowness of the rulers of their day and age.

These thinkers supported their ethical claims with arguments and examples meant to appeal to as wide an audience as possible. The philosopher Mencius devised a famous thought-experiment in which a passerby sees a baby teetering on the edge of a deep well. He argues that all human beings will have an impulse to rush over and rescue the baby from danger; anyone who does not have such an impulse is not a human being. Such claims are relevant to all of us; they address, as Roetz says, "a world of recipients that is open in time and place."[13] In the third-century BCE, the classic text known as the *Master Lü's Spring and Autumn Annals* was thought to be so comprehensive that it was displayed in the marketplace of the city of Xianyang with a reward of one thousand pieces of gold hanging above it, offered to anyone who could add or subtract even a word.[14]

When we read these works today our goal should be to reconstruct their universal themes. The Axial Age period of "Chinese Enlightenment" can be an important source of guidance and inspiration not only for contemporary

Chinese, but for the rest of us as well. It is a matter of respect for these thinkers and texts that we take them seriously as philosophy.

Roetz believes that it is scholars who maintain that cultural differences are ineradicable who are forcing contemporary notions like "incommensurability" or "projection" onto the classic texts. It is itself the height of projection to say that whereas classical Chinese philosophers thought they were making claims that applied to all humanity, these claims have no application beyond the cultural context in which they were made. Mencius himself gives no indication of thinking that boundaries of time and space pose any barrier to the accumulation of learning:

> Mencius said to Wan Zhang, "That scholar, whose goodness is most outstanding in the village, will become a friend to all the good scholars of the village. That scholar, whose goodness is most outstanding in the state, will become a friend to all the good scholars of the state. That scholar, whose goodness is most outstanding in the world, will become a friend to all the good scholars of the world. When he feels that being a friend to all the good scholars of the world is not enough, he will go back in time to consider the people of antiquity, repeating their poems and reading their books."[15]

The important distinction is not between one culture and another, but rather between those who care about learning and those who do not. If we are devoted to learning, we are part of a community that transcends culture and time-period.

Synthetic universalism

The second type of comparative universalism involves the construction of a world philosophy by means of synthesis of prominent global traditions. The goal is to develop a more global philosophy that can serve as the foundation of a transnational political community.[16]

Synthesis was widely discussed in the early stages of comparative philosophy as an independent discipline in the 1940s and 1950s. A prominent advocate was the American comparativist F.S.C. Northrop (1893–1992), who envisioned a "new philosophy" that would unite East and West. Such a philosophy, he wrote,

> by enlarging the outlook and values of each part of the world to include those of the other, may well serve as a trustworthy criterion of the good for a truly cosmopolitan and international world order, in which the diverse basic conceptions and resultant valuations of two great cultures are combined into a single world civilization, the richer and better because it includes in

complementary harmony with balanced emphasis the most profound and mature insights of each.[17]

Proponents of this approach were marked by their great idealism, envisioning a "world-wide spiritual renaissance, when human consciousness will take a great stride forward."[18] They emphasized the social relevance of comparative philosophy, believing the cross-cultural dialogue it facilitated could contribute to global peace.

Some prominent criticisms emerged early on. In a 1951 symposium devoted to comparative synthesis, the American philosopher John Dewey reminded his interlocutors that a category such as "East" contained great diversity, including China, Japan, Indonesia, India, and parts of Russia. If comparative philosophers really want a meeting of cultural-philosophical traditions, he argued, their most important task should be to "help break down the notion that there is such a thing as a 'West' and 'East' that have to be synthesized."[19]

Other critics argued that the attempt to fuse distinct cultural philosophies leads to principles devoid of meaningful content.[20] Suppose someone were to suggest that the spirit of the great philosophical traditions can be expressed in the maxim "be kind to others." The question would be, what is involved in being kind? Does it mean to treat everyone equally, or to regard our family and friends with special care? What if being kind to some involves harming others? These are issues on which the great traditions have differed. Without being rooted in one tradition or another, our maxims may slide into meaninglessness. If we attempted to combine the signature dishes from different cultures—sushi and spaghetti, biryani and bulgogi—we would end up with flavorless mush.

The various attempts at synthesis, in any case, did not appear to lead to a more universal philosophy. In combining two traditions, the comparativist must consciously choose which elements to combine and which to leave out. As a consequence, the systems constructed tend to reflect nothing so much as the particular interests of their creators. Many comparative philosophers came to look upon synthesis with suspicion, and by 1970, the approach had largely died out.[21]

In recent times, comparativists have found a more limited application for synthesis in their work. For Chad Hansen, the goal of synthesis is an outgrowth of moral tradition respect (Chapter 3). When we encounter a philosophical tradition with moral beliefs that strike us as impressive and intellectually rich, yet different from our own, we begin to doubt that our own tradition has a monopoly on the truth. We wonder whether we could combine the best features of our own tradition with the best features of the other in some new moral system.[22]

Yet if synthesis occurs, argues Hansen, it should be as the result of a gradual process of evolution on the part of each tradition, with each side judging from within its own perspective what is valuable about the other. This process may lead to convergence, but there is no guarantee. Comparative philosophers will also play a more subdued role than in earlier accounts. Rather than being "moral prophets" whose insights into the culture-philosophical traditions in question enable them to predict points at which they will converge, their goal is to lay the foundations for respectful engagement.

Challenges and criticisms

Let us now turn to some puzzles and problems for the comparative universalist. Why would anyone think there are cross-cultural philosophical universals? Can we avoid mistaking our own particular beliefs for universal ones? Is genuine universalism possible?

Grounding the search for universals

Differentialists argue that since cultural forces shape everything a person thinks, makes, and does from very early on in life, we can take it for granted that the mental lives of members of isolated cultures will be entirely unique. Universalists in turn must develop some basis for their belief that culturally distinct traditions will converge on certain points. What grounds the search for cross-cultural philosophical universals?

Often universalists appeal to the biology.[23] Are we not all human? The philosopher and historian of science G.E.R. Lloyd has pointed out some complications with this view, however. First, there is biological diversity as well as cultural diversity. Even though all human eyes share the same basic anatomy, some humans may be dichromatic (having two different types of cones) or tetrachromatic (four different types), while most are trichromatic (three different types). Additionally, the commonalities established by biological considerations are often minimal. The capacity to feel fear, for instance, has played an important evolutionary role in protecting human beings from predators. But early on in our development our culture instills us with both a distinctive language for describing such feelings and acceptable ways of expressing them. As Lloyd concludes, "What is common, and what is subject to variability across human populations, in this domain can certainly not be settled by *a priori* assumptions."[24]

We could also try to ground the search for universals in psychology. Roetz appeals to Kohlberg's six-stage theory of moral development: in the first stage, an individual relies only on selfish considerations of reward or punishment; in the last, on the conscientious commitment to universally valid principles. From research in different parts of the world, Kohlberg determined that these stages of development were cross-culturally applicable. Roetz thinks the theory can provide a universally valid framework for assessing different cultures' moral development, enabling us to measure East Asian societies on the same scale as Western ones. Even so, the differentialist may draw on the number of critics who have contended that Kohlberg's theory reflects Western biases, especially in its higher stages.

A third possibility lies in what the philosopher Martha Nussbaum calls "grounding experiences."[25] Regardless of culture, all humans have to deal with certain realities. Because we are mortal, we have to think about our impending deaths and shape our lives accordingly; because we have bodies, we must vie with hunger and thirst and desire; because we are social creatures, we have to learn to manage our relations with others. While human beings do not all respond to these experiences in the same ways, the fact that we share them can provide a starting point for cross-cultural reflection. The differentialist, on the other hand, may point to the sheer diversity of cultural responses to such experiences.

We can also try to ground the search for universals in the fact of cross-cultural communication. If there were no universals, cross-cultural communication would be impossible; but cross-cultural communication is possible, so there must be universals.[26] This strategy recalls Davidson's argument about interpretation (Chapter 4). Like Davidson, comparativists can always turn the challenge back to the differentialist: "If the cultures in question are really so different, how is it possible that you can explain these differences so clearly?"[27]

This is not a complete list of the possibilities, nor an exhaustive discussion of any of them. The grounding question shows the potential connection of comparative philosophy to a range of fields outside philosophy.

Separating the universal from the particular

Yet even if there is reason to think that our comparisons may uncover philosophical universals, how will we know that we have uncovered them?

What if we have mistaken accidental features of particular traditions for components of philosophy everywhere?

On the historical approach, a philosophical view is seen as universal if it is held to be true by cultural traditions that developed in isolation from one another. That the traditions converged independently on the view in question is taken to mean that it transcends cultural boundaries. The focus is on traditions rather than individual thinkers and texts in order to prevent us from cherry-picking a few similar-sounding passages and maintaining that they are evidence of a philosophical universal. Even if we find similar-sounding views in works of philosophy from different cultures, these views may serve entirely different purposes in the broader contexts in which they were formulated. They also may be isolated instances of a position not generally found in the traditions in which the texts were written. This holistic focus, as we saw in Chapter 3, is representative of comparative philosophy at large.

Yet remember that comparative philosophers generally limit their comparisons to two cultural traditions. Can we really draw conclusions about "the philosophical table of elements" on this basis? How many traditions must be included before we know what is elemental and what is not?

Probably the most substantial example of historical comparison is the Israeli philosopher Ben-Ami Scharfstein's *Comparative History of World Philosophy*. Weighing in at around 700 pages, this work encompasses *three* traditions: the Chinese, Indian, and Western ones. Scharfstein argues that these are the *only* three major philosophical traditions; philosophy, he says, "had just three territorial origins, three beginning languages, three historical pasts, and three webs of self-reference. That there have been just three major philosophical traditions is, therefore, a fact, a brute fact, I would say."[28] While other cultures may have possessed some kind of "wisdom," these were the only three that developed philosophy in the strict sense, namely, that which is articulated in the form of principles and defended through rational argumentation.[29]

If philosophy is limited to three traditions, then the sort of examination needed to find universals is at least possible, though it would require Herculean effort. Still, as we have discussed (Chapter 1), the definition of philosophy Scharfstein employs as his standard is not the only one available for comparative purposes. And even if we do limit the development of philosophy to three parts of the world, how do we know that all possible philosophical traditions would develop along the same lines?

In synthetic universalism, a principle is thought to have universal application if it combines features of certain traditions in a way that can appeal to all humanity. Yet while it does seem plausible that by working across multiple cultural traditions we are less likely to mistake norms particular to our own society for universal ones, how do we know that principles we have constructed in this manner are universally valid?

Kwasi Wiredu proposes that a principle is universal if a society that does not recognize its observance is unable to survive in a tolerable condition. His own candidate for such a principle is what he calls "sympathetic impartiality": that before we act we are able to imagine ourselves in the position of those who will be affected and welcome the act from their perspective.[30] In asking whether others would welcome the act, we counteract our tendency to impose on others the values we take to be universal. Wiredu points to the Golden Rule found in the major world religions, Kant's Categorical Imperative, and the traditional ethical code of his own native Akan culture as evidence that many cultures have in reality accepted a principle like this one. If any culture were to forgo such a principle, considering only naked self-interest, it would quickly be reduced to a Hobbesian state of nature.

Other principles, such as "Everyone should practice monogamy," do not pass the test. We can imagine circumstances in which the population of one sex vastly outnumbered the population of the other, and the practice of polygamy or polyandry was necessary to remedy this unbalance.[31] When Christian missionaries tried to enforce the practice of monogamy on the African societies they encountered, it was a result of their own cultural biases.

The differentialist will argue, however, that what counts as a "tolerable condition" may vary from society to society. Instead of striving to determine principles that can guide all humanity, we should try to show how different ethical foundations may be justified, or to establish shared norms of action based on these different foundations. We will explore these possibilities further in the next two chapters.

One-sidedness again

Opponents have also argued that comparative universalism is inherently biased toward the more dominant tradition. Suppose that humans are divided equally among five cultures, with cultures A, B, C, D, and E each having 20 percent of the population. Yet because of culture A's great wealth, they have a disproportionate amount of universities with philosophy departments, outnumbering all of the other cultures by a ratio of 10 to 1. When philosophers from all the cultures get together to discuss cross-cultural philosophical universals, inevitably the members of B, C, D, and E are going to be treated as if they are the exception rather than the rule. What is deemed "universal" in their cultural traditions will be whatever matches the standard set by culture A.

The main challenge of comparative philosophy is to go beyond our own conceptual structure, to gain access to the "alternate realities" to be found in the conceptual structures of other traditions. The universalist approach glosses over this challenge by allowing us to remain comfortably within our own categories. In the varieties of universalism considered above, you may have noticed a tendency to use Western concepts as the basis for engaging other cultures: the idea that philosophy is the defense of abstract principles through rational argumentation, that the ultimate goal of ethical development is to achieve autonomy, or that the ancient Chinese experienced an "Enlightenment." If the universals we uncover match so neatly with concepts in our own cultural tradition, one wonders how comparative universalism is any improvement on its Enlightenment predecessor. A greater focus on difference could change comparative philosophy from what it has been, the imposition of one culture's values onto all the others, into what it ought to be.[32]

"Soft" universalism?

Recently, several comparative philosophers have advanced more restrained versions of universalism that aim to avoid such objections. *Soft universalism* focuses on similarities between philosophical traditions from different cultures while at the same time rejecting attempts to ground these similarities in some deeper foundation.

Lin Ma and Jaap van Brakel contend that for us to interpret a text from a distant cultural tradition, we have to assume that the author is a human like us who engages in what we recognize as human practices. Consider the following passage from the *Daodejing*: "By adding and removing clay we form a vessel./ But only by relying on what is not there, do we have use of the vessel."[33] While we may not understand the philosophical meaning of this passage or know the exact context in which it was written, we at least recognize the practice of shaping clay in order to make a cup or a bowl.

However, there are a couple of qualifications about what this recognition involves. First, we need not assume that the ancient Chinese method of forming a clay vessel is *identical* to ours—only that it has certain points of similarity. It is these "family resemblances" (see Chapter 1 and Chapter 6 for earlier discussion) between their practice and ours that provides the initial basis for comparison. Second, we need not think that this practice is a human universal, but only that it is recognizable to us from our own standpoint.

The most important task of the comparative philosopher, according to Ma and van Brakel, is to construct *quasi-universals* that link together concepts from different cultures.[34] Based on our initial recognition of similarity, we take a concept from our own philosophical tradition and extend it to include certain features of the practice we have recognized. For example, we might think that certain features of the concept of "thing" found in Western philosophy overlap with the notion of thing (*wu* 物) found in the text of the *Daodejing*.[35] Recognition of similarities will lead us to see important points of difference as well, and our map of these features will grow more refined as we proceed.

Quasi-universals are distinct from universals proper in that we hold them open to revision as we discover more in the process of interpreting a text such as the *Daodejing*. They are also "quasi" (from the Latin word for "almost") in that they connect a limited number of traditions (often just two) of traditions rather than applying to all humanity. A comparative philosopher does not need to start from the assumption of "universal" human categories to initiate a constructive dialogue with a culturally distant tradition.

It is possible to apply the framework of soft universalism to our concept of comparative philosophy itself. As Saranindranath Tagore, a philosopher at the National University of Singapore, writes, "The project of comparative philosophy requires the recognition that multiple philosophical traditions have developed in different geographies throughout human history. This recognition is possible only if points of intersection can be cataloged … across traditions."[36] In granting recognition to philosophical traditions outside our own, we aim to broaden the scope of philosophical inquiry in a way that allows for constructive differences to emerge. Tagore envisions a conception of world philosophy in which different cultural traditions are "like liquid flows connecting with each other already and always."[37] While there are recognizable points of overlap, however, there is no transcendent point of departure for comparative philosophy. Rather, it is an ever-evolving enterprise that must be approached from within each of the world's traditions.

Soft universalism enables comparative philosophers to avoid the pitfalls of standard universalism without at the same time sliding into relativism. However, it is likely that the standard universalist approach will consider this approach to be more soft than it is universalism. Without any deeper basis for our judgments of similarity, what distinguishes an accurate recognition from a totally arbitrary one? More work is needed on behalf of the soft universalist approach to reply to this type of objection.

Conclusion

For better or worse, universalism played a central role in the early development of comparative philosophy as a discipline. In spite of strong criticism in the time since, the approach continues to find proponents today. The aspiration of a philosophy that transcends cultural boundaries lives on in aspects of the consensus and global-philosophical approaches that we will consider later on (Chapters 10 and 11, respectively).

9

Pluralism

Suppose you are the lead designer of the experiment on Planet Phi looking down at Phase II of the simulation. While you can't help but feel excited by the various attempts of humanoid philosophers to create a common morality, you also experience a bit of remorse. The philosophical traditions on the Planet have taken generations to develop, a testament to the effort and creativity of its countless residents. Is the world you designed really better off with a single universal philosophy?

It's possible that a diversity of philosophical traditions, like a diversity of cuisines, will make our own life better off in the long run. As one comparative philosopher writes, "A world in which irreducibly different forms of moral life stand up on their own two feet, shoulder to shoulder, is immensely more interesting and a greater testament to humanity than any homogenized conception of morality ever could be."[1] The pluralistic view maintains that, while not all moralities are equal, more than one of them can be true.

On the pluralist approach, the purpose of comparative philosophy is not merely to identify cultural differences, but to show how these differences are both justified and irreducible to one another. Comparison is worthwhile insofar as it "teaches us about the diversity and richness of what human beings may reasonably prize, and about the impossibility of reconciling all they prize in just a single ethical ideal."[2] Instead of a final morality that synthesizes elements from different cultures, the pluralist looks toward a future in which a number of different visions of the human good flourish alongside one another.

The case for pluralism

The most comprehensive defense of pluralism is given by David Wong, a philosopher at Duke University, whose 2006 book *Natural Moralities* contains a rich account of the relationship between value, culture, and philosophy.[3] In this section we will begin with Wong's account of cultural morality, and then turn to his argument on behalf of pluralism.

Understanding cultural moralities

According to Wong, an adequate morality must answer to deeply rooted human needs and desires, while at the same time helping to ensure social cohesion. In serving this dual function, it must identify goods that human beings can devote themselves to seeking, provide the right kind of balance between concern for self and concern for others, and set forth a way to accommodate disagreement within a society about moral matters. Societies that endure have sophisticated ethical codes that have evolved over long periods of time. Those who live in nations like the United States, Wong writes, are the beneficiaries of a composite moral tradition with roots in many different cultures that has taken shape over centuries.[4]

Wong rejects the ideas that cultures are integrated wholes in favor of a more nuanced understanding:

> Sometimes "cultures" are thought to be rather simple affairs in which people share the same values and practices and ways of making meaning of their worlds. I want to suggest that a culture can to some extent consist of commonly recognized values, but that these values provide a counterpoint to one another. The identity of a culture is in part defined by which values are the most salient and which ones serve as counterpoints to others.[5]

A value like individual autonomy, for instance, only carries weight when it is contrasted with the value of serving the interests of one's community. Societies that prioritize autonomy over community do so because they are wary of what happens when this order is reversed. The value of community is always present in such societies, but generally confined to the background. The same goes for societies that value community over autonomy; it is not that the latter value is absent, just that the former is prioritized. Distinct cultural moralities contain many of the same basic values but arrange them in different orders.

The counterpoint model of culture has important consequences for understanding other societies' values. As we have seen (Chapter 5), proponents of foundational incommensurability argue that what we can understand is relative to our worldview; the differences between our cultural morality and theirs run so deep that we cannot make sense of them. According to Wong, however, this view does not account for the fact that we sometimes experience another culture's morality as presenting a genuine alternative to our own. When a member of a more community-oriented society criticizes our own as too individualistic, we can understand this criticism and take it to heart, because we share to some extent the values that motivate it. The complex nature of our own cultural backgrounds gives us a flexibility and openness toward other moral configurations. We realize that members of other cultures confront the same conflicts we do but choose to resolve these conflicts in different ways.

Moral ambivalence and the case for pluralism

A well-known passage from the *Analects* shows how different societies can emphasize opposing values:

> The Duke of She said to Confucius, "Among my people there is one we call 'Upright Gong.' When his father stole a sheep, he reported him to the authorities."
>
> Confucius replied, "Among my people, those who we consider 'upright' are different from this: fathers cover up for their sons, and sons cover up for their fathers. 'Uprightness' is to be found in this."[6]

Whereas the Duke of She's society emphasizes the impartial application of justice, Confucius lives in one that foregrounds duties between family members. The Confucian tradition is built on the latter foundation. Other passages in the *Analects* teach that respect for one's elders when one is young instills a reverence for one's superiors later in life; that this respect requires obedience to one's parents even when they are in the wrong; and that it should continue to guide one's actions after they are dead. Confucius' disciple Mencius defended filial piety against critics who advocated an ethics of impartiality in its place by arguing that regard for one's father is the feature that separates humans from beasts.[7]

For the moral universalist, one of these moralities must be superior to the other. The utilitarian will argue, for instance, that the morality described by Confucius will benefit Upright Gong's sheep-thieving father at the expense of the greater good; more parents will be led to steal, enabled by their children's protection. Utilitarian ethics might account for more limited duties toward our parents by saying that doing good things for those closest to us can help us to be more unselfish people. But what ultimately matters is the greater good of all, and aiding our parents is worthwhile insofar as it contributes to this good.[8] The right morality is that exemplified by Upright Gong.

Yet a single principle like the utilitarian one does not seem to capture all the things that matter to us. Should parents and children really take care of each other only because it furthers the overall human good? When we ask ourselves why we love our family members, "for the sake of the overall human good" is probably the furthest answer from our minds.[9] This does not mean that the overall good is not important to us; if one night we see pictures on TV of impoverished children in other countries we may experience sadness and guilt. But we recognize that dedicating ourselves to the pursuit of this good may conflict with our duties to the people we love.

While important strands of American cultural heritage emphasize honoring and caring for one's parents, many Americans will reject attempts to make filial piety the basis of society. A recent Chinese law, entitled "Protection of the Rights and Interests of Elderly People," requires children to visit their parents and employers to give their employees time off for such visits. After a seventy-seven-year-old mother in one eastern Chinese city sued her daughter and son-in-law for neglect, a court ordered that the couple must visit her at least once every two months.[10] In other parts of East Asia, laws mandating financial support for elderly parents are widely approved; in some cases, the right to be cared for by one's children is enshrined in the country's constitution.[11]

We can easily recognize the value of such laws in an increasingly industrialized China where there is an increasing number of people over the age of sixty and living apart from their children.[12] We might also see that greater emphasis on filial obligation would have value in Western societies as well. During the European heat wave of 2003, nearly 15,000 French citizens died from heat-related causes, largely elderly citizens neglected by their children and neighbors. At the same time, however, we understand that a law mandating filial care is unlikely to become a reality anywhere in Europe of North America, because of the premium we place on personal freedom.

When we see the appeal of another value or way of life yet at the same time realize that we cannot accept it because it conflicts with our own, we experience what Wong refers to as "moral ambivalence":

These sorts of conflict pose special difficulties because we can understand both sides. Even if we are firm in taking a side, we can understand that something of moral value is lost when we act on that side, and the loss is of such a nature that we cannot simply dismiss it as a regrettable though justifiable result of the right decision.... We see that reasonable and knowledgeable people have made different decisions, and any prior convictions we might have had about the superiority of our own decisions gets shaken.[13]

The pluralist maintains that the basic values at stake in moral conflicts cannot be reduced to one of them or another. It is good to help your family members *and* good to promote the overall welfare of humanity. It is also good to respect individual rights; to do one's best to realize one's talents; and to be attuned to the world around us. If we try to condense all these different goods into one category, chances are that we will leave something important out of the picture. As the twentieth-century political philosopher Isaiah Berlin once wrote, "Not all good things are compatible, still less all the ideals of mankind."[14] Our experience of moral ambivalence supports the pluralist case.

When we recognize that in emphasizing personal freedom above all else our society gives up on other things that matter, that another society might pursue these things by placing more emphasis on values like social responsibility or filial obligation, and that each of these societies might be better off than the other in certain respects, we will be suspicious of the idea that one system is best. People who have lived in both East Asian and Western societies can enjoy the greater sense of family and community in the former while at the same time appreciating the greater independence available in the latter.[15]

Zhuangzi and the value of pluralism

To see how the pluralist mind-set can lead to a richer life, take a moment to read the following story from the classical Chinese philosopher Zhuangzi, recounting an exchange between the author and his friend Huizi:

Huizi said to Zhuangzi, "The king of Wei gave me some seeds of a huge gourd. I planted them, and when they grew up, the fruit was big enough to hold five piculs. I tried using it for a water container, but it was so heavy I couldn't lift it. I split it in half to make dippers, but they were so large and unwieldy that I couldn't dip them into anything. It's not that the gourds weren't fantastically big—but I decided they were no use and so I smashed them to pieces."

Zhuangzi said, "You certainly are dense when it comes to using big things! In Song there was a man who was skilled at making a salve to prevent chapped hands, and generation after generation his family made a living by bleaching silk in water. A traveler heard about the salve and offered to buy the prescription for a hundred measures of gold. The man called everyone to a family council. 'For generations we've been bleaching silk and we've never made more than a few measures of gold,' he said. 'Now, if we sell our secret, we can make a hundred measures in one morning. Let's let him have it!' The traveler got the salve and introduced it to the king of Wu, who was having trouble with the state of Yue. The king put the man in charge of his troops, and that winter they fought a naval battle with the men of Yue and gave them a bad beating. A portion of the conquered territory was awarded to the man as a fief. The salve had the power to prevent chapped hands in either case; but one man used it to get a fief, while the other one never got beyond silk bleaching—because they used it in different ways.

"Now you had a gourd big enough to hold five piculs. Why didn't you think of making it into a great tub so you could go floating around the rivers and lakes, instead of worrying because it was too big and unwieldy to dip into things! Obviously you still have a lot of underbrush in your head!"[16]

From our ordinary point of view, we see only the value that we are used to seeing. When some object does not conform to the purpose we have in mind for it, we react with frustration, like Huizi with the giant gourds. Zhuangzi's solution to this problem is to expand our perspective, recognizing that any item has a multitude of uses. A thing that doesn't fit well in one domain can have a perfect place in some other, a material that is of no value to one person can lead another to riches. If it seems of little worth to us, it is the result of our own failure of imagination.

Sometimes we take for granted that the preeminent values in our society are the only values that anyone should have. If we see societies that do not emphasize these values, our tendency is to react the way Huizi does. The pluralist reminds us that our ordinary perspective on value is limited. Our society represents one possible configuration of values in one particular part of the world at one particular moment in human history. Because our chance circumstances provide access to limited ways of life, we experience only a small portion of the goods that are possible for humans to experience.[17]

A perspective that recognizes a multiplicity of values is better than one that does not in that it allows us to get more out of life. We can never know all the potential uses of an object, nor can we know all the possible ways of organizing and giving meaning to human life. Nonetheless, the ability to recognize that different ways of life have value can help us lead lives that are more capable of adapting to changing circumstances. In the process, we may increase the stock of values that we have at our disposal.[18]

Zhuangzi's story does not imply that all uses for a thing are equal. Since the gourd's size, shape, and surroundings all put limits on its possible uses, we will not find a use for it simply by making one up.[19] Still, if we can find multiple uses for an object like a gourd, think of all the possibilities for something such as a human life.

Epistemic pluralism and the new age of philosophy

Up until now in this chapter, we have been discussing pluralism about value. Yet, we can also apply the pluralist framework to ways of thinking about reality. Jonardon Ganeri, a philosopher at the University of Toronto, connects epistemic pluralism with a new era of philosophy. In its first stage, philosophy is defined by what Ganeri calls "the colonial use of reason": a way of thinking that claims to be impartial and universal while at the same time denying any other approach can attain this standard. Prominent in eighteenth- and nineteenth-century Europe, this way of thinking demands of other traditions that they "make your use of reason like ours . . . or admit that you are outside reason and not actually engaged in philosophy at all."[20] Ultimately, the demand is reinforced by colonial power and violence.

In a more recent stage, "comparative philosophy" emerges, with thinkers from colonized traditions engaged in a struggle to be recognized by the dominant form of reasoning, hoping to have their own perspectives included in the debate. While these philosophers made great progress in putting forth their own traditions' perspectives, the colonial use of reason still remains the standard by which all else is measured. As we examined in Chapter 6 of this book, the asymmetrical use of Western ideas and categories remains a central problem in comparative philosophy today.

However, Ganeri sees philosophy today as entering an "age of re-emergence." There is an opening up of philosophy around the globe coupled with attempts to address the inequalities inherited from colonialism:

First, philosophies from every region of the world, locally grounded in lived experience and reflection upon it, are finding new autonomous and authentic forms of articulation. *Second*, philosophical industry, leaving behind a centre-periphery mode of production, is becoming again polycentric: the philosophical world is returning to a plural and diverse network of productive sites. *Third*, Europe and other colonial powers have been provincialised, no longer mandatory conversation partners or points of comparison but rather unprivileged participants in global dialogue. *Fourth*, philosophers within the largely anglophone international academy are beginning to acknowledge their responsibility so to arrange international institutions as to enable wide and open participation.[21]

Re-emergent philosophy resists the coercion of the colonial use of reason as well as the lingering bias towards the colonizer's standards and methods of comparative philosophy. In the new stage, we witness a free exchange of novel ideas and concepts drawn from the different world philosophies. Rather than one dominant paradigm of philosophy, there is a movement toward diverse and innovative forms of reasoning.

Whereas Wong's approach to pluralism is based on ethical values, Ganeri focuses on methods of inquiry. Re-emergent philosophy, he says, "embodies a type of pluralistic realism, a commitment to the claim that there are many ways to investigate a reality whose existence is independent of human inquirers, a plurality of ways of thinking that cannot be reduced to any single mode of interrogation (least of all to the colonial use of reason)."[22] Under this new paradigm, scholars work to retrieve ways of thinking from traditions that have been marginalized by colonialism. The new age of philosophy thus requires work within traditions as much as it does work across them.

One example of a use of reason that is not beholden to colonialism is drawn from Ganeri's research in classical Indian philosophy. Rather than reasoning by means of applying a general rule to each particular situation, thinkers in Indian traditions cite a particular example and then apply it to the case at hand. Ganeri gives the following example:

> Look, it is going to rain (*pakṣa*: proposed thesis). For see that large black cloud (*hetu*: sign). Last time you saw a large black cloud like that one (*dṛṣṭānta*: exemplary case), what happened? Well, it's the same now (*upanaya*: application). It is definitely going to rain (*nigamana*: decision).[23]

Instead of relying on a universal rule, the mode of reasoning is dependent on the context. If you want to convince your interlocutor that is going to rain, you find an example that is familiar to them, and use it as an exemplary case.[24] Ganeri sees such case-based reasoning as especially useful in the age of re-emergence, because it frees us from the necessity of a general rule to mediate encounters between different traditions.

While Ganeri's *epistemic pluralism*—the idea that there are many, irreducible ways of knowing reality—differs from the pluralism defended by Wong, it has similar implications for cross-cultural philosophy. Without a single, universal approach to guide us, we look to different culturally bound traditions for new forms of philosophical reflection.

Criticism and evaluation

So far, we have been exploring the main claims of pluralism and the underlying justification for these claims. But does the pluralist approach hold up to scrutiny? In this section we will discuss some problems with this approach.

Value pluralism and evaluative incommensurability

A main problem arises from pluralism's acceptance of evaluative incommensurability. If we are faced with a conflict between a tradition that emphasizes community and one that prioritizes the rights of individuals, the value pluralist will contend that it is impossible to resolve. Wong writes that "no judgment of superiority can be made here.... [E]ach sort of ethic focuses on a good that may reasonably occupy the center of an ethical ideal for human life."[25]

While pluralism shows us how to appreciate diverse approaches to the human good, the critic may argue that it leaves us with little to do after that. How can societies with different moralities engage one another? Suppose Confucius and the Duke of She were to continue their conversation. The Duke of She argues that the morality found in Confucius' society leads to a disregard for the sufferings of nonfamily members, to a breakdown of the rule of law, and to nepotism and corruption. When he asks Confucius to respond to these criticisms, the latter tells him he should more appreciative of alternative moral configurations.

This is not an imaginary problem. Some pluralists have reacted negatively to attempts by philosophers based in the West to impose one model of human rights on the rest of the world, emphasizing the different conceptions of rights to be found in different cultures. This line of thought has seeped into statements made by those in positions of power. As the leader of the Chinese delegation to the 1993 United Nations Conference on Human Rights argued, countries with different cultural backgrounds "have different understanding and practice of human rights. Thus, one should not and cannot think of the human rights standard and model of certain countries and demand all countries comply with them."[26] The assertion of difference is the first step in the argument, the second is cutting oneself off from criticism.

Think too of the many people in the modern world who have roots in more than one cultural tradition. The film *The Joy Luck Club* (based on a novel of the same name by Amy Tan) tells the story of two generations of women, the older made up of four friends who immigrated to the United States from China, the younger their American-born daughters. The values of the two generations are in constant and sometimes bitter conflict. The mothers want their daughters to follow traditional Chinese values, but the daughters have caught the spirit of American independence. They respond to their mothers' demands for obedience by saying things like, "This isn't China. You can't make me!"

As we have seen, the pluralist can give us a subtle way of understanding the competing values at stake in the mother-daughter interactions. But what can it tell us about how the mothers or daughters should act? Which cultural morality should they prioritize? Suppose we grant the pluralists are correct that there is more than one good, and that the different goods are incompatible with one another. After they have shown us examples of these goods, like caring for one's parents, emphasizing individual autonomy, and so on, what is there left to do?

Engagement with other true moralities

In response, the pluralist will argue that we must first refine our notion of what is philosophically productive. Progress does not necessarily mean that one morality has to win out over the others. In thinking that there must be a single solution to every difficult moral issue, we presuppose a universalist conception of morality. A single morality might ease our confusion by telling us how to act in every situation, but it will exalt one good at the expense of others.

Instead, forward movement could take place *within* each morality. On a pluralist account of progress, a number of ethical traditions continue to exist alongside one another, with each constructively advancing its own conception of the good as a result of exposure to and reflection on the others.

Adherents of different cultural moralities might learn, for instance, how to attain a more careful balance between goods. If it is true that different values form a counterpoint to one another, then when we emphasize one value, we lose something of the value it is set against. Looking at other cultural traditions can serve as corrective to the excesses of our own.

In one essay, Wong examines the values of "competition" and "harmony" in ancient Greece and ancient China.[27] Though the Greeks emphasized competition, and the Chinese harmony, in neither case did these values exclude their opposites. Since athletic contests in ancient Greece were part of a cultural striving for excellence, the Greek focus on competition presupposed the background value of harmony. The Chinese value on harmony in turn entailed a kind of competition between diverse points of view, since it required that individuals air their disagreements with their superiors when it would help them determine the best policy to implement.

Wong thinks that at the midpoint between these two values, we would not find a perfect balance, but rather a kind of "bland mediocrity." A cultural morality has to emphasize one value or another to serve as a motivating ideal for a society's members. Nonetheless, he believes modern-day Chinese and Westerners can learn from each other about how to avoid too much of one extreme or the other. If we lose sight of the common striving for excellence, then competition becomes nothing more than individuals pursuing their own private goods at everyone else's expense. If we forget about the importance of disagreement, then harmony turns into mindless conformity.

A cultural morality might also learn how to confine its focal values within their proper spheres.[28] Confucianism and Daoism, the two most prominent philosophical traditions which emerged in ancient China, have very different visions of human ethical practice. Yet the maxim, "Confucian in public life, Daoist in private life" has been widely accepted. Perhaps a similar compromise could be found for other competing values. A full human life could find a place for competition and harmony, obedience and independence, familial obligation and care for strangers. The goal of the comparative pluralist would be to map the correct scope of each tradition's values.

There are other possibilities for mutual exchange.[29] Adherents of one cultural morality could use standards internal to the alternative one to raise questions about its configuration of goods. The two moralities could also share concepts with one another that enrich the ways in which each can distinguish various goods, just as the Confucian conception of "filial piety" can give twenty-first-century Americans a new category for thinking about relationships with family members. And not all interaction between opposed cultural traditions has to be philosophical in nature. Adherents of different moralities can learn from viewing each other's art, films, literature, customs, and the like. Even if we accept the evaluative incommensurability of these moralities, we will still have plenty to accomplish.

Epistemic pluralism vs. relativism

We also find objections to the idea that there are many incompatible yet equally valid epistemic systems. One problem with this idea, as Contemporary philosopher Paul Boghossian writes in his book *Fear of Knowledge: Against Relativism and Constructivism* (2006), is that we tend to defer to one of these systems, science, when we want to know what the facts are. If we wish to determine who the first people in America were, for example, then "we have a variety of techniques and methods—observation, logic, inference to the best explanation and so forth, but not tea-leaf reading or crystal ball gazing— that we take to be the only legitimate ways of forming rational beliefs on the subject."[30] Epistemic pluralism tells us, however, that there are no facts that make science more correct than any other epistemic system. Why should we accept anything on this view?

To ward off this criticism, Ganeri clarifies that his pluralism is about "stances" rather than "systems." An epistemic system is a set of norms that tells us when a particular belief is justified. A stance is more akin to a "style of inquiry," a strategy or policy that we adopt to arrive at factual beliefs. "One such policy," Ganeri writes, "might be to attend only to what is immediately present in experience, another might be to enumerate everything one encounters without making any categorial distinctions, another to attend to stasis rather than flux, or vice versa."[31] While these stances may be genuinely different from each other, more than one may be equally valid. He gives the analogy of traveling different paths up a mountain, where more than one path can be useful for reaching the top.

At the same time, Ganeri is careful to distinguish his pluralism from relativism. Stance pluralism, he contends, is compatible with the idea that "there is a single reality to be explored, a multi-aspectual, multidimensional, multiply essenced one."[32] While each climber views the mountain differently, what each sees can be claimed to represent the mountain. On the other hand, stances such as the colonial use of reason are illegitimate if they deny that other stances exist or engage in violence to suppress them.

Strengths of the pluralist approach

A great advantage of the pluralist approach lies in its ability to respond to the problems discussed in the last part of the book. As we have seen, a common criticism of comparative work is that it assimilates diverse philosophical traditions into a single Borg-like entity. Pluralism can be an important corrective to the "thrust toward homogenization" that has characterized much of comparative philosophy.[33]

Incommensurability and relativism are also problems for the comparative philosopher. In response to proponents of foundational incommensurability, the pluralist is able to show how different cultural traditions can understand each other's values, since these values answer to the common standard of human needs and desires. Unlike the relativist, the pluralist can assert that some of these values are good or bad depending on whether they fulfill human needs and allow for social stability. And while the pluralist does subscribe to an evaluative incommensurability between traditions containing true moralities, these traditions can still make internal philosophical progress by engaging with one another.

The counterpoint model of cultural values also helps us avoid reducing a philosophical-cultural tradition to one value or another. Pluralists eschew a model of cultural difference in which societies embodying incompatible values are engaged in a struggle for world dominance. The problem with this model is that it treats the different cultures as "complete and closed systems" which are only now beginning to open themselves up to dialogue, rather than pluralities which have always been characterized by internal debate. What is happening now is not a "clash" between cultural competitors, but rather a growing awareness that each society contains within itself the same basic conflicts of values as all the others.[34] Societies have much to learn from one another about how to resolve these conflicts. As the Beninese philosopher Paulin J. Hountondji puts it, "What we must recognize today is that pluralism does not come to any society from outside but is inherent in every society."[35]

Conclusion

Pluralism gives us an outlook on where we are now with respect to the many living philosophical traditions around the world, but also on where we would like to be in the future. This outlook appears well adapted to the world we inhabit today. Responding to different ways of life modes of inquiry by asserting the superiority of one's own can cut a person or a society off from growth. The goal of comparative philosophy, in the pluralist view, is to understand and preserve the different cultural perspectives on human reality, and enable communication between all.[36]

Still, we might think that we can get beyond an irreducible plurality of cultural perspectives in our quest for the good life. Without common values to appeal to in cases of conflict, the world will not be a very secure place. We must therefore consider approaches that, while sympathetic to the different shapes cultural moralities can take, try to go further than pluralism.

10

Consensus

The consensus approach combines elements of universalism and pluralism. The goal is to establish a set of norms shared by multiple traditions while at the same time allowing for diversity of acceptable philosophical foundations for these norms. A consensus approach to human rights tries to find support for rights within a particular cultural-philosophical tradition, acknowledging that each tradition may have its own reasons to support norms respecting rights. The goal of the consensus approach is to achieve a more stable global society, one in which incommensurable philosophical foundations are no barrier to agreement on the essentials of human conduct.

Consensus not only offers a way for comparative philosophers to resolve the tension between universalism and pluralism, but also gives us a concrete goal to work toward. This goal finds its realization in documents such as the Universal Declaration of Human Rights that serve as standards for governments worldwide. While the goal of consensus has been most frequently articulated by political philosophers, because the work of identifying grounds for common norms involves the scrutiny of the metaphysical and ethical foundations of different traditions, it can include comparativists interested in other areas as well.

There are both theoretical and practical obstacles to the consensus approach. Will adherents of different cultural moralities be able to "agree to disagree" on the foundations of the good life? Will the agreement in question be anything more than platitudes? Additionally, what is the philosophical value of consensus? Does consensus only tell us which norms are agreed upon by particular traditions at a particular moment in human history, or does it establish something more enduring?

Consensus in theory and practice

In the first part of this chapter, we'll look at the underlying theory of consensus and how this theory has been adopted by cross-cultural philosophers. We'll also consider a well-known example of the consensus model and some lessons it provides.

Rawls' overlapping consensus

The consensus approach takes for granted a certain picture of the different worldviews present in the modern world, as well as a particular means of ensuring a stable coexistence of these worldviews. In both aspects, it draws on the later work of the great twentieth-century political philosopher John Rawls.

According to Rawls, the diversity of moral doctrines is a fact of contemporary political life. The many different worldviews present within modern democracies involve "conflicting and indeed incommensurable comprehensive conceptions of the meaning, value, and purpose of human life."[1] Think for a moment of all the different conceptions of the good life that exist within a nation like the United States. From Amish to Zoroastrian, the different communities of Americans find roots in incomparable religious, philosophical, and cultural backgrounds. This diversity will not go away as time passes, but will persist and possibly even increase.

The problem is how to get all of these people to live together. As Rawls puts it, "How is it possible for there to exist over time a just and stable society of free and equal citizens, who remain profoundly divided by reasonable religious, philosophical, and moral doctrines?"[2] It's easy enough to see how a family whose members have incompatible belief-systems would fall into disarray. How can a society composed of a multitude of such belief-systems avoid such a fate?

Making one of the worldviews applicable to everyone would be possible only through the use of force, and a society that depends on force will not be just or free, and probably not stable either. Another option is what Rawls refers to as a *modus vivendi* (literally, "way of living"), a kind of treaty that maintains a balance of power between groups with opposed points of view. Yet this arrangement does not ensure long-term stability either, since when the balance of power shifts, the dominant group will try to assert its superiority over the others.

Rawls himself defends the pursuit of an "overlapping consensus," wherein adherents of different religious or philosophical worldviews converge on a set of shared norms based on their own individual reasons that are not necessarily compatible with one another. In particular, they must reach agreement on how the basic social and political institutions of their society are to be structured. Rawls maintains that the consensus model is the best answer to his question about how to achieve an enduring and just society. Instead of using coercion, consensus achieves social stability through "free and willing agreement." And since each group has reasons within its own moral doctrine to support the agreed-upon norms, it is more stable than a *modus vivendi*. Breaching the norms due to shifts in balance of power would mean violating one's own beliefs.

Consider a norm stating that a society should be set up so that all its citizens have an equal chance at advancing themselves. We can find different reasons for agreeing to this norm: we may believe that people are all created equal in the eyes of God; that we are by nature equally capable of developing our talents; or that a society set up in some other way will end up treating some of its members as mere means for the good of others. If we want everyone to agree on one of these reasons, we will not get very far, since they arise from different religious or philosophical commitments. In establishing consensus, we remain neutral with regard to the underlying foundations, so that acceptance of the norm emphasizing equal opportunity does not imply adherence to any particular larger doctrine.

The consensus approach in comparative philosophy

The theory of overlapping consensus presupposes a pluralist conception of morality. If there were a single scale by which we could measure the diverse values found in all the different moral worldviews, we would be able to say which of these worldviews was best; but since there is no such scale, we are left with a number of competing moralities that cannot be reduced to one another. Nonetheless, the search for generally acceptable norms that are independent of commitment to any particular worldview recalls attempts by comparative universalists to construct a globally applicable morality.

Some cross-cultural philosophers have adopted the consensus approach as a means of convincing other cultures to adopt norms they think should apply universally. Different premises, as Rawls reminds us, can result in the same conclusion. If there is widespread agreement within our culture on a norm C, supported by premises P1, P2, and P3, we approach other cultural-philosophical traditions with the goal of determining what premises within it can be used to support C. Once we have learned enough about the basic premises accepted by that culture, we can construct a chain of reasoning linking one or more of these premises and C. We then use this chain of reasoning as a means of persuading the other culture to accept C. It is much more likely that we will convince these cultures to adopt the norms we think are important if we do so on their own terms.[3]

Human rights discourse in contemporary Western societies involves both a set of norms that are enshrined in law and an underlying system of values. Consensus advocates contend that while we may be able to convince others to accept the norms, it is difficult and perhaps impossible to get them to adopt the particular values that support them. Different cultures prioritize different goods, which become entrenched in their social customs and political institutions. While some Western theorists think that human dignity is a universal value, others may believe that this value is in fact particular to the Judeo-Christian worldview, in which human beings are seen as created in the image and likeness of God. Values such as the achievement of spiritual well-being or realization of familial relationships may appear more important to members of other societies.

East Asian societies in particular may reject Western human rights discourse not because they disagree with the set of norms, but because they are suspicious of the underlying premises. As Charles Taylor points out in an essay defending the consensus approach, Western views of rights are clustered at one end of the individualism/collectivism scale, focusing on the importance of the individual person's consent. In societies with a more collectivistic outlook, the worry is that the Western model "focuses people on their rights, on what they can claim from society and others, rather than their responsibilities, what they owe to the whole community or its members. It encourages people to be self-regarding and leads to an atrophied sense of belonging."[4] Leaders such as Lee Kuan Yew, the former prime minister of Singapore, reject the "total package" that comes with human rights norms because they believe it will lead to the breakdown of civil society.

Rather than trying to establish the universality of human rights by basing them on certain principles we think all rational people should accept, the consensus approach looks for agreement on human rights from within different cultural perspectives.[5] Tradition A may condemn slavery because it teaches that all humans are equal, Tradition B because it prizes the virtue of humaneness. If the one tradition has no concept of humaneness, and the other thinks that differences between people are a fact of life, the point is that they both agree that slavery is wrong. Such agreement not only makes a more compelling case for extending rights across cultural boundaries, but also gives us a less ethnocentric account of these rights. In forcing us to find grounds for common norms within different cultural traditions, the consensus approach prevents these traditions from being nothing more than passive receptacles of our values.

Taylor points to the example of Thailand, where attempts at social reform have looked to the Buddhist tradition as a foundation. Of particular interest to the reformers is the tradition's belief that individuals must take responsibility for their own enlightenment; Buddhists also advocate a doctrine of nonviolence (*ahimsa*), which forbids us to coerce others. In using these values rather than imported Western ones to provide a foundation for democracy and human rights, "A rather different route has been travelled to a similar goal."[6]

A Buddhist foundation for democracy and human rights may even be an improvement in some respects. Taylor notes that the commitment to nonviolence in Buddhism extends to the environment; Thai Buddhists have fought to defend rural lands against exploitation by the government and big business. The worldview also condemns greed as one of the causes of violence. The great political heroes in the Buddhist tradition are not revolutionaries who overthrow oppressive governments by force, but peaceful reformers.

The consensus approach can lead to a stronger philosophical foundation for rights than that which is available in any one culture. We think of many pillars holding up the same edifice. The discovery that other traditions have reason to support the norms we think are important can be an exhilarating one, giving us confidence that these norms are not merely a matter of our own culture's biases.

The universal declaration of human rights

An important example of consensus in practice is the Universal Declaration of Human Rights, adopted by the United Nations in 1948. In the aftermath of the Second World War, there was a deeply felt need to reestablish norms concerning respect for human rights in response to the ideologies of Nazism and Fascism that had led to the conflict. The resulting Declaration has set the Guinness World Record for the "Most Translated Document" of all time (currently it appears in over 500 different languages and counting); it has its own holiday, "Human Rights Day," celebrated on the anniversary of the signing. While the drafting process was carried out by political delegates rather than philosophers, it illustrates both the challenge and the promise of the consensus approach

The Preamble of the UDHR proclaims it to be "a common standard for all peoples and all nations." Its thirty articles include the following protections:

The right not to be held in slavery or servitude.
The right not to be tortured.
The right not to be arbitrarily arrested, detained, or exiled.
The right to move freely within a country, and to leave or return.
The right to marry and start a family.
The right to work, and to receive equal pay for equal labor.
The right to a standard of living that ensures one's health and well-being.
The right to an education, to be free at least in its elementary stages.

The document as a whole provides a kind of "moral anchor" for international organizations like Amnesty International and Human Rights Watch that attempt to enforce human rights norms worldwide.

While the UDHR is quite concise (under 1,800 words in its entirety), it was the product of long discussion, taking place in seven drafting stages between January 1947 and December 1948. Just the drafting process for Article 1, recounted by Johannes Morsink in his fascinating book *The Universal Declaration of Human Rights: Origins, Drafting, and Intent*, gives us a sense of the difficult and sometimes tense debate.[7] The final version of the article states: "All human beings are born free and equal in dignity and rights. They are endowed with reason and conscience and should act towards one another in a spirit of brotherhood."

But endowed *by whom*? Originally two competing versions of the second sentence were proposed. The first said, "endowed *by nature* with reason and conscience," the second, "*Created in the image and likeness of God*, they are endowed with reason and conscience." When delegates from Latin American countries, who saw belief in God as a moral foundation shared by the vast majority of humanity, argued for the latter version, those from the USSR and China objected that this language would represent Western intolerance. The phrase "by nature," on the other hand, although originally inserted as a reference to the Christian idea that a natural law is implanted in the hearts of all humans, was taken by some delegates to suggest a purely materialistic view of human beings that denied their spiritual origin.

In the end, the drafters left out both phrases. As the French delegate René Cassin wrote, this allowed them "to take no position on the nature of man and of society and to avoid metaphysical controversies, notably the conflicting doctrines of spiritualists, rationalists, and materialists regarding the origin of the rights of man."[8] The final language of the article allows those who subscribe to these conflicting doctrines to interpret the idea of being "endowed with reason and conscience" as they see fit.

This compromise did not satisfy everyone. The delegate from the Netherlands, a Roman Catholic priest and politician named L.J.C. Beaufort, arguing that a secular foundation for rights was no foundation at all, insisted on adding language about the divine origin of the recognition of human rights into the Preamble of the Declaration. Past experience, he warned, has shown "the danger of allowing the monstrous materialistic conception of man as a mere tool in the service of the State."[9] Without a spiritual basis for rights recognition, leaders in Communist countries could not be expected to take rights seriously. Ultimately though, even delegates from non-Communist countries rejected Beaufort's proposal, in one part because they recognized the possibility of nonreligious foundations for rights and in another because they did not want to be drawn into deep theological disputes. The final version of UDHR contains no reference to God or the divine.

To its authors, the Declaration illustrated the awesome power of consensus. As the Chilean delegate Hernan Santa Cruz wrote:

> I perceived clearly that I was participating in a truly significant historic event in which a consensus had been reached as to the supreme value of the human person, a value that did not originate in the decision of a worldly power, but rather in the fact of existing—which gave rise to the inalienable right to live free from want and oppression and to fully develop one's personality. In the Great Hall ... there was an atmosphere of genuine solidarity and brotherhood among men and women from all latitudes, the like of which I have not seen again in any international setting.[10]

Nonetheless, questions about the universality of the UDHR have been around from very early on, commencing even before the final draft was finished.

As Morsink recounts, late in 1947 the UN Human Rights Committee received a memo from the American Anthropological Association. Starting from the premise that values are "relative to the culture from which they derive," the memo cautioned the Committee's members that their efforts would lead to an ethnocentric code rather than a universal one. What is considered a human right in one culture, its authors maintained, may be considered barbarism in another. Rather than trying to impose one culture's standards on all the rest, we should allow each to come up with its own distinctive means of ensuring the good of the individual and society. These charges of ethnocentrism have continued throughout the history of the document.

Writing fifty years after the signing of the UDHR, Morsink points out that these critics often seem to be ignorant of the debates that informed the drafting process. As we have seen in the case of Article 1, the authors of the UDHR took great care not to impose a set of Western foundations on the rest of the world. Further evidence of the Declaration's universal appeal is its subsequent affirmation in various forms by non-Western societies. As one author writes, "[the UDHR] and subsequent treaties have since been adopted, adapted, expanded, and deployed by peoples throughout the world in pursuit of their own locally defined objectives.... [I]t cannot seriously be argued that these rights are still the exclusive product of Western societies."[11]

Even so, there remains plenty of work to be done in establishing a global consensus on rights. Some Islamic nations, for instance, have opposed Article 18 of the UDHR, which guarantees freedom of religion, on the grounds that the Koran prohibits Muslims from changing their religion. The forty-five member-states of the Organization of the Islamic Conference ratified an alternative document, the Cairo Declaration of Human Rights in Islam, in 1990. Contemporary critics have pointed out that the UDHR reflects the balance of power present in 1948, when some nations in Africa and Asia had not yet gained independence of colonial rule.

Consensus theorists emphasize that documents such as the UDHR are imperfect but necessary starting points. As Onuma Yasuaki writes, these documents

> are no more than a first clue to identifying transnational and inter-civilizational human rights. They are essentially political products, generally taking the form of normative consensus among national governments. Yet, we have no other choice but to accept them as today's most authoritative expression of the normative consciousness of the global community on human rights. No other instruments, whether they be the statement by the US or Chinese government, claims of leading human rights NGOs, or views

of leading scholars, can claim that they represent the global consensus more legitimately.[12]

To promote an enduring respect for human rights, comparative philosophers must work to find further foundations for consensus in the world's many different cultural-philosophical traditions, as well as to clarify the methods that are used to arrive at shared norms.

Evaluating the consensus approach

Critics have questioned the *possibility* of consensus, its *meaningfulness*, and its *philosophical value*. In this section we will explore these criticisms and some possible replies. Like other approaches to comparative philosophy, consensus faces many obstacles.

Is consensus possible?

Some philosophers have found problems with the theory of overlapping consensus. The contemporary Confucian political philosopher Jiang Qing criticizes Rawls' view for presupposing its own comprehensive moral doctrine, namely a liberal democratic one that takes values like freedom and equality to be foundational.[13] When Rawls asks, "How is it possible for there to exist over time a just and stable society of free and equal citizens?" he already takes for granted a certain picture of how society should be. These democratic values are not open for negotiation when we try to reach a consensus among the plurality of ethical and religious worldviews present in modern societies. Jiang sees Rawls' theory as hypocritical, claiming to be neutral between worldviews when it is anything but. Similarly minded critics have seen the theory as "not a principled and self-limiting moral position but a political device with a large hidden agenda"—to spread liberal values to all sectors of society.[14]

Others have taken issue with the practice of consensus. Within a single country like the United States there is little agreement about norms concerning abortion and euthanasia. People who dispute these issues appear to have little shared background, drawing on incompatible perspectives—religious, secular, conservative, liberal, libertarian, feminist, utilitarian—that influence their judgments. What would a consensus on norms regarding abortion or euthanasia even look like?

The prospect of consensus on these issues looks worse when we turn to the international arena. As one prominent philosopher sums up the situation at the beginning of a book on global bioethics: "It is not just that there is a failure of consensus on all the major issues of human life, ranging from the significance of human sexuality, human reproduction, early human life, the allocation of scarce resources, and the nature of governmental authority, to the significance of suffering, dying, and death, but that no resolution of our controversies appears in sight."[15] If we can find little overlap within our own society, what should we expect when we bring together societies from different parts of the world? People may not be able to ignore their most basic commitments in order to reach a global consensus.[16]

As the persistent controversy surrounding the UDHR illustrates, particular instances of consensus are always open to the charge that they are attempts by one group to impose its values on the others. The possibility that certain factions will dominate the conversation is another barrier to the practical realization of consensus. Even if the arrived-at norms are adequately representative of the groups around the table, what about those who aren't given a seat in the first place? Consensus among the world's major cultural-ethical traditions may come at the expense of the less prominent ones.[17]

While we need to be aware in advance of the immense practical difficulties in achieving consensus, these difficulties should not prevent us from the attempt. Without some agreement on the basic issues surrounding human life and death, we live in a realm of moral anarchy in which the most powerful impose their views on everyone else. To prevent a situation in which only the representatives of major constituencies have a say, some have defended a "horizontal" model of consensus in which the subgroups within each society reach across cultural boundaries to establish agreement with like-minded others.[18] Feminists in China, for instance, could attempt to establish consensus with women's rights advocates in other countries. While agreement on all the major ethical issues is a goal far in the future, documents like the UDHR show that some degree of consensus can be achieved.

Nor do all attempts at consensus fully accept Rawls' model. On an alternative view, advocated by the political theorist Bhikhu Parekh, we reach consensus not by leaving our moral, religious, and philosophical values at the door, but rather through dialogue about these values and our reasons for holding them with members of other cultures. Contrary to the drafters of the UDHR, Parekh believes that this approach is the only way to ensure that the values we arrive at are genuinely universal.[19]

Is consensus meaningful?

But even supposing we can attain an adequately representative set of norms, what about the content of these norms? Other opponents of consensus claim that its conclusions are so broad that they are meaningless, glossing over significant areas of disagreement.

We have seen a version of this criticism already in Beaufort's opposition to the language of Article 1 of the UDHR. Without God, he asked, what do rights really mean? The vague content of more recent documents has led some observers to pessimism about the potential of the consensus model. Critics have pointed out that the 2005 UNESCO Declaration on Bioethics and Human Rights invokes concepts like "justice" and "equality" without defining them, and what is worse, ignores issues like abortion altogether. "The Declaration," writes one author, "is marked by a general vacuity of its principles, as well as a failure to take seriously the moral difference characterizing the age."[20] Political theorists have similarly disparaged the 1997 Universal Declaration of Human Responsibilities, a proclamation on the part of former heads of state including Jimmy Carter, Mikhail Gorbachev, and Lee Kuan Yew, for indulging in empty moralizing. One article states that "Everyone has the responsibility to promote good and to avoid evil in all things," another that "Every person has a responsibility to behave with integrity, honesty and fairness." The document leaves it unclear how such behavior will help us confront the issues of our time: climate change, population growth, income inequality, and famine.

The inability of consensus to achieve substantive values may be seen as a consequence of the model itself. If you have ever tried to get a bunch of individuals to take a position on some matter, you know that the more varied these individuals' interests, the more watered-down their conclusions as a group will be. Since the more specific the recommendation, the greater chance there is that someone will object to it, the incentive is to make the language of the final product as vague as possible. "Our students should be able to communicate orally, in writing, and through other formats," agreed the General Education committee at my university after long discussion among representatives of all its departments.

In seeking cross-cultural consensus, the more we incorporate our foundational values into the final list of statements, the more we are guilty of ethnocentrism; the less we do so, however, the less meaning these conclusions will have to us. When we just agree on the name for a norm, but nothing else, what have we really achieved?[21] As the comparative political philosopher Daniel A. Bell sums things up, "In short, the aspiration to develop values of more universal scope with substantive content may not be realizable. Cross-cultural dialogue will lead to either empty platitudes or politically controversial conclusions likely to be rejected by affected constituents."[22]

Few of the norms listed in the Universal Declaration of Human Rights, however, could be considered devoid of content. Reading the document as a whole one is inclined to agree with Hernan Santa Cruz that these norms represent a leap forward in our collective conception of human morality. If these norms did not have any content, why would the governing bodies of many countries continue to resist implementing them? And while we could pick out a few weak points in the Universal Declaration of Human Responsibilities, many of the norms in that document—that well-off people have a responsibility to work to end poverty and inequality, that freedom of the press must be balanced out by conscientious reporting, or that members of particular religious traditions should avoid prejudice against those of different beliefs—are quite substantial.

Honest disagreement should be given its due, of course. The consensus approach is not a replacement for ongoing debate and criticism between members of rival traditions. Yet although documents like the UDHR may be faulted for glossing over significant areas of disagreement, the points of agreement they identify can serve as a foundation for worldwide progress on issues that matter.

Does consensus have philosophical value?

A final objection concerns the philosophical value of consensus. In philosophy, the objection goes, it is justification that matters. We cannot provide justification for a view simply by showing that some other tradition has reasons for affirming it; what matters is that these are *good reasons*. But consensus by its very nature leaves out any evaluation of the reasons we have for supporting a norm; all it tells us is whether certain groups of people will agree to it at this moment in time. As a result, as one author puts it, "The approach is either anthropological or sociological (in that it may be of empirical or historical interest) or else political (in that it may represent a path to social stability or accommodation), but it is of no inherent philosophical or ethical interest."[23]

We can easily think of cases in which the consensus view is morally unacceptable. While gender inequality has been a matter of consensus throughout most of recorded human history, such agreement should not give the view any weight in ethical debates.[24] Without some independent standard by which to evaluate the norms at issue, how do we know that today's consensus is any improvement?

The proponent of consensus will question, however, whether our standard of evaluation really is "independent." If we accept that there is a plurality of foundations for the good human life, judgments about the strength of our reasons will depend on which of these foundations we adopt. Attempts to assert our moral principles in the cross-cultural arena will end in failure, since members of different traditions may be equally certain that they already have the best ones available. If we want to convince those who do not share our own cultural-philosophical framework that we are in the right, we must appeal to standards they accept.

As Parekh's approach illustrates, philosophers who adopt the consensus approach do not have to be entirely neutral with regard to competing moral foundations. We have reasons for why we value what we do, and we should expect that others have reasons as well. But because we are shaped by our culture, we cannot guarantee that those reasons are free of ethnocentric bias. We must submit them to the test of cross-cultural dialogue to make sure that others can comprehend and accept them.[25] Consensus does not have to mean giving up on finding reasons for the norms we accept, but simply accepting that our attempts at providing such reasons are limited in important ways.

Non-Western approaches to consensus

Most of our discussion up until this point has been based on a Rawlsian model of consensus. Yet philosophers working in non-Western traditions have also developed ideas about consensus that challenge the dominant model. In this section, we will examine two of these approaches.

Consensus in Chinese philosophy

Many Chinese political thinkers will reject Rawls' idea that pluralism is inevitable, instead tending to see all differences as reconcilable.[26] Rather than overlapping consensus between mutually incompatible points of view, the focus is on achieving *harmony*, which aims "to combine the diverse elements of the many members of society at a particular time into a single cohesive whole."[27] In Chinese society, it is not uncommon for a single person to practice Confucianism, Daoism, and Buddhism in different elements of their life, without seeing any contradiction in moving from one to the other.[28]

The notion of harmony (*he* 和) has deep roots in Chinese culture. A passage in the *Zuozhuan* text says that "Harmony is like making soup. One needs water, fire, vinegar, sauce, salt, and plum to cook fish and meat. One needs to cook them with firewood, combine them together in order to balance the taste."[29] As this metaphor suggests, harmony is not about achieving sameness, but about balancing different elements in order to achieve a fine result. According to the Confucian tradition, this harmony can occur at different levels: in the individual person, within the family, between different groups in society, and between human beings and the natural world.[30]

Due to the influence of these ideas, some scholars argue that the idea of consensus takes on a different meaning in Chinese culture. The traditional model of consensus in China, as Hall and Ames put it, is "not an agreement about how individuals ought to behave, but a consensus at the level of aesthetic feeling and common practice."[31] Whereas the *rational* model of consensus attempts to arrive at "sameness of belief," the Chinese *aesthetic* model attempts to coordinate differences in harmonious action. The ruler's function is to find creative ways in which diverse interests may be put together so as to produce a harmonious society.

Western models of consensus presuppose a certain type of society— driven, as Hall and Ames argue, by the "need to find abstract or general principles to accommodate differences among diverse populations."[32] In China, however, theorists of consensus can assume a shared background to help resolve disputes. Practices such as ritual allow for differences while at the same time expressing the shared life of the community.

Consensus in African philosophy

Kwasi Wiredu points to the traditional practice of consensus in African society, where elders "sit under the big trees and talk until they agree."[33] The faith in consensus as a form of decision-making is supported by life in a communal culture where cooperation among members is more characteristic than a winner-take-all competition between them. While community members may often think of themselves as having different or opposed goals, ultimately their interests converge. This notion of society is reinforced by the Ghanaian symbol of the Siamese crocodile, with two separate heads competing for food, not realizing that the food in the end goes to the same stomach.

Consensus in Wiredu's understanding is pragmatic in nature. It does not mean everyone must share the same beliefs about the world or matters of right and wrong. Members of a society who disagree with one another still need to act together. Consensus, as Wiredu writes, "is an affair of compromise, and compromise is a certain adjustment of the interests of individuals ... to the common necessity for something to be done."[34] Such compromise does not settle disagreement, but instead is a dynamic affair where debate is always ongoing.

Wiredu contrasts government by consensus with the oppositional style of politics found in the US and UK, where different parties compete in a zero sum game for dominance. Imitation of this adversarial majoritarian style of politics in African countries has led to growing division and the marginalization of smaller ethnic groups by larger ones. A consensus-based political structure would also restore the communal culture that was found in traditional societies and has been disrupted by the forces of colonialism and industrialization.

In both of these types of consensus, we see frameworks that not only predate Rawls and Taylor by many centuries, but which also are motivated by distinctive notions of how to achieve agreement within a community. While the Rawlsian model of consensus is useful for understanding global dialogue on human rights, it also may entail uniquely Western assumptions about the structure of this dialogue.[35] More work needs to be done concerning non-Western theories of consensus.

Conclusion

The consensus approach illustrates further how comparative work might be done across traditions with incommensurable foundations. Even if we cannot decide which cultural morality is best, we can at least attain agreement on basic norms. Universalists and pluralists alike can commit themselves to the goal of furthering this agreement.

Since the process of achieving consensus often involves investigation of the underlying foundations for the norms in question, as well as a reconstruction of the chain of reasoning between this foundation and the norm, we need philosophically trained experts to assist the effort. Comparative philosophers in particular can help determine the degree to which norms found in different cultural-philosophical traditions can be described as "shared." If we want meaningful and enduring consensus between different cultural moralities, comparative philosophers should get involved in the process.

11

Global Philosophy

Suppose that in place of stand-alone courses in comparative philosophy, philosophy departments offered all their usual courses—Ethics, Epistemology, Philosophy of Mind—but added comparative dimensions to each. In the Ethics course, the professor might briefly describe a Confucian account of the virtues during the unit on virtue ethics. In Philosophy of Mind, you could learn Buddhist accounts of consciousness alongside Western ones. For the last few weeks of a course, perhaps you would study one or two ideas from non-Western ethical traditions in their own right.

Global philosophy means "engaging in philosophy in a way that is open ... to the insights and approaches from philosophers and philosophical traditions around the globe."[1] While remaining within our own philosophical tradition, we look to thinkers and texts from other traditions to expand the philosophical resources at our disposal and submit our own ideas to external criticism. The goal is not to compare fixed historical traditions, but rather for these traditions to creatively interact at specific points in the contemporary philosophical arena. Some global philosophers even reject the title of "comparative philosophy," since they think it implies we are merely pointing out similarities and differences between philosophies of the past.

The theory behind global philosophy is still a work in progress, having been articulated in various forms by philosophers working in different traditions.[2] The following chapter is more exploratory in nature than the ones that have preceded it, drawing on these different accounts to reconstruct the case for the global approach.

The challenge of global philosophy

Even as the global approach aims to make comparative philosophy less focused on the past, it also attempts to make contemporary philosophy more cross-cultural. Let us take a look at each of these challenges in turn.

Fusion philosophy

In the introduction to their book *Comparative Philosophy Without Borders* (2016), Arindam Chakrabarti and Ralph Weber offer one of the best articulations of the global-philosophical approach, which they refer to as "fusion philosophy." In their view, the approach means

> just doing philosophy as one thinks fit for getting to the truth about an issue or set of issues, by appropriating elements from all philosophical views and traditions one knows of but making no claim of 'correct exposition,' but just solving hitherto unsolved problems possibly raising issues never raised before anywhere.[3]

Rather than aiming to understand a particular philosophical tradition, the fusion philosopher focuses on working out a solution to a specific philosophical problem. In working out this solution, the practitioner "forgets" about the source and tries to extend a certain idea or argument in way that is novel and relevant to the issue at hand.[4] If someone objects that they are lifting the idea or argument out of its original context and then reshaping it and mixing it with other concepts in a way that makes it unrecognizable, the fusion philosopher will respond that, "well, that's the whole point."[5] The focus is on getting at the truth about the issue and not on the authority of this or that thinker or tradition. (In this regard, the "fusion" is different from the attempts at synthesis of traditions that we explored in Chapter 8, in that it does not try to preserve the truth found in multiple traditions.)

According to Chakrabarti and Weber, fusion philosophy aspires to *do* philosophy in a way that is *borderless*, crossing different geographic and cultural boundaries, leaping across boundaries in time, and relying on a mixture of philosophical methods.[6] The traditional comparative philosopher who attempts to understand similarities and differences between different cultural traditions ends up reaffirming the boundaries between these traditions: *The Chinese Confucian view is this, while the Greek tradition represented by Aristotle views it as that.* These borders put us in philosophical "comfort zones," where we become entrenched in familiar ways of thinking.[7]

Chakrabarti and Weber hope to push the boundaries of cross-cultural inquiry into a realm beyond comparative philosophy. They look toward a future in which the philosophical aspect triumphs over the comparative aspect: "Our dream is that future fusion philosophy will shed its local epithets, even the epithet 'comparative.' All good philosophy should be unapologetically, and, eventually, unselfconsciously, comparative and culturally hybrid."[8] In this vision, the comparer of cultures will make way for the *global philosopher*.

The need for interaction

The global-philosophical approach is best considered as a variety of what the philosopher of social science Brian Fay calls "interactionism."[9] What universalism and differentialism have in common, according to Fay, is that they treat "self" and "other" as fixed concepts, imagining them as two circles alongside one another. This image of cultural engagement leaves us with a limited range of options: either combine the circles in some way or keep the boundaries of each intact. As an alternative to these two views, interactionism

> conceives of the relation of the self and the other dialectically; it denies that "at bottom" the self and the other are essentially distinct and fixed, or that a particular identity means utter difference from that which it is not. Instead, it insists that the identity of the self is intimately bound up with the identity of the other (and vice-versa), that self and other are constantly in flux, and that they are both similar as well as different.[10]

To visualize the interactionist view of self and other, Fay gives the image of two spirals ascending upward with various points of contact with one another. The point is "a dynamic commingling in which parties constantly change."[11]

The interactionist is interested most of all in the points of contact between the parties in question. These "exchanges" can be both creative and destructive. In some cases, both cultural traditions may learn from another, while in others, one may be forced to give up ways of thinking that have long been part of it.

To be sure, all the approaches to comparative philosophy that we have considered thus far emphasize interaction between traditions in one form or another, but the traditions themselves tend to be treated as already finished products. Both the pluralist and consensus-builder often seem to take different cultural values for granted, rather than things that are subject to forceful negotiation. The universalist in turn looks to construct a view that goes beyond the particularities of tradition. On the interactionist view, however, as we have already seen in the case of "fusion philosophy," the goal is neither to overcome differences nor to preserve them, but rather to challenge or alter them.[12] Global philosophers emphasize the need for *constructive engagement* between philosophers working within different traditions, claiming that the mutual exchange of criticism and argument can not only enrich the traditions themselves, but also contribute to the advancement of contemporary philosophy as a whole.[13]

Philosophers in non-Western traditions have recognized the necessity of interaction for some time. In his essay, "Global Philosophy and Chinese Philosophers," Stephen Angle cites many examples of twentieth- and twenty-first-century Chinese thinkers who have called for greater engagement with Western philosophy. Their central argument is that such engagement would lead to the development of Chinese culture and its philosophical traditions. If ancient philosophies such as Confucianism are to survive in the modern world, they must be able to hold their own in confrontations with outsiders. As Fay puts it, "The principle lesson of the ethic of interactionism is: engage, learn from, adapt—or perish."[14] This recognition has not been limited to Chinese philosophers, but is also found in many recent works of Indian philosophy that attempt to connect with Western ideas and audiences.[15]

Making Western philosophy global

A main challenge is to convince Western philosophers to take the global approach. As it happens, very few courses in Western philosophy departments make any attempt to incorporate a comparative dimension. Comparative philosophy, Chinese philosophy, Indian philosophy, etc., tend to be taught independently of everything else that is covered in these departments, if they are taught at all.

Sometimes the case for making Western philosophy global takes the form of circular reasoning. It is assumed that because we are now living in a global era, philosophy must take account of traditions from different parts of the world. The next move is to accuse contemporary Western philosophy of failing to do this, of being close-minded, narrow, and out-of-date, with the conclusion that contemporary Western philosophy must change its ways.

The problem is that while the initial step in the argument will be quite appealing to those already engaged in comparative philosophy, it may not ring true for everyone else. Suppose that I am a philosopher interested in the problem of whether knowledge is justified true belief, a puzzle that goes back to Plato's *Theaetetus*. Why should the recent event of globalization necessitate that I change my approach to this problem? How we define knowledge is a question independent of whatever historical events are taking place in the outside world.

Accusations of close-mindedness will not be enough to convince such a philosopher. Instead, we must show how engagement with other cultural-philosophical traditions can make our own work more philosophically productive. In the rest of this chapter, we will examine further the case for global philosophy, focusing on the aspects of external criticism and problem-solving introduced in Chapter 2.

External criticism

Philosophical traditions are characterized by vigorous internal debate, often extending to the fundamental ideas within them. In the Confucian tradition, there is a long-standing question about how the values of *ren* ("humaneness") and *li* ("ritual"), two central concepts in the *Analects*, fit together. In the tradition of Western liberalism, we find a debate about how to understand the concept of "liberty." Adherents of the just war tradition dispute the connection between *jus ad bellum* ("justice in declaring war") and *jus in bello* ("justice in waging war"). These debates have helped form the development of each tradition.

However, traditions are also shaped by the need to justify themselves to outsiders. Often the most progress is made when we are forced to defend a view we take for granted against a challenging interlocutor. Mohist critics have questioned the value that Confucians place on *li*, communitarians the centrality of individual liberty in the liberal tradition, and realists and pacifists the coherence of the idea of a "just war."

The global-philosophical approach extends these challenges to the cross-cultural level. What challenges can East Asian political traditions provide to Western liberalism (or vice versa)? What would a Buddhist have to say about the just war tradition? On this conception, comparative philosophy is "built on the fundamental premise that the conversation across traditions will burn away some dross and refine and confirm some truths."[16]

In its broadest sense, cross-cultural criticism means making evaluative judgments about the basic claims put forward by the tradition in question (the word "critical" itself is rooted in the Greek *kritikos*, meaning "capable of judgment"). While this may in principle include both positive and negative judgments, it is often when we are challenged by others that we are most philosophically productive.

The Boddhisattva's mind

In 1987, the Dalai Lama initiated the Mind and Life Dialogues, which he conceived as "a joint quest between scientists, philosophers and contemplatives to investigate the mind, develop a more complete understanding of the nature of reality and promote well-being on the planet."[17] The dialogues addressed specific topics of interest to the Tibetan Buddhist tradition, emphasizing how Western science and philosophy could inform the tradition's understanding of these topics as well as what the tradition could contribute to Western science and philosophy. Questions for discussion at some of the meetings included the following[18]:

> What are the significant differences in the Buddhist and Western approaches to emotions? How do Buddhist and Western thought differ in their approaches for working with emotions, particularly in methods for ameliorating destructive emotions?
>
> What kinds of techniques might be used to discover the nature of minds and brains? In what ways can Tibetan understandings about the control of conscious states be measured by Western science? How can Western methods of state control be incorporated into Tibetan practices?
>
> How do Western theories of the "natural" state of human beings compare with Tibetan Buddhist ones? What are their different senses of what must be done to cultivate higher moral thinking and action? What might Western science learn from Tibetan traditions about how to become more compassionate?

As you can gather from these topics, the discussions not only aimed to learn about differences between Tibetan Buddhism and Western philosophy and science, but also anticipated the exchange of methods and philosophical resources.

One of the invitees to the 2000 Dialogue was the American philosopher of mind Owen Flanagan. His experience inspired him to write *The Bodhisattva's Brain* (2011), a book that examines the 2,500-year-old Buddhist tradition according to the standards of contemporary analytic philosophy and scientific naturalism. In particular, Flanagan wants to challenge aspects of Buddhism that he sees as understandable given the historical circumstances in which they developed, yet nonetheless indefensible within the modern world: the belief in karma and reincarnation, heavens and hells, deities, and so on. Stripping away such doctrines would yield what he calls "Buddhism naturalized," a version of Buddhism that is consistent with our best modern scientific theories.

Flanagan's approach to Buddhism illustrates the "dynamic commingling" that is characteristic of global-philosophical interactionism. In the book's acknowledgments, he thanks the "strange mix of straight-arrow analytic philosophers, neurophilosophers, comparative philosophers, psychologists, neuroscientists, Buddhist laypersons, monks, nuns, and Buddhist studies scholars" who helped him along the way, showing how global philosophy can be used as one approach among others to shed light on living philosophical issues.[19] The conversation is also open across time. At the beginning of the book, Flanagan asks his readers to allow for the kind of dialogue that would "invite Confucius, Siddhārtha Gautama, Mohammed, Joan of Arc, Catherine the Great, Karl Marx, Thomas Jefferson, Sojourner Truth, or any other interesting or wise dead person with a view, or who is representative of a tradition, into our conversations about our problems ... and listen to what they say."[20] Buddhism in particular can make a significant contribution to conversations taking place in the modern West, he thinks, though only after we get rid of some of its accumulated superstitions.

Consider the belief in karma, the idea that one's actions will bear fruit in the future.[21] On what Flanagan calls a "tame" interpretation, karma refers to the idea that sentient beings engage in purposeful actions, and these actions have important consequences. Since it does not appeal to any supernatural explanations for why sentience exists, but simply tries to make sense of the phenomenon of intentional action, this understanding of karma is compatible with modern science. According to Flanagan, it even seems to support the Western division between the social and natural sciences, with the former being devoted to understanding human actions and their consequences.

The robust or "untame" understanding of karma, on the other hand, claims that when a person dies their immaterial consciousness is reborn in the body of some other sentient being, the status of which is determined by the merit of one's actions in the previous life, and that this cycle of birth, death, and rebirth can go on for many lives. If we believe in this kind of karma, Flanagan argues, we must presuppose some sort of "hidden causality" that is undetectable by our best scientific instruments. He criticizes modern Buddhists who accept such a presupposition for not holding their beliefs to high standards of evidence, standards that are necessary if we want to make progress in our understanding of the world. If countless generations of people in Asia and elsewhere have held such a belief without any evidence supporting it, it is only because of its ability to provide social stability and psychological comfort.

Flanagan also contends that Buddhist teachings about the mind contradict the best hypotheses in philosophy and neuroscience. The Dalai Lama has defended a dualistic view, maintaining that the mind cannot be reduced to mere matter. Yet it is naturalistic explanations of phenomena that have proven over time to be the most reliable, replacing supernatural explanations in numerous other domains. For states of mind to cause things to happen in the world around us, the best available explanation is that they are reducible to brain states. As Flanagan concludes, "There is no longer any need for bewilderment, befuddlement, or mysterianism from Buddhism or any other great spiritual tradition in the face of the overwhelming evidence that all experience takes place in our embodied nervous systems in the world, the natural world, the only world there is."[22] A naturalized understanding of Buddhism is, in any event, more in keeping with the spirit of the original Buddha's teachings.

Much contemporary work on Buddhist philosophy consists in providing interpretations of its main doctrines. But those attracted to Buddhism may also want to find out whether, given all that we know at present, the doctrines can be considered true. If we take Buddhist philosophy seriously then we should hold it to the same standards of evidence and argumentative rigor that we apply to our best contemporary theories.

Making criticism hit the mark

Cross-cultural philosophical criticism can go wrong in many ways. It can be based on a shallow understanding of the target tradition or arise from assumptions about the superiority of one's own tradition or defensiveness regarding its perceived shortcomings. If I criticize you personally, you might feel that I have missed the mark, that I possess an ulterior motive, or that the criticism stems from an intellectual or moral deficiency on my part. There is all the more potential for these reactions when cultural boundaries are added to the mix, as we may feel that the critic knows little about our values or way of life. The inclination is to go on the defensive, making the exchange into a series of *tu quoque* ("you too!") arguments. To avoid these failings, we need to think about the basic features that allow critical exchanges between traditions to be philosophically productive.

When we see a contemporary philosopher criticize an ancient and venerable tradition, it may strike us as arrogant or disrespectful. We may suspect the philosopher does not fully understand—or does not care about understanding—the cultural-philosophical tradition they are criticizing, for if they did understand, they would not be so quick to criticize. In the history of Western philosophy, we can find plenty of examples of hasty or uninformed criticism of philosophical traditions in other cultures.

One thing we learn from Flanagan's engagement with Buddhism is that strong criticism of another tradition is compatible with great respect for it. Noting that its combination of metaphysics, epistemology, and ethics is one that rivals Plato in its comprehensiveness, yet improves on the ancient Greeks with its emphasis on the virtues of compassion and loving-kindness, Flanagan thinks Buddhism has great potential as a modern philosophical worldview. Recall that "moral tradition respect" (Chapter 3) is the standard that draws comparative philosophers to engage other traditions in the first place, giving them the impetus to acquire knowledge of their histories and main teachings and concepts. If a tradition struck us from the outset as lacking in depth, we would have no reason to engage with it any further. In philosophy, strong criticism can even be *an indication of* respect, insofar as it aims at developing the view that is criticized.

Respect for another tradition does not mean treating its beliefs as sacrosanct. One participant in the Mind and Life Dialogue held at MIT in 2003 expressed his disappointment at the deference with which the attendees treated the Dalai Lama. "Perhaps the scientists' reverence for His Holiness," he said, "was incompatible with their typical style of argument and debate. Alas, respect has a place in the quest for truth, but reverence does not. The meeting would have been more useful if it had been more irreverent."[23]

The question is what evaluative criteria we should use in such encounters. Flanagan seems to think that conversation with representatives of other traditions has to be "ethnocentric"; we must be allowed to respond to others "with our own reflective standards of cogency, wisdom, and breadth and depth, feeling free to judge their answers as helpful or inadequate for our time."[24] He does not base his critique on standards internal to Buddhism, such as whether the doctrines in question contribute to human enlightenment, but rather on if they are acceptable to contemporary analytic philosophers and scientific naturalists.

In reading the most negatively critical parts of Flanagan's book, we may run the risk of reducing Buddhism to a series of antiquated doctrines revolving around karma and rebirth. We have to remember that the central doctrines in any traditions have been subject to vigorous debate over the centuries, that there are many competing interpretations of these doctrines, and that the tradition has a wide array of philosophical resources apart from them. "All-or-nothing" judgments about the value of a tradition's central concepts have a high burden of proof.

Since global philosophy means remaining rooted in our own tradition, the problem of one-sidedness is a special worry for this approach. With only our own standards to go on, we will end up seeing other traditions mainly in terms of what they offer us, rejecting whatever does not meet our preestablished conditions. To counteract this danger, global philosophers emphasize that the engagement must take place in both directions. Many comparative philosophers in recent years have used ideas from non-Western cultures as a source of critique of the basic assumptions of the Western philosophical tradition. In the last decade, for example, there have been a number of books that use classical Chinese philosophy to challenge basic assumptions of Western ethical and political theory—books such as *Against Individualism: A Confucian Rethinking of the Foundations of Morality, Politics, Family, and Religion* (2016) by Henry Rosemont, Jr., *The China Model: Political Meritocracy and the Limits of Democracy* (2015) by Daniel A. Bell, and *Against Political Equality: The Confucian Case* (2019) by Tongdong Bai.

Flanagan's more recent book, *The Geography of Morals: Varieties of Moral Possibility* (2016), argues that contemporary philosophers should open themselves up to challenges from non-Western traditions:

> Otherwise, one is not aware of the full range of moral sources, not sensitive to the "varieties of moral possibility," and in danger of being "imprisoned by one's upbringing." Often we don't see the possibilities for becoming better than we are or the possibilities for better ways of achieving our ends. The space of possibilities divides into real and notional possibilities, changes that I could make in myself or my world, and changes that are practically or conceptually impossible for me or for people like us. But if I see no possibilities, then effectively there are none.[25]

Cultural critique, Flanagan goes on to say, is essential if we hope to make progress in our ways of thinking and living ethically.[26]

The potential for misunderstanding is not unique to cross-cultural criticism, but is rather a feature of philosophical criticism in general. Socrates' opponents accused him of merely wanting to win the argument rather than caring about the truth. Philosophers today often accuse colleagues in their own tradition of misconstruing their views. If this possibility does not stop us from engaging in philosophical debate, why should it stop us from cross-cultural criticism? Given the potential benefits, we should be willing to take the risk of criticizing others and of opening ourselves up to their criticism.

Problem-solving

Inviting representatives of other cultural-philosophical traditions into our philosophy discussions may not only strengthen our ability to defend our basic principles. It can also give us access to a wider range of resources for approaching the issues that matter to us.

The limits of our intuitions

Suppose our cultural surroundings shape the way we think about some of these issues in ways we are not aware of. These surroundings could be compared to the all-powerful but malicious demon that Descartes conjures up in the First Meditation, implanting ideas in our minds that we cannot help but think are true. How certain should we be of the answers we usually take for granted?

Recent evidence from experimental philosophy suggests that members of other cultures have different ways of responding to some of the central problems of philosophy. We have seen this phenomenon already in the case of the "Magistrate and the Mob" scenario (Chapter 5). If we want to make sure that we are thinking about such problems in as unbiased a manner as possible, we need to take into consideration the possibility of culturally variable intuitions.

If you have taken a philosophy of language course, then you will be familiar with the puzzle of how a proper name *refers* to the person it names. When we use a name like "Nero," how is it that the name "picks out" or "points to" the first-century CE Roman emperor? On the *descriptivist* view, a person who uses the name has a certain description in their head, such as "ancient Roman emperor who fiddled while Rome burned." If the actual emperor Nero is the unique or best match for this description, the name successfully refers to the emperor; whereas if the description matches with many individuals or none at all, it does not refer to anything. On the competing *causal-historical* view, first formulated by Saul Kripke in the 1970s, the description we associate with the name plays no role in determining its referent. The name "Nero" only refers to the actual figure if the person using it is linked to a chain of previous users that extends all the way back to the person who first gave it to the child emperor-to-be.

Philosophers of language in the Western hemisphere have come to accept that certain examples devised by Kripke raise significant problems for the descriptivist view. Take a moment to think about the following case:

> Suppose that John has learned in college that Gödel is the man who proved an important mathematical theorem, called the incompleteness of arithmetic. John is quite good at mathematics and he can give an accurate statement of the incompleteness theorem, which he attributes to Gödel as the discoverer. But this is the only thing that he has heard about Gödel. Now suppose that Gödel was not the author of this theorem. A man called "Schmidt," whose body was found in Vienna under mysterious circumstances many years ago, actually did the work in question. His friend Gödel somehow got hold of the manuscript and claimed credit for the work, which was thereafter attributed to Gödel. Thus, he has been known as the man who proved the incompleteness of arithmetic. Most people who have heard the name "Gödel" are like John; the claim that Gödel discovered the incompleteness theorem is the only thing they have ever heard about Gödel.

Now try to answer the crucial question. Who is John talking about when he uses the name "Gödel"? Is it (a) the person who really discovered the incompleteness of arithmetic, or (b) the person who got hold of the manuscript and claimed credit for the work?[27] Whereas descriptivism suggests he is talking about person (a), Kripke maintains that he is talking about person (b). Most philosophers of language, including descriptivists, have accepted that (b) is the correct answer.

In the early 2000s, a team of researchers led by Edouard Machery of the University of Pittsburgh wanted to see if this intuition was shared across cultural boundaries. They gave the above case to two groups of students, one at Rutgers University and the other at the University of Hong Kong. Their research, published in their paper "Semantics, Cross-Cultural Style," found that the American students were more likely to agree that John was talking about person (b), whereas their Hong Kong counterparts were more likely to think he was talking about person (a).

Machery et al. believe these findings should lead to an "end of innocence" for Western philosophers. The latter can no longer assume that their intuitions about puzzles involving reference are universal. Conclusions based on these intuitions do not have application to philosophy of language as such, but rather to philosophy of language as based on the culturally contingent beliefs of Western academics and their colleagues.

Experimental philosophy, it should be noted, is a recent development in philosophy that has stirred up much controversy. Some critics have held that there is nothing novel or interesting about cross-cultural research on philosophical intuitions, since philosophers already know from talking to their colleagues and students that intuitions vary. In this particular case, Machery and his team admit that their work is not the final word on the issue of reference across cultures, calling for more experiments to test and develop their findings.

Nonetheless, in cases where a certain response to a philosophical puzzle is the consensus view, the discovery of cross-cultural variance can be significant. It can lead our discussion in unanticipated directions, forcing us to take into account a wider set of possibilities in defending the views we hold. More recently, there have been studies in experimental philosophy testing intuitions from members of different cultures on other classic philosophical problems such as the "Ship of Theseus," the belief that one's "true self" is motivated towards the good, moral objectivism, and others.[28] Figuring out which of our philosophical intuitions fall short of universality does not necessarily mean traveling to another part of the world and collecting data from the students we find there. Rather, it could simply involve incorporating views from non-Western thinkers and texts into our classroom discussions.

Cultural resources

Even if we do not accept the argument from culturally variable intuitions, another reason to adopt a more global approach to philosophical problem-solving is because we have reason to believe that other cultural-philosophical traditions have developed methods and concepts that may be of use to us in our own discussions.

We find a conceptual foundation for this idea in the work of Manuel Vargas, a philosopher who writes on moral agency and Latin-American thought. Vargas starts from the idea of *cultural resources*: the epic poems, forms of music, birthday ceremonies, and many other such items that have meaning and power in the shared mental life of a group of people.[29] These resources help the group flourish in the world it inhabits, strengthening social relations among its members, and connecting them to their past.

Although often attached to long-standing traditions, any given cultural resource is "renewable" in the sense that it can inspire the production of novel resources. Vargas cites the phenomenon of sampling in contemporary hip-hop to show how older cultural creations can be used to produce new ones that both refer to the older ones and transform them.

Some cultural creations are *complex* in that they bring together in an illuminating way a diverse array of the basic resources of that culture, offering unlimited possibilities for reuse. A film such as *The Godfather* drew together many elements of the experience of Italian immigrants in America, becoming a touchstone for later films and television series, as well as for emcees, video-game makers, and restaurateurs. People commonly quote well-known lines from the script in different contexts (a student filling out my teacher evaluation form advised his peers to "Leave the gun. Take the Connolly."). Social critics have noted the ways in which the film helped to Italianize American culture, the so-called "Godfather effect."

An important mission of the modern university, according to Vargas, is to produce and preserve such complex cultural resources. Philosophy in particular is concerned with maintaining resources for dealing with problems that we have no reliable and widely shared method of resolving. One reason that Western philosophy departments incorporate the history of philosophy into their curricula is so that we may keep track of the resources that have already been developed, keeping them close at hand in case they may be useful to us. Other cultural-philosophical traditions may also be worth preserving for the same reason.

To take one example, recent work in the global-philosophical vein has argued that the Buddhist tradition can make important contributions to contemporary debates about personal identity. In 1984 Derek Parfit, considered one of the most important moral thinkers of the late twentieth and early twenty-first centuries, published *Reasons and Persons*. The work defended a reductionist view of identity, in which a person is nothing more than the existence of a brain and a body accompanied by a series of interrelated physical and mental events.[30] Though the book was widely read, most philosophers did not accept Parfit's account. Cross-cultural thinker Mark Siderits has argued, however, that reductionist accounts of personal identity in the Buddhist tradition, refined through countless debates over the centuries, can help Parfit and his supporters respond to their non-reductionist critics.[31]

In another instance, contemporary advocates of virtue ethics have started to expand their gaze beyond Western thinkers like Aristotle and Hume to resources found within the Confucian tradition. Working in collaboration with scholars of Chinese philosophy, they have found ways in which Western and Confucian views of virtue can enrich one another.[32] Many centuries before their Western counterparts, thinkers like Mencius formulated ideas about virtue that centered on feelings of empathy for the suffering of others. These ideas could be supported further by taking into account the recent psychological work on empathy that informs some contemporary Western theories of virtue. Confucian thinkers also developed views about moral humility, emphasizing the need to examine oneself in the face of another's misbehavior, which we do not find in Aristotle. Perhaps discussions of virtue ethics in Western classrooms will eventually incorporate this broader range of ideas.

Brian Bruya, a scholar of Chinese philosophy and editor of the 2015 collection *The Philosophical Challenge from China*, points out that ideas have an "inherent plasticity":

> ... [W]hen efficient horse harnesses made their way from China to Europe, it is safe to say that no one objected that they should not be used on the ground that they had come from a different context. The same goes for many other Chinese inventions—the seed drill, the printing press, the fishing reel, playing cards, the compass, gunpowder, porcelain, the metal stirrup, and so on. Chinese ideas were adapted to their new contexts. Just as these ideas changed the course of European history, there is no reason that more abstract ideas cannot also make contributions. Some already have.[33]

Even after being interpreted and developed outside of their original contexts, cultural resources can be of further use to their originators. After Jimi Hendrix's electric version of Bob Dylan's "All Along the Watchtower," Dylan began performing a version of the song based on Hendrix's arrangement rather than his own. Ramen noodles originated in China and then developed into the national dish of Japan that is now popular in China. Perhaps philosophers in other traditions can take Western concepts of virtue, transform them within the framework of their own tradition, and then offer new uses of the concepts to Western philosophers.[34] Global philosophy is full of possibilities.

Balancing the interpretive and constructive dimensions

A main challenge of the global approach is to balance its focus on advancing contemporary philosophy with the emphasis comparative philosophy has traditionally placed on studying traditions in their entirety. Without looking at individual thinkers and texts within their larger traditions, the worry is that our understanding of them will remain superficial. Critics have accused fusion philosophy of a "methodological naïveté" that ignores the challenges of cross-cultural comparison in favor of a misguided optimism about the possibility of transcending the boundaries between culturally distinct philosophical traditions.[35] As one reviewer of Chakrabarti and Weber's *Comparative Philosophy Without Borders* puts it, "can we actually 'philosophize *without* borders'? The fact that the authors intentionally modify, shift and fuse classical or established borders in a creative way does not mean that they do not unintentionally erect new borders. Are we not therefore crossing borders only to encounter new ones?"[36]

Some representatives may respond negatively to those who read their culture's traditions in a way that it is too loose. One of the philosophers discussed in Angle's essay on global philosophy in China is the Confucian political theorist Jiang Qing. In his attempt to develop a Confucianism capable of meeting the challenges of the modern world, Jiang nonetheless emphasizes that any legitimate understanding of the tradition must be rooted in its ancient texts. "The Classics are Chinese culture," he writes, "depart from the Classics and it's [simply] not Chinese culture."[37] Adopting ideas piecemeal from other traditions can also lead to charges of cultural appropriation.[38]

Yet the focus on traditions can often hinder interactions with philosophers at large. If it is solving the problems that matters, why worry about whether the answers faithfully represent the traditions from which they are derived? Imagine a philosopher who says, "Who cares about this tradition or that tradition? I only want to find productive solutions in what I am reading. If it helps to solve the problem, that's enough for me."[39]

Yet in severing the solution of a problem from its context within a cultural-philosophical tradition, we may deprive ourselves of the full wealth of resources that the tradition offers. Reading a few passages of an ancient Chinese text in translation may indeed inspire us to think of a new solution to a problem. But chances are that we will only understand the full meaning and potential of this solution once we have dug a bit deeper, figuring out what issue these passages are trying to resolve, how this issue fits within the broader concerns of the text, in what respects the issue is similar or different to the one we have in mind, and so on. The more we understand about the text and the tradition of which it is part, the better prepared we will be to derive solutions from it. This means that it will not be enough to take issues-based classes like those envisioned at the beginning of this chapter; we must also complete ones that study the texts and traditions directly and in detail.

The global-philosophical approach must manage to address both kinds of critics. One recent work actually incorporates two kinds of scholarly notes: footnotes that answer readers concerned with whether the solution is philosophically viable, endnotes to address those wondering if it is faithful to the tradition.[40] While this challenge arises for any historian of philosophy who attempts to address contemporary issues, it is magnified in global philosophy because of the added differences in language and culture in the worldviews being brought together.

Conclusion

Some thinkers have suggested that the global-philosophical enterprise may eventually transcend the boundaries of tradition altogether, culminating in a "transnational philosophical community" that provides its own standards of philosophical evaluation.[41] Such a suggestion leads us to wonder about the long-term prospects of comparative philosophy. Suppose the researchers on Planet Phi were to speed up their simulation so that, instead of studying how intertribal philosophical counters take place in approximate real time, they could see how the shape of these encounters changes across many generations of interaction. Will the future residents of Planet Phi need cross-tribal philosophy any more, or was it just a temporary phenomenon of a transitional period in the experiment? Global philosophy puts us at the edge of where comparative philosophy meets something new.

Part IV

The Practice of
Comparative Philosophy

Study and Teaching Resources for Doing Philosophy Comparatively

Chapter Outline

Chapter 1 Is There Such a Thing as Comparative Philosophy?

Exercise 1.1 Defining "philosophy" for the purposes of comparative philosophy

One of our concerns in this chapter has been with arriving at a definition of philosophy that is inclusive of thinking from non-Western cultures yet at the same time still meaningful as a definition of philosophy. In this exercise, we will reflect on some conceptions of philosophy found in some popular introductions to the subject.

First, read through the definitions. Which features of philosophy are emphasized by each?

Then, answer the following questions. Which definition do you think is most useful for studying philosophy from non-Western traditions? Which is least useful? Why? Do we need a single definition of philosophy for the purposes of studying philosophy from different cultures?

(A)

"Philosophy is all about our beliefs and attitudes about ourselves and the world. Doing philosophy, therefore, is first of all the activity of stating, as clearly and convincingly as possible, what we believe and what we believe in. . . . It is the effort to appreciate the differences between one's own views and others' views, to be able to argue with someone who disagrees and resolve the difficulties that they may throw in your path." (Solomon and Higgins, *The Big Questions: A Short Introduction to Philosophy, 8th Edition*)

(B)

"The word 'philosophy' carries unfortunate connotations: impractical, unworldly, weird. . . . I would prefer to introduce myself as doing conceptual engineering. For just as the engineer studies the structure of material things, so the philosopher studies the structure of thought. Understanding the structure involves seeing how parts function and how they interconnect. It means knowing what would happen for better or worse if changes were made." (Blackburn, *Think: A Compelling Introduction to Philosophy*)

(C)

" Philosophy means thinking as hard and as clearly as one can about some of the most interesting and enduring problems that human minds have ever encountered. What makes acts right or wrong? What is it to be conscious? Is there anything wrong with a woman renting out her body? Is it immoral to get an abortion? (Perry, Bratman, and Fischer, *Introduction to Philosophy: Classic and Contemporary Readings, 7th edition*, with slight editing)."

(D)

"Philosophy is an activity: it is a way of thinking about certain sorts of question. Its most distinctive feature is its use of logical argument.

Philosophers typically deal in arguments: they either invent them, criticize other people's, or do both. They also analyze and clarify concepts. The word 'philosophy' is often used in a much broader sense than this to mean one's general outlook on life, or else to refer to some forms of mysticism. I will not be using the word in this broader sense here. (Warburton, *Philosophy: The Basics*, 3rd Edition).

Exercise 1.2 Making sense of the category "Chinese philosophy"

In this chapter we also have explored the question of the legitimacy of the category of non-Western philosophy. In her paper "Is There Such a Thing as Chinese Philosophy? Arguments of an Implicit Debate," Carine Defoort lays out two main positions that we might take with respect to the category of "Chinese philosophy." The arguments she discusses for each position are summarized below. Based on these arguments, which position do you think is most plausible, and why? Are some of the arguments more convincing than others?

Position 1: Chinese philosophy does not exist.

(A) *Philosophy as a discipline did not originate in China.* Philosophy as a specific discipline emerged in ancient Greece, and classical Chinese thinkers such as Confucius and Laozi did not think of themselves as practitioners of this discipline. So it would be historically inaccurate to refer to Confucius and Laozi as Chinese philosophers.

(B) *Chinese thinkers do not meet the definition of philosophy.* Philosophy is a systematic inquiry that includes sub-disciplines such as metaphysics, theory of knowledge, and logic. Confucius and Laozi did not engage in the kind of systematic argumentation that one finds in Plato, Aristotle, Aquinas, etc., so they should not be considered philosophers.

(C) *Philosophy is unnecessary for us to appreciate Chinese thought.* Philosophy is not universal, but a Western cultural product that just happens to have spread to other parts of the world. While the discipline of philosophy is closely tied to systemic inquiry, thinkers like Confucius and Laozi are concerned with the personal, familial, and social. We can understand the richness of these ancient Chinese masters without having to bring philosophy into it.

Position 2: Chinese philosophy absolutely does exist.

(A) *The name "philosophy" is Western in origin, but the practice is found the world over.* Regardless of how Confucius and Laozi understood themselves (and were understood in China for centuries before the term "philosophy" was introduced), they still are motivated by similar concerns as philosophers in ancient Greece.

(B) *Chinese thinkers do meet the definition of philosophy.* While Confucius and Laozi may not explicitly engage in philosophical system-building, their works still contain an implicit system, and it is up to us to draw out that system and understand its meaning. While it may not include all the elements of philosophical systems found in Western thinkers, it may contain some elements not found in thinkers like Aristotle and Aquinas, which gives it its own distinctive richness as philosophy.

(C) *Studying Chinese thought can help us advance the discipline of philosophy.* While thinkers like Confucius and Laozi are concerned enough with the enduring questions of human life that they can be considered philosophers in the same sense as Plato, Aristotle, and Aquinas, they are also different enough in their ways of thinking that they help us question many of the basic assumptions of mainstream Western philosophy. Since questioning our basic assumptions is one of the aims of philosophy (see, for instance, the first definition in Exercise 1.1 above), studying Chinese thought or other non-Western philosophical traditions has immense philosophical value.

Exercise 1.3 Incorporating non-Western philosophy into the curriculum

As discussed in this chapter, most philosophy programs in the English-speaking world have tended to exclude non-Western philosophy from their basic curriculum. If there is any hope for changing this state of affairs, according to Bryan W. Van Norden (whose "Multicultural Manifesto" we discussed in this chapter), it will come from the emerging generation of philosophers:

"For many years, I was very pessimistic about the study of the Less Commonly Taught Philosophies (including East Asian, South Asian, Africana, and Indigenous American). However, in the last few years I am increasingly optimistic about the future because I have met so many undergraduate and graduate students, and assistant professors who are much more open-minded about philosophy."

(pers. comm.)

As mentioned in this chapter, students at SOAS University in London gained attention for their recent attempts to "decolonize" the philosophy curriculum at their university, making it more inclusive of thinkers from non-Western philosophical traditions. Van Norden encourages similarly motivated students to challenge their departments to offer more courses in these areas (he provides a collection of resources on his website: bryanvannorden.com), as well as to start a local chapter of MAP (Minorities and Philosophy), an organization dedicated to improving the climate in philosophy for members of marginalized groups.

What courses on Non-Western traditions does your own department offer? What additional courses would you like to see offered? If you were designing your own philosophy curriculum, roughly what proportion of it would you devote to non-Western thinkers and texts? How would you justify their inclusion?

Suggested readings for this chapter

Allinson, "The Myth of Comparative Philosophy or the Comparative Philosophy *Malgré Lui.*"

Defoort, "Is There Such a Thing as Chinese Philosophy? Arguments of an Implicit Debate."

Dotson, "How Is This Paper Philosophy?"

Krishna, "Comparative Philosophy: What It Is and What It Ought to Be."

Lloyd, "What is Philosophy?" (Chapter 1 of *Disciplines in the Making*).

Further questions for discussion

1. What are the different conceptions of philosophy that Lloyd discusses within the tradition of Western philosophy? How does the meaning of philosophy grow more complicated as we consider non-Western traditions?

2. Why does Allinson argue that comparative philosophy is a "myth"? What paths forward does he offer for comparative philosophy in spite of this status?

Chapter 2 The Goals of Comparison

Exercise 2.1 Comparing in order to understand: thinking it through

Charles Taylor writes that our understanding of another culture will depend not just on the thing we are studying,

> but it will also vary with the student, because the particular language we hammer out in order to achieve our understanding of them will reflect our own march toward this goal; it will reflect the various distortions that we have had to climb out of, the kinds of questions and challenges that they in their difference pose to us. It will not be the same language in which members of that culture understand themselves; it will also be different from the way members of a third culture will understand them, coming as they will to this goal through a different route, through the identification and overcoming of a rather different background understanding.
>
> (Taylor, "Understanding the Other," 30)

Thus, he notes, how twenty-first-century Americans understand the writing of Roman history will be different from how twenty-fifth-century Chinese or twenty-second-century Brazilians understand it.

1. What do you think is distinctive about the philosophical ideas and assumptions that you will bring to your understanding of thinkers and texts from a distant time and place?

2. Based on these distinctive ideas and assumptions, what particular stumbling blocks to understanding a culturally distant philosophy would you expect to arise in the course of your study?

3. What specific steps can you take to get over these stumbling blocks? How can you avoid distorting the thinker or text you are studying with the ideas and assumptions from your own culture? (More on this issue in Chapter 6.)

Exercise 2.2 External criticism: further examples

Here are some additional examples of comparative philosophy providing an external standpoint from which to assess the Western philosophical tradition. What is the criticism in each passage? What features of Western philosophy do they point out? Have you noticed these features before?

(1)

Here I make an extremely bold and possibly very contentious observation: that Western philosophy has become too name-centric, where the great thinkers have become too pivotal to thinking. . . . I speculate that indigenous philosophy, as it appears in the literature, does not draw heavily on particular individuals so vehemently as Western philosophy does. Written indigenous philosophy engages instead more with, and drills deeply into, a fundamental cultural phenomenon—not through the lens of another individual, but with the writer bringing together the spheres of lived experience, intellect, and the unknown. Whilst this difference between the two could just be the result of a cultural nuance, to the indigenous thinker it may also signal a divergence in focus, where dominant (not all) Western scholarship defaults to the prized and comfortable zone of previous thinkers. If my suspicions here are credible, then thought in this vein is barred from entering into the endless possibilities that a thing offers. One just draws on the same paradigm to tell another story. (Mika, "Counter-Colonial and Philosophical Claims," 1140)

(2)

As we have seen, [the Chinese philosopher Zhuangzi] unambiguously advocated the need to "be natural": to act according to intuition rather than by deliberately taking thought and working out pros and cons; in other words, to follow yin *rather than* yang. *In Western philosophy, as in Western culture generally, this side of human nature has, on the whole, been neglected, and, in some schools (such as Logical Positivism), even been judged to be non-philosophical because unverifiable. Yet most of the important decisions made by human beings spring from intuition rather than reason: relationships, interests, loves, jobs, even putting flowers in vases.* (Billington, *Understanding Eastern Philosophy*, 109)

(3)

Yet, in spite of these obvious limitations, the dialogues [found in the Upanishads and other Indian philosophical texts] may provide an interesting take-off point for exploring those possibilities of thought that have been so brusquely or casually rejected in the text. In a sense, the Indian philosophical texts provide a far greater opportunity for such an exercise than most philosophical texts written in the Western tradition, as they provide in the very format of their presentation the possible argument or arguments against their position and their reply to them. The counter-positions are, therefore, there in the open and the reader is continuously aware of them. He does not have to hunt for them, or try to find them by delving under the surface of the text, as it is the case with most of the philosophical texts written in the West or in the Western tradition. The suppressed text, so to say, is more exposed in the Indian tradition of philosophical writing than in most other traditions. (Krishna, "Thinking versus Thought," 30–1)

Exercise 2.3 Comparative philosophy and philosophical problem-solving

Pick a problem from the column on the left, and then pick a non-Western tradition from the column on the right that you think might offer a fruitful or interesting approach to that problem. Next, do a quick online search to see what has already been written on that problem from the perspective of the tradition in question. Did your search turn up anything? If so, what has been written about the philosophical problem in the particular tradition you chose? Do you see any major differences between how this tradition approaches the issue and how it is approached generally in Western philosophy? (More on this approach in Chapter 11.)

Table 12.1 Problems of philosophy in non-Western traditions

What is the nature of reality? Does reality exist independently of our minds?	Chinese Philosophy Japanese Philosophy Indian Philosophy
What is required to have knowledge of something? Is there anything we know for certain?	Tibetan Philosophy Korean Philosophy Arabic and Islamic Philosophy

What is the mind and how is it related to the body? What is the self? What makes you the same person over time?

What does it mean to have free will? Is free will real or just an illusion?

Does God exist? (*Do gods* exist?) What is the nature of the divine?

How does language have meaning? How do words refer to things? What does it mean for a statement to be true?

What makes an action right or wrong? How should we think about ethics in relation to business, medicine, or the environment?

What is the best way for a society to be structured? What makes a particular society just or unjust?

African Philosophy
Afro-Caribbean Philosophy
Latin-American Philosophy
Indigenous Philosophy in the Americas
Indigenous Australian Philosophy
Polynesian Philosophy
(this is not a comprehensive list; for more categories, take a look at this link: https://philpapers.org/browse/philosophical-traditions)

Suggested readings for this chapter

Cline, "Why Compare?" (*Confucius, Rawls, and the Sense of Justice*, 29–47).
Garfield, "Two Truths and Method."
Struhl, "No (More) Philosophy without Cross-Cultural Philosophy."
Taylor, "Understanding the Other."

Further questions for discussion

1. Taylor writes that "The great challenge of this century, both for politics and for social science, is that of understanding the other." Why is understanding the other so difficult, according to his Gadamer-based view? What sort of understanding of other cultural traditions is possible, and how can we achieve it?

2. Cline, Garfield, and Struhl all advance arguments for why philosophy should include a cross-cultural dimension. What are these arguments? Which is most successful in your view?

Chapter 3 The Role of Tradition and Culture

Exercise 3.1 Exploring philosophical traditions

In the first part of the chapter, we discussed the importance of tradition in philosophy. For this exercise, pick one specific philosophical tradition, either Western or non-Western (a list of different philosophical traditions can be found at the PhilPapers database: https://philpapers.org/browse/philosophical-traditions). Once you have selected a tradition, try and answer the following questions:

1. What are the basic texts that make up this tradition? What languages are used in these texts?
Example: "European existentialism": Kierkegaard's *Fear and Trembling*, Heidegger's *Being and Time*, Sartre's *Being and Nothingness*, Beauvoir's *The Second Sex*. Languages include French, German, Danish.

2. What are the distinctive concepts or values that are central to this tradition?
Example: Freedom, authenticity, being-in-the-world, being-towards-death, the absurd, anxiety.

3. What arguments or debates or fundamental differences occur within this tradition?
Example: Some existentialist thinkers embrace theism (Dostoevsky, Kierkegaard, Marcel), while others reject the transcendent realm (Nietzsche, Sartre). We also find competing conceptions of the meaning of values such as "authenticity" among the various existentialist thinkers.

4. If you had to choose a philosophical tradition from another culture with which to compare the tradition you picked, which tradition would you choose? Why? After you've answered this question, do a quick search to see if there has been any comparative work bringing the two traditions together.
Example: Since I study Chinese philosophy, I'm always interested in how Western traditions that I teach in some of my courses have parallels in Chinese traditions. The relation between existentialism

and Chinese thought has been a longstanding topic of interest in comparative philosophy, continuing up until the present day. (Interested readers can take a look at the recent book, *Cross-Cultural Existentialism: On the Meaning of Life in Asian and Western Thought*, by Leah Kalmanson.)

Exercise 3.2 Debate: approaches to culture within Latin American philosophy

In this chapter, we addressed the question of how philosophy and culture are related. In this exercise, we will explore a range of answers to this question that have been offered by scholars working in Latin American philosophy. Which perspective do you think gets it right? (Note the similarities between this debate and the one explored in Exercise 1.2 above.)

1. *Philosophy is universal and excludes culturally contingent features*
Philosophy is best understood as an abstract inquiry on a par with physics or mathematics. There is just one philosophy, that aims at universal truths, and exists independently of the contingencies of culture, language, history, etc. While it makes sense to talk about philosophy that is done within Latin America or by people of Latin American heritage, there is nothing to justify a distinctive branch of "Latin American philosophy." (For discussion, see Pereda, "On Mexican Philosophy," and Nuccetelli, "Latin American Philosophy")

2. *Philosophy is always bound up with culture and there's no escaping that fact*
Since philosophy aims at confronting one's everyday reality, philosophical ideas and theories are always reflective of the particular cultures in which they have originated. As the Mexican philosopher Leopold Zea once wrote, "Even though being, God, etc., are issues appropriate for every man, the solution to them will be given from a Latin American standpoint" (Zea, "The Actual Function of Philosophy in Latin America"; quoted in Nuccetelli, "Latin American Philosophy"). Latin American Philosophy is a cultural product that focuses on issues that are relevant to people in this particular region.

3. *The core of philosophy is universal, but it also branches out to include culturally specific questions*
Philosophy is made up of a core of universal problems, such as the nature of knowledge or the connection between mind and body. But at the same time, it has many different branches that stretch out from this core and deal with specific topics. For example, in addition to timeless topics in ethics such as the nature of duty, there also the more applied questions of biomedical ethics that attempt to address specific questions of contemporary relevance (such as a just global distribution of a pandemic vaccine). Latin American philosophy can be thought of as a branch of philosophy that responds to specific problems that have emerged in Latin American contexts. (See Nuccetelli 2002: 246–7)

4. *The opposition between universal and culturally particular philosophy is a false one*
In fact, the more abstract and general aspects of philosophy inform the particular and culturally embedded ones, and vice versa. Concrete experiences found in particular cultures can be used to challenge abstract views in ethics, epistemology, and metaphysics. On the other hand, there are universal ideas and norms defended by philosophers that can serve as restrictions on cultural practices in Latin America. (See Pereda, "On Mexican Philosophy," 195–6 for this view)

Suggested readings for this chapter

Hansen, "The Normative Impact of Comparative Ethics."
Ikuenobe, "The Parochial Universalist Conception of 'Philosophy' and 'African Philosophy.'"
Ivanhoe, "Moral Tradition Respect."
MacIntyre, "The Virtues, the Unity of a Human Life and the Concept of a Tradition" (Chapter 15 of *After Virtue*).
Pereda, "On Mexican Philosophy, For Example."

Further questions for discussion

1. What is a tradition, according to MacIntyre? What does he see as some misconceptions about tradition?
2. What are the strengths and weaknesses of viewing culture as a unity or diversity? What are some implications of each approach for comparing the philosophies of different cultures?

3. As mentioned, some critics have thought that Hansen's third criterion of moral tradition respect is lacking. If so, what should we put in its place? Is there some other basis for engaging other traditions that we haven't thought of?

Chapter 4 Linguistic Incommensurability

Exercise 4.1 Recognizing different problems of incommensurability

In each of the following passages, what type of incommensurability (linguistic, foundational, or evaluative) does the author appear to have in mind? What specific philosophical problem is the author using the concept to address?

(1)

Incommensurability can be characterized as a lack of a certain kind of semantic contact between the languages of two competing theories due to changes in either the semantic values (meaning or reference) of the non-logical constituents of sentences or the semantic values (factual meaning, truth-values, or truth-value status) of sentences themselves in these languages. (Wang, *Incommensurability and Cross-Language Communication*, 9)

(2)

Incommensurability, by admitting that productions may belong to qualitatively different worlds, disables judgment by a common standard. . . . Consequently, incommensurability as a political position may go furthest toward respecting the force of other groups' differencing by putting a check on the epistemological-cum-political intrusions of worldly scholarly formations and their valuations. (Klausen, "Civilization and Culture in Anticolonial and Comparative Political Theory," 670–1, with slight edits)

(3)

What is true for us, given the meaning we attach to moral concepts such as the right thing to do, may not be true for others, given the meanings they attach to those concepts. The relativity of moral truth comes down to our having somewhat different meanings from moral concepts and the terms we use to express those concepts. (Wong, *Natural Moralities*, 72)

(4)

By 'commensurable' I mean able to be brought under a set of rules which will tell us how rational agreement can be reached on what would settle the issue on every point where statements seem to conflict. (Rorty, *Philosophy and the Mirror of Nature*, 316)

(5)

For more and more people, the fundamental presuppositions that inform their conception of political morality are accordingly incommensurable with the presuppositions formally embraced by the societies in which they live. And unfortunately, whenever this happens—whenever people feel that they can no longer describe their most closely held values in a way that those who disagree with them can appreciate and understand, things do no usually end well. (Reiff, "Incommensurability, Cultural Relativism, and the Fundamental Presuppositions of Morality," 189)

Exercise 4.2 The language of being: further perspectives

As mentioned in this chapter, because classical Chinese is a language that developed outside of Indo-European languages, some scholars have seen it as a good test of the linguistic relativity hypothesis. One case study we discussed was the use of the English terms "being" and "non-being" to translate the Chinese characters *you* 有 and *wu* 無. Consider the following passage from the *Daodejing* (Chapter 40), along with five different English translations:

天下萬物生於有，有生於無。

All things in the world come from being;
And being comes from non-being. (tr. Wing-Tsit Chan)

The myriad creatures in the world are born from Something, and Something from Nothing. (tr. Lau)

The world and all its creatures arise from what is there;
What is there arises from what is not there. (tr. Ivanhoe)

The events of the world arise from the determinate,
And the determinate arises from the indeterminate. (tr. Ames and Hall)

The things of the world are generated from presence.
Presence is generated from non-presence. (tr. Moeller)

1. What is unique about the terms that each translator uses to render *you* and *wu*? Which ones do you think make the text sound most like Western philosophy? Which are least familiar?

2. Some scholars have argued that we should reject the translation of *you* and *wu* as "being" and "non-being," since these translations do not allow us to see the important differences between the ancient Chinese concepts and those found in Western philosophy (Lacertosa, "For a philosophy of comparisons," 332; Yu, "The Language of Being," 451). Others contend that these translations are acceptable, as long as we understand that *you* and *wu* have meanings that do not overlap with being and non-being (Liu, "The Notion of *Wu* or Nonbeing as the Root of the Universe and a Guide for Life," 153). Based on what you've read in this chapter, do you think we should use "being" and "non-being" to translate *you* and *wu*? Why or why not?

Exercise 4.3 Davidson vs. MacIntyre: weighing the debate

Which of the two main approaches to the problem of linguistic incommensurability discussed in this chapter is more plausible, in your view? Why? Is there a third possibility?

Response 1 (Davidson): The idea of incommensurability does not make sense. This is because we cannot even begin to comprehend others' language and how it differs from our own without assuming a shared background against which we understand these differences. When proponents of linguistic relativity offer examples in support of this view, they are able to describe very well the various ways terms are used in different languages, something they could not do if the view were true. For example, even if the name "Doire Columcille" is difficult to translate, MacIntyre can explain in clear English what this name means to the people who used it.

Response 2 (MacIntyre): In fact, the challenge of incommensurability is a real and present one. Comprehending another language is not just about grasping the meaning of a particular term or phrase, but rather understanding the whole set of beliefs that is shared by the particular community of people that use that language. For example, people who use the name "Doire Columcille" share a particular history, geography, religion, etc. that gives meaning to this particular name. To understand what the name means we have to learn this language as well as we know our own native one; but even so the meaning of the name may be closed off to us.

Suggested readings for this chapter

Davidson, "On the Very Idea of a Conceptual Scheme."
Graham, "The Relation of Chinese Thought to the Chinese Language" (Appendix 2 of *Disputers of the Tao*).
Kuhn, "The Resolution of Revolutions" (Chapter 12 of *The Structure of Scientific Revolutions*).
Ma and van Brakel, "Preliminaries—Philosophy and Language" (Ch. 1 of *Fundamentals of Comparative and Intercultural Philosophy*).

Further questions for discussion

1. What is the process by which one scientific paradigm replaces another, according to Kuhn? How does this process illustrate the incommensurability of the new paradigm and the old one?
2. What are some of the differences between the Chinese language and Indo-European ones, according to Graham? What impact do these differences have on philosophical discussions carried out in each?

Chapter 5 Foundational and Evaluative Incommensurability

Exercise 5.1 The presuppositions of the Western philosophical tradition

In the area of Chinese philosophy, the scholars David L. Hall and Roger T. Ames are well-known for their claim that comparative philosophers cannot understand Chinese thought without first attaining an awareness of the basic assumptions that they bring along with them. On their view, "all scholars tend to swim in a set of assumptions they can neither see nor challenge. They are like fish that do not know they swim in water because they have never experienced air" (Frisina, "Thinking Through Hall and Ames," 570–1). If we do not recognize these assumptions, then we will not be able to make sense of thinkers and texts from other traditions. Among these assumptions, Hall and Ames mention the following ideas that have characterized the Western tradition since its inception in Ancient Greece:

- Western philosophers have tended to appeal to transcendent principles (Plato's Forms, Aristotle's Unmoved Mover) to explain the reality in front of us.
- Western philosophers think in terms of dualism that separates the higher from the lower.
- Western philosophers (beginning with Socrates) seek fixed definitions that lay out the essential features of basic philosophical concepts.
- Western philosophers seek the underlying "substance" that makes a thing what it is, rather than focusing on its relationships with other things or looking at reality in terms of events and processes.
- Western philosophers focus on the individual person and their traits, rather than seeing the person in terms of their relationships with others.

1. Based on your study of philosophy so far, do you think it is true that these assumptions are inherent to Western philosophy? Why or why not? Are there others that you would add to the list?

2. How much of a barrier do these assumptions pose to our understanding of thinkers and texts to other traditions? What steps can we take to counteract them? (More on this question in the next chapter!)

Exercise 5.2 Taking a position on evaluative incommensurability

As mentioned in this chapter, Alasdair MacIntyre argues that *there are no neutral standards by which we can assess the competing claims of philosophical traditions against one another*. Below are some responses that comparative philosophers have made to MacIntyre. Which of these responses do you think gets it right? Why? Are there other possible responses?

1. *MacIntyre is right about evaluative incommensurability, and contemporary Western philosophers especially should pay attention.* Non-Western traditions have their own standards of justification, and we should be careful about foisting our own standards onto these traditions. Even if another cultural-philosophical tradition possesses a standard that is incommensurable with our own, we can still learn from dialogue with this tradition. (Bussanich, "Ethics in Ancient India," 33–4)

2. *MacIntyre is wrong about evaluative incommensurability, because we do not need a neutral standard in order to compare different traditions.* Just because there are no neutral standards, this does not mean that we cannot compare these traditions against one another. When we translate between two languages, we do not need to rely on a third, neutral language for our translation to be successful, but instead, we just translate directly from one to the other. Similarly, we can assess the competing claims of philosophical traditions by comparing them with one another directly. Such a comparison might expose limitations or errors, as well as strengths, in one or both traditions. (Huang, *Why be Moral?* 2–3)

3. *Even if MacIntyre is correct that two traditions possess incommensurable standards, this is only a temporary state of affairs, and we can find common ground for comparison by learning another tradition from within.* Two different traditions may have incommensurable standards, but someone from Tradition A who takes the time to learn Tradition B from within and becomes at home in that tradition, understanding it as well as their own, can serve as a "bridge" between the traditions, offering grounds for assessment between them. (Sim, *Remastering Morals with Aristotle and Confucius,* 9–10)

Suggested readings for this chapter

Doris and Plakias, "How to Argue about Disagreement."
Moody-Adams, "Taking Disagreement Seriously" (Chapter 1 of *Fieldwork in Familiar Places*).
Winch, "Understanding a Primitive Society."
Wong, "Three Kinds of Incommensurability."

Further questions for discussion

1. In the first part of this chapter, we examined several cases in which differing standards of justification are a barrier to cross-cultural understanding. What are some other possible cases you can think of? What are some methods we can use to overcome this barrier?

2. What is descriptive cultural relativism, according to Moody-Adams, and how does it relate to ethical relativism? Why does she think descriptive cultural relativism is underdetermined?

3. How are the three kinds of incommensurability related, in Wong's view? What does he think is the most interesting argument for evaluative incommensurability?

Chapter 6 One-sidedness

Exercise 6.1 Reflection: comparative philosophy as it ought to be

In a paper published in 1986, Daya Krishna (whose critical stance we discussed in Ch. 1) argues that there is a gap between *what comparative philosophy is*—"the imposition of the standards of one dominant culture upon the others"—and *what comparative philosophy ought to be*: "the mutual liberator of each philosophical tradition from the limitations imposed on it by its past." As we have seen from the discussion in this chapter, the problem of one-sidedness has persisted into the present day.

In your view, what are some practical steps that may be taken in our comparisons to in order to counteract the problem of one-sidedness? Which of the methods discussed in the last part of this chapter do you think is most useful? What can we do to close the distance between what comparative philosophy is and what it ought to be? (The next two exercises discuss a couple of recent proposals.)

Exercise 6.2 Is the name "comparative philosophy" part of the problem?

In a recent book, Monika Kirloskar-Steinbach and Leah Kalmanson argue that the title "comparative philosophy" reinforces a narrow conception of the work that this field is capable of producing. They likewise criticize names such as "cross-cultural philosophy" and "global philosophy" for suggesting that philosophy is just one thing across different contexts. While the goal of comparison is to result in a broader conception of philosophy, these names "unwittingly reinscribe the very box such scholarship seeks to escape from" (*A Practical Guide to World Philosophies*, 6). Instead, they suggest the title "World Philosophies," which they think has the following advantages:

- The plural "philosophies" suggests an openness to different conceptions of the field and diverse practices, which may overlap but do not need to share any essential features.
- The name shows that philosophy does not belong to any particular group or culture, but instead is the common property of all humans; thus, it captures "the ubiquity of philosophical activity as it relates to our being in the world" (8).
- It contrasts with the standard conception of philosophy, which tends to be Eurocentric in its practices.

What do you think about these arguments? Is it time to abandon the name "comparative philosophy" in favor of one that suggests a more inclusive approach?

Exercise 6.3 Should comparative philosophers be deliberately one-sided in a way that favors non-Western traditions?

Some comparativists have maintained that the remedy for one-sidedness is not to try to be neutral in our comparisons, but rather to undertake them in a way that challenges the dominance of Western philosophical categories and ideas. Here are a couple of arguments for this kind of counter-asymmetrical style of comparison (if there is a better term for it, let me know!):

1. In comparative philosophy, as we have seen in this chapter, there has been a long history of asymmetrical interpretation, where

Western ideas and categories set the standard by which to describe and evaluate thinkers and texts from non-Western traditions. It is not enough to strive for neutrality in our comparisons, but rather we should try to counteract the hegemony of Western philosophy. One way to accomplish this is through counter-asymmetrical comparison.

2. One of the fundamental tasks of philosophy is to challenge our most basic assumptions about the world and our place within it. Comparative philosophy is supposed to help us achieve this task by exposing us to alternative ways of thinking about reality, knowledge, and ethics. By setting up our comparisons in a way that deliberately foregrounds the insights of non-Western traditions, we are better able to achieve this basic goal of philosophy.

Are these arguments convincing? Do you think comparative philosophy should be undertaken in a way that deliberately favors concepts and arguments from non-Western sources?

(For further discussion of these questions, see Ames and Rosemont, Jr., "Were the Early Confucians Virtuous?"; Angle, "Building Bridges to Distant Shores"; Ni, "Deliberate One-Sidedness as a Method of Doing Philosophy"; and Rosemont, Jr., *Against Individualism*.)

Suggested readings for this chapter

Clarke, Introduction to *Oriental Enlightenment.*

Kirloskar-Steinbach and Kalmanson, "Why World Philosophies?" (Chapter 1 of *A Practical Guide to World Philosophies*).

Shun, "Studying Confucian and Comparative Ethics: Methodological Reflections."

Tuck, "The Philosophy of Scholarship" (Ch. 1 of *Comparative Philosophy and the Philosophy of Scholarship*).

Wiredu, "Toward Decolonizing African Philosophy and Religion."

Further questions for discussion

1. What are some of the possible remedies for one-sided comparison? Which of these remedies is most effective, in your view?

2. Why does African philosophy need to be decolonized, according to Wiredu? What is involved in the process of decolonization?

3. What is "orientalism," according to Said? What are the strengths and weakness of Said's analysis, according to Clarke?

4. As mentioned in the chapter, one possible cure for one-sidedness is to use the less dominant tradition's categories to interpret or evaluate the more

dominant one's. What concepts from non-Western traditions do you think could be fruitfully applied to Western thinkers and texts?

Chapter 7 Generalizations

Exercise 7.1 Two recent perspectives on cultural generalizations

The use of generalization in cross-cultural philosophy continues to be a topic of debate. Based on your own view after having read the discussion in this chapter, which of the views below do you agree with, and why? Is there some third possibility that combines the insights of both?

When engaging in cross-cultural comparison, to think that interpreters of foreign texts approach those texts with beginners' eyes or with the same set of concerns as the original authors and direct descendent commenters is a hermeneutic mistake. . . .
None of this is to say that cultural differences are absolute, essential, eternal, or insurmountable. However, there are differences. Our cultural gulfs are the product of subtle conceptual differences and the implicit connotations of certain metaphors developed across a long accretion of cultural transmission. With careful investigation and critical scrutiny, certain generalizations about these differences can take shape. Hermeneutically responsible interpreters will use these generalizations as a starting point for deeper investigation.
(Mason, "Generalizations, Cultural Essentialism, and Metaphorical Gulfs," 495–6)

I, on the other hand, tend to see even continuous historical traditions as incredibly internally heterogeneous and complex, even on the relatively shortest of historical timeframes, not to mention in the long run of civilizational development. And so, attempts to accentuate generalities of whatever type runs the risk of marginalizing quite important aspects of cultures, and worse, sub-traditions and sub-populations of those cultures. When we then turn around and compare two traditions or more, the risks for distortion and marginalization and cultural chauvinism only increase. The more specifically focused a comparative study is, with respect to definite thinkers, texts, timeframes, themes, and so forth, the more informative and illuminating I tend to believe a comparative study will be.
(Berger and Kramer, "Lessons from Intercultural Philosophy," 138)

Exercise 7.2 Chinese Philosophers Generalize About Western Thought

Here are some broad generalizations about Western philosophy and religion from the part of contemporary Chinese philosophers. Are they accurate? Do we evaluate generalizations differently when they are about our own cultural traditions? If so, why?

(1)

In Western religion, when people are about to fight a war, everybody prays to God. Hitler prayed to God, Roosevelt prayed to God. Who exactly is God to help? That is why if you want to win in war it is best to look at the people, see whether they will follow you, and that requires looking at yourself. That has been the attitude of the Chinese since ancient times. By the time of Confucius it was already very clear and very concrete. The Westerner on the other hand never looks at himself but always prays to God. That is the point of divergence between the East and West. (Mou Zongsan, *Nineteen Lectures on Chinese Philosophy*, Lecture 3)

(2)

Relatively speaking, by questioning human nature and human dao *[way], Chinese philosophy emphasizes a focus on human nature or the question of human existence, whereas Western philosophy stresses the question of heaven and the true reality of the world . . . .*

Both affirm that philosophy, or the study of human nature and dao, *provides guiding tools for accomplishing the self [i.e. personal development] and accomplishing the world [i.e. transforming our natural and social environments]. Chinese and Western philosophy, however, emphasize these two aspects differently.*

Chinese philosophy focuses on accomplishing the self, or in other words, it observes more the process of accomplishing the self. Western philosophy, on the other hand, systematically observes the process of accomplishing the world. (Yang, *Philosophical Horizons*, 125–6)

(3)

In Western modernity, heaven and humans are distinct and mutually opposed, and one of the major themes of society and culture is human's struggle with and contrast with nature. This is particularly clear in the way in which Western epistemology is fascinated by the relationship between subject and object. This approach in epistemology is a historically rooted reflection of the industrial revolution and contemporary Western civilization. In contrast to agricultural society and its close accord with nature, the Western approach uses science and technology to transform nature and create new things. (Li, A History of Classical Chinese Thought)

Exercise 7.3 Country comparisons

Try out the "Country Comparison" tool found at Hofstede Insights (a website based on the research of psychologist Geert Hofstede discussed in this chapter): https://www.hofstede-insights.com/country-comparison/

Which two countries did you compare? Did you find any surprising or otherwise interesting results? Do you see any links between these results and philosophical texts that have been produced in those countries?

Suggested readings for this chapter

Ames, "The Necessity of Informed Generalizations in Making Cultural Comparisons" (*Confucian Role Ethics*, 20–35).
Mason, "Generalizations, Cultural Essentialism, and Metaphorical Gulfs."
Nisbett, *The Geography of Thought* (especially Chapters 4–7).
Oyserman et al., "Rethinking Individualism and Collectivism."
Slingerland, "Body and Mind in Early China: An Integrated Humanities-Science Approach."

Further questions for discussion

1. What are some prominent examples of generalizations about different cultural philosophies? What methods can we use to determine whether these generalizations are valid?
2. What is the difference between cultural generalization and cultural essentialism? What are Ames' arguments in favor of using informed generalizations in our comparisons? How does he respond to critics of the use of generalizations?
3. What evidence does Nisbett offer on behalf of his claim that East Asians and Westerners have opposed ways of viewing the world around them? How do philosophers from each culture fit into this picture of cultural difference?

4. What do Oyserman et al. conclude from their meta-analysis of studies on individualism and collectivism? What are some of the strengths and limitations of the individualist/collectivist framework?

Chapter 8 Universalism

Exercise 8.1 Moral universalism in the twenty-first century—a recent debate

As mentioned in this chapter, a common form of universalism is *moral universalism*, or the belief that there are certain moral principles that apply to all humanity. In 2021, scholars debated the merits of moral universalism in a symposium published in the *Journal of World Philosophies*. After reading the account of the debate below, answer the questions at the end to determine where you stand on the issue.

To begin the debate, the political philosopher Kok-Chor Tan sets forth a position known as *cosmopolitan liberalism*, which holds that the principle of respect for individual autonomy applies to all human beings regardless of their culture or citizenship. One objection to this position is that it is a kind of "moral imperialism," taking an idea that is prominent in the Western political tradition and trying to inflict it on other cultures, and judging these cultures as "backwards" if they do not live up to the standard of one's own values.

Tan responds to this objection by saying its target is really moral dogmatism, rather than moral universalism. Moral dogmatism asserts without argument that one's own moral views are superior to all other contenders, relying on force rather than persuasion to convert others to these views. But the cosmopolitan liberalism that Tan envisions uses reason and dialogue to make its case. It opens itself up to critique from members of other cultural traditions, and is committed to reforming or abolishing practices with liberal societies that fail to live up to their own standard.

The problem, then, is not with thinking that one's moral views are universal, but doing so in a way that cuts off the possibility of dialogue. As Tan writes,

> . . . [T]his presumption of the truth of one's own view is not necessarily parochial—we must access the moral world from a particular point of view. . . . What is required is that cosmopolitan

liberals be ready to offer reasons for their convictions, reasons that they can reasonably believe that others can accept, and be prepared to receive and respond to criticisms in turn.

("Globalizing Cosmopolitanism," 102)

He advocates the virtue of *moral modesty*, where we accept that our own moral point of view may be limited in certain ways and open ourselves up to broadening our ideas through the engagement with other cultural traditions. There is nothing wrong with moral universalism when it is accompanied by this humble attitude.

Steve Coutinho, a scholar of Chinese philosophy, offers some counterarguments to Tan's view. To begin, he questions whether the moral universalist can be genuinely open to learning from other cultural traditions. The cosmopolitan liberal may learn from engagement with other traditions how to argue more persuasively for the principle of autonomy, or to notice practices in their own society that do not live up to it—but they are unlikely to give up the principle itself. "To be genuinely open to learning something new," Coutinho points out, "we must be prepared for it to challenge what we take to be most obvious. If both sides are to be genuinely open to dialogue, then the liberal must also risk having their own sacred ground challenged" ("Mutual Openness and Global Justice," 106).

Countinho argues that there are good reasons to challenge the individualist foundation of cosmopolitan liberalism. One problem is that it treats the individual in isolation, not accounting for the ways in which our own good is entwined with the good of others. "People are not purely separate individuals," he writes, "but biologically and psychologically, we exist and flourish through interactions with others, and depend on each other for growth and support" (ibid.). Even liberal societies set certain limits on the pursuit of individual autonomy, recognizing that it must involve some degree of compromise with the interests of others. In practice, societies structured around individual autonomy still permit economic exploitation and other forms of injustice, both domestically and in their relations with other countries.

At bottom, what the moral universalist fails to recognize is that there are other fundamental values at stake in the global debate. For cultures that prioritize values such as human relationality and social harmony, the appeal to individual autonomy is going to ring hollow. Being truly open to dialogue with other cultural traditions means giving equal consideration to the values that are most important to them. As Coutinho puts it,

. . . [I]t might even be the case that we come to recognize that their societies based on a different set of values (mutual nurturing, perhaps) enable their citizens to flourish in ways that our own citizens do not. Their people may live fulfilled lives, enjoying what they do, despite not thinking of themselves as separate individuals whose rights to choose cannot be infringed. And yet, they may be seen to flourish, either in similar ways to us . . . or in ways that we autonomous individuals may fail to flourish.

(Ibid.,107)

The trouble with moral universalism is that it cuts us off from the possibility of discovering ways of flourishing that that are equal to or better than our own. Coutinho's argument points us in the direction of pluralism rather than universalism—a position which we will consider further in the next chapter.

Given the arguments, which side do you think gets it right? Why? Are there other possibilities than the ones mentioned above?

Exercise 8.2 Weighing the objections to universalist approaches to cross-cultural philosophy

Here is a summary of some main objections to universalism:

1. Universalism has a disreputable past, often having served as a cover for narrow-minded and exclusionary readings of non-Western traditions on the part of Western philosophers.

2. Universalism is biased in favor of the dominant philosophical tradition, so that the "universal" tends to be whatever fits its standard.

3. Belief that certain philosophical categories are universal can lead us to miss important differences between traditions.

4. There is no agreed upon standard by which comparativists can determine which philosophical views are universal and which are not.

5. Judgments of similarity are often laden with assumptions on the part of the comparativist, so that the similarities between different cultures' philosophies can be more imagined than they are real.

Are some of these objections more convincing than others? Which do you find unconvincing? Overall, do you think these objections should lead us to give up on the universalist approach?

Suggested readings for this chapter

Nussbaum, "Non-Relative Virtues."

Roetz, "Methodological Considerations: A Universalistic Heuristic of Enlightenment" (Chapter 3 of *Confucian Ethics of the Axial Age*).

Tan, "Globalizing Cosmopolitanism."

Wiredu "Are There Cultural Universals?" (Chapter 3 of *Cultural Universals and Particulars*).

Zhao, "A Defense of Universalism: With a Critique of Particularism in Chinese Culture."

Further questions for discussion

1. What is comparative universalism? How does it try to avoid the perceived failings of Enlightenment universalism?

2. What are the central features of Chinese cultural particularism, according to Zhao? What reasons does he see for defending the universalist view?

3. Nussbaum, Roetz, and Wiredu each put forth a unique framework within which comparative universalist inquiry might proceed. What are these frameworks? Which is the most appealing, in your view?

Chapter 9 Pluralism

Exercise 9.1 Evaluating Wong's argument for pluralism

As discussed in this chapter, David Wong offers an argument for pluralism based on our experience of moral ambivalence, in which we understand both sides of a disagreement and see that there is something lost in taking our own side. Here are several criticisms of his argument (all adapted from the book *Moral Relativism and Chinese Philosophy: David Wong and His Critics*). Do you think any of the criticisms are accurate? Which ones?

Criticism 1. In cross-cultural encounters, many members of a culture do not experience moral ambivalence, but rather the conviction that their view is the correct one

In debates between one culture that values human rights and another that values social harmony, members of the former culture may think that members of the latter are simply mistaken. Perhaps some members of culture may experience moral ambivalence, but it does not appear to be the only or even the most common response to moral conflict. (See Gowans, "Naturalism, Relativism, and the Authority of Morality," 108)

Criticism 2. Our experience of moral ambivalence does not necessarily mean that pluralism is true

There could be other explanations, apart from the truth of pluralism, for why we experience moral ambivalence. Such reasons might include lack of conviction in our own way of life, or the fact that the ultimate source of value is difficult to discern. And the experience of moral ambivalence in itself does not have to undermine our own views about right and wrong. As Chad Hansen writes, "The experience of appreciating another's view reminds me that in their shoes, I would find their views as appealing and my present ones strange. It does not give me any basis for doubting my actual reasons for my present views, nor absent constructive argument, that theirs is *true*" (Hansen, "Principle of Humanity vs. Principle of Charity," 90).

Criticism 3. Moral ambivalence might be a stage in the search for a universal morality

Our experience of moral ambivalence might lead us to try and combine our morality with other moralities. Lawrence Blum writes that "appropriate confrontations with alternative moralities will quite frequently result in *new* moralities that are regarded by their possessors as preferable and superior to the original one(s)" (Blum, "Human Morality, Naturalism, and Accommodation," 42). Pluralism, then, is not the end of the journey, but the beginning of a search for the best possibility morality.

Criticism 4. Wong's account of pluralism doesn't encompass everything that we would want from a morality

Consider the moral idea of the "human being." We use phrases such as "treat me like a human being!" or talk about "dehumanization" or "inhumanity." This indicates that there is a dimension of morality that does not begin from a particular group, but is rooted in humanity itself. Wong's account of pluralism does not do enough to take into account this dimension of morality. (See ibid., 38–9)

Exercise 9.2 Pluralism and Personal Experience: A Reflection

In his book *To Be an American: Cultural Pluralism and the Rhetoric of Assimilation*, Bill Ong Hing describes growing up in an extended Chinese-American family in Superior, Arizona, working in the family grocery store next to his house. To his parents, he speaks Cantonese; to his siblings, English. To the majority of the store's customers in a majority Mexican-American community, he speaks Spanish (though to Navajo and Apache customers, he speaks English); to the neighborhood children, Spanish and English. His family celebrates holidays from many different cultures, and his friendship and personal growth involves interactions with people from multiple backgrounds.

As Hing writes, "I learned values and approaches to life from people of all backgrounds, from my Catholic Mexican American playmates to my Jewish high school history teacher, from Navajo and German customers to the chief administrator of the local mine" (11). In his book, Hing, now a professor at the University of San Francisco, explores the meaning of cultural pluralism in an increasingly diverse society, with pressures towards both assimilation, on the one hand, and separatism, on the other. One theme of the book is how our own personal experiences will inevitably shape our views about these issues.

Reflection: Is your own worldview informed by more than one culturally bound set of values? What have you learned from each culture? How do you balance these values against one another?

Exercise 9.3 Pluralism and Gender

As Ann A. Pang-White writes in her introduction *The Bloomsbury Research Handbook of Chinese Philosophy and Gender*, the pluralistic framework can also be applied to issues of gender. Chinese philosophers in the Buddhist, Confucian, and Daoist traditions have used resources from these ancient schools to address issues debated by contemporary feminists in Western countries. Pang-White suggests that "Perhaps, the very concept of 'feminism' and 'gender' (vocabularies originated from the West) needs to be broadened and redefined. Such a pluralistic and genuinely multicultural approach is to be welcomed for the future growth, the deepening, and the health of gender discourse. . . ." (17)

For this exercise, take a look at one of the following articles that addresses the topic of gender from the perspective of a philosophical tradition in China. What is different about the conceptual framework that is used to address the topic? Does the author arrive at conclusions about gender that are different from those that might be accepted by contemporary Western philosophers? How does studying the tradition in question broaden our notions of gender?

"Toward a Confucian Feminism—Feminist Ethics In-the-Making," by Li-Hsiang Lisa Rosenlee (Chapter 7 of her book *Confucianism and Women*).

"Yinyang Gender Dynamics: Lived Bodies, Rhythmical Changes, and Cultural Performances," by Robin R. Wang.

"Buddhist Nondualism: Deconstructing Gender and Other Delusions of the Discriminating Mind through Awareness," by Sandra A. Wawrytko.

Suggested readings for this chapter

Hountondji, "True and False Pluralism" (Chapter 8 of *African Philosophy: Myth and Reality*).
Ivanhoe, "Pluralism, Toleration, and Ethical Promiscuity."
Wong, "Pluralism and Ambivalence" (Chapter 1 of *Natural Moralities*).

Further questions for discussion

1. How does pluralism differ from synthetic universalism in its approach to values? What are the strengths and weaknesses of each position?

2. What are some of the possible responses to pluralism discussed by Ivanhoe? Which does he think is the best one? Do you agree?

3. What does Hountondiji mean by "true pluralism"? Why does he think a return to true pluralism will enrich the African philosophical tradition?

Chapter 10 Consensus

Exercise 10.1 Human rights in non-Western traditions

Read one of the following papers that discusses the basis for human rights within a non-Western tradition (this is by no means an exhaustive list):

An-Na'im, Abdullahi A. "Islam and Human Rights: Beyond the Universality Debate."

Carozza, Paolo G. "From Conquest to Constitutions: Retrieving a Latin American Tradition of the Idea of Human Rights."

Chan, Joseph. "A Confucian Perspective on Human Rights for Contemporary China."

Metz, Thaddeus. "*Ubuntu* as a moral theory and human rights in South Africa."

What is the general approach to discussing rights within the tradition in question? What concept(s) from that tradition does the author invoke to make the case for human rights? What is unique about how rights are understood within that tradition?

Exercise 10.2 Case study: a norm of caring for one's elderly parents

Cross-cultural dialogue about human rights should lead us not just to find support in non-Western traditions for rights we think are important, but also to expand our own notions about which rights matter. In the Confucian philosophical tradition, one important norm concerns the duty of children to take care of their aging parents. As the fourth-century BCE Confucian thinker Mencius says, "Of all forms of service, which is the greatest? It is serving one's parents. . . . There are many services one must perform, but the serving of one's parents is the root of all of them." (4A19) In countries influenced by the Confucian tradition, this emphasis on care of parents is often reflected in law. For instance, in Singapore, the "Maintenance of Parents Act," enacted in 1995, *provides elderly or needy parents, who are unable to maintain themselves adequately, with a legal channel to seek maintenance from their children, who are capable of supporting them, but are not doing so.*

Contemporary scholars of the Confucian tradition point out that these laws will be surprising to many Westerners. While Western human rights laws may protect the rights of children, they do not have much to say about the rights of elderly parents (Chan, "A Confucian Perspective on Human Rights for Contemporary China," 235). Yet in China and other East Asian countries, filial care is a deep and longstanding value. Chenyang Li writes that, "Unlike in the West, where filial morality is rarely a philosophical topic, in China it has long been at the center of philosophical discourse. One cannot understand traditional Chinese culture without understanding the role of filial morality" (Li, "Shifting Perspectives," 218–19).

If we want human rights discourse to be a genuine dialogue rather than a tool of Western hegemony, we must entertain this notion of the rights of the elderly. Doing so will mean taking it up for possible inclusion in the agreed-upon list of basic rights. As Daniel A. Bell argues,

> During the course of cross-cultural dialogue, it is not inconceivable that non-East Asian states may also come to regard the right to be cared for by adult children as a fundamental human right. For example, Western participants may come to question the assumption that relatively fit elderly parents can be committed to nursing homes. More pragmatically, the promotion of filial piety

can be seen as advantageous in an age when Social Security payments are no longer economically sustainable at their current level. If these arguments are sufficiently persuasive to non-Asian participants, perhaps all parties can agree that the right to be cared for by adult children should be included in the unforced consensus on human rights.

("Which Rights are Universal?", 853)

Now suppose a member of the Chinese delegation proposes the right of elderly parents to be cared for by their adult children for inclusion on the list of fundamental human rights. What support for the norm of elderly care do we find in Western philosophical traditions? Are there resources in Western traditions that would reject such a norm? Should we include the rights of elderly parents on the list of basic rights?

Exercise 10.3 The consensus approach to comparative philosophy—yea or nay?

As discussed in this chapter, there are many potential problems with the consensus approach to cross-cultural philosophy. This approach may be a guise for spreading Western values to the rest of the world, rather than achieving meaningful agreement. Such agreement may not be possible in any case, since people from vastly different worldviews may not be able to set aside their basic moral frameworks in order to reach consensus around a list of minimal norms. The approach may be biased toward the most established philosophical or religious traditions around the world, while leaving out less prominent ones. And regardless of these concerns, would there be any moral or philosophical weight to an agreement reached by consensus? The list goes on.

And yet, the approach has its appeal. As the philosopher Owen Flanagan writes in a recent article:

Philosophically, convergence of expert opinion, an unforced consensus about the good life or the range of lives that are good, especially among independent traditions, would provide some basis for confidence that there are universal and objective answers to the deepest, and also shared, existential questions. It would support the view that these answers are accessible across otherwise different cultural traditions, and not esoteric or accessible only by way of the right culturally parochial metaphysics or theology. Practically, such consensus would offer some basis for hope that peoples of different traditions might find a healthy and respectful *modus vivendi* centered on the deep structure of shared values, and not see reason to be at each other's throats over more superficial differences in culture, customs, and habits.

(Flanagan, "Confucian Excellence," 190)

In other words, the consensus approach may be our best hope for achieving a meaningful set of norms to help people from around the world live together—by the results of philosophical inquiry rather than by superstition, and in harmony rather than suspicion and discord.

Given the discussion in this chapter, do you agree with Flanagan about the promise of the consensus approach? Or do you see reason to reject this approach in light of the many objections?

Suggested readings for this chapter

American Anthropological Association, "Statement on Human Rights" (1947).
Parekh, "Non-Ethnocentric Universalism."
Rawls, "The Idea of an Overlapping Consensus."
Taylor, "Conditions of an Unforced Consensus on Human Rights."
"The Universal Declaration of Human Rights."

Further questions for discussion

1. What is the consensus approach to comparative philosophy? How does Taylor adapt Rawls' theory of overlapping consensus to cross-cultural dialogue on human rights?

2. What does consensus have in common with either universalism or pluralism? Why does Parekh call his theory of consensus "pluralist universalism"?

3. What concerns does the American Anthropological Association raise about the universality of the proposed declaration of human rights? Are these concerns valid, in your view? Why or why not?

Chapter 11 Global Philosophy

Exercise 11.1 Exploring the problem-solving approach

Here are some recent articles in Chinese philosophy that take a global-philosophical approach:

Chen, Xunwu. "The Problem of Mind in Confucianism."

Bruya, Brian J. "The Rehabilitation of Spontaneity: A New Approach in Philosophy of Action."

Huang, Yong. "Confucius and Mencius on the Motivation to be Moral."

Kim, Richard. "Human Nature and Moral Sprouts: Mencius on the Pollyanna Problem."

Lai, Karyn. "Confucian Reliability and Epistemic Agency: Engagements with Feminist Epistemology."

Liu, JeeLoo. "Confucian Moral Realism."

Slingerland, Edward. "The Situationist Critique and Early Confucian Virtue Ethics."

Take a look at one of the articles, and then answer the following questions. What is the main philosophical problem that is addressed in the paper? How is the Chinese tradition used to approach this problem? Does the author make any statements about the methods they are using? Do you agree with their approach to the issue?

Exercise 11.2 Fusion philosophy vs. comparative philosophy

Near the end of this chapter, we discussed the debate between adherents of a new post-comparative fusion philosophy and proponents of established approaches to comparative philosophy. The following chart captures some of the significant differences:

Table 12.2 Comparative philosophy vs. fusion philosophy

Comparative Philosophy	Fusion Philosophy
Uses comparative methods as a means of understanding texts from different cultures and uncovering assumptions of different cultural traditions	Uses philosophical methods (phenomenology, analysis, etc.) on texts from different cultures to find creative solutions to contemporary philosophical problems
Focus on nuances of language, historical context	Focus on attaining the truth about some philosophical issue
Shows the significance of cultural boundaries	Aims to produce philosophy that transcends cultural boundaries
Critique of fusion philosophy as methodologically naïve and failing to make sustained engagement with texts and tradition	Critique of comparison as an outmoded form of cross-cultural philosophy that has failed to convince mainstream philosophers of its value

What do you see as some of the strengths and weaknesses of each approach? Overall, which do you think is the better approach to cross-cultural philosophy?

Exercise 11.3 Design your own research in experimental philosophy

Step 1. What is a well-known problem or puzzle in philosophy that you think will elicit different intuitions across cultural boundaries? What makes you suspect that intuitions will differ?

Step 2. What is a simple and comprehensible scenario that you could give to participants in a study that would test whether intuitions in fact differ?

Step 3. Has any research already been done on this philosophical problem? Check out the archive of recent papers at https://philpapers.org/browse/experimental-philosophy-crosscultural-research.   What would your proposed study do to develop already existing research? (Perhaps this exercise should be done in teams!)

As an example, remember the famous Ship of Theseus puzzle? In a recent paper, a team of forty-six researchers from around the world collected intuitions about this puzzle from some 2,700 participants in twenty-two different countries in North and South America, Europe, the Middle East, South Asian, and East Asia. In their variation of the puzzle, translated into seventeen languages, there is a builder named John who made a rowboat named "Drifter" thirty years ago. Over time he has replaced every single one of the original boards. Last month, he took the original boards from his shed and uses them to build a second rowboat with exactly the same design. Which boat is Drifter, the one resulting from the replacement of parts over time, or the one he built last month? More importantly, do the answers to this question vary by geographical region? Check out the paper "The Ship of Theseus Puzzle" (Rose, Machery, et al.) for the results.

Exercise 11.4 Reflection on approaches to comparison

(A) Of the various approaches discussed in this part of the book—universalism, pluralism, consensus, global philosophy (and the different variations of each)—which do you think is the most useful for advancing cross-cultural philosophy? Why? Which do you think is least useful?

(B) Are there other possible approaches to cross-cultural philosophy that you believe have been left out in the discussion? If so, what are they?

Suggested readings for this chapter

Angle, "Chinese Philosophers and Global Philosophy."
Brooks, "How Global is Global Justice?"
Bruya, "Introduction: Chinese Philosophy as a Resource for Problems in Contemporary Philosophy" (from *The Philosophical Challenge from China*)
Chakrabarti and Weber, "Introduction" and "Afterword" to Comparative Philosophy without Borders.
Siderits, "Comparison or Confluence?"

Further questions for discussion

1. What are the main assumptions of the global-philosophical approach? How does it differ from comparative philosophy as traditionally conceived?
2. What are some arguments for taking a global approach to philosophy? Which of these arguments is most successful, in your view? Least successful? Are there other arguments not touched on in this chapter or the above readings?

Conclusion

The ultimate aspiration of comparative philosophy is not just to develop new philosophies, but to produce a new kind of philosopher.[1] This philosopher, in addition to being trained in logic and conceptual analysis, skilled at the careful reading of difficult texts and the construction of written arguments, and dedicated to exposing dogmatism in all its forms, would be adept at comparing and evaluating diverse ways of thinking and living. Comparative philosophy is not a replacement for all the other types of philosophy, but an additional tool we may bring to the pursuit of wisdom.

Anyone interested in philosophy can learn to use comparison as one method among others to advance philosophical discussion. At a minimal level of commitment, this means simply taking a look at what philosophers from a culturally distinct tradition have to say about some issue. If you are interested in philosophy of mind, for instance, what do Buddhist philosophers have to say about the mind? If you are interested in the ethics of war, what do the early Chinese philosophers have to say about aggressive war? At a higher level of commitment, comparative research may involve learning about the broader history and philosophical development of the tradition in question, or even trying to master its language. I hope the discussion we have undertaken in this book may serve as a starting point for those who want to pursue any area of philosophical interest at the cross-cultural level.

Philosophy is not just an academic pursuit, but one that prepares its practitioners to thrive in the world around them. As the American Philosophical Association says in its recently adopted statement on the philosophy major, "The study of philosophy serves to develop intellectual abilities important for life as a whole, beyond the knowledge and skills required for any particular profession."[2] These include the ability to engage in rigorous intellectual debate, to think about problems with no obvious answers, and to fulfill the responsibilities of citizenship and public life.

In the Fall of 2021, as I was finishing up work on the second edition of this book, I attended a conference on "Justice between Generations" at Concordia University in Montreal. Crossing the international border between Champlain, New York, and St-Bernard-de-Lacolle, Quebec, few other vehicles were present, due to the travel restrictions in place because of the COVID-19 pandemic. Many of the conference participants presented via Zoom, fielding questions from other online contributors as well as from a masked audience of local attendees made up mainly of students and faculty from the university. While the set-up of the conference was something no one would have predicted in January 2020 when it was first announced, and comprised an extraordinary logistical challenge for its organizers, it was inspiring to see philosophers joining in from Addis Ababa and Auckland, Shanghai and Seattle, to talk about different approaches to climate change and other ethical issues impacting future generations. These issues are global issues and coming to terms with them will require all of the resources at our disposal.

Navigating these different cultural perspectives requires a unique set of skills. The greatest thinkers from other traditions put us face-to-face with the limits of our own foundational beliefs, forcing us to defend what never struck us before as needing defending. Since comparative philosophers deal on a daily basis with vast differences in language, philosophical foundations, and value configurations, they as much as anyone recognize the difficulties involved in overcoming them and have developed sophisticated tools for coping with these difficulties. As negotiating these differences becomes an increasing part of public life and the responsibilities of citizenship, training in comparative philosophy will gain in value.

Finding one's place as a member of the global community, as Martha Nussbaum writes, "is often a lonely business. It is, in effect, a kind of exile— from the comfort of assured truths, from the warm nestling feeling of being surrounded by people who share one's convictions and passions."[3] Our encounters with alternative conceptual frameworks can be disorienting, alienating us from the beliefs cherished by members of our own society. The hope is that by developing the right sorts of skills and abilities, we can learn to flourish as philosopher-citizens of the world.

Notes

Introduction

1. Mill, *Principles of Political Economy*, 174.
2. Mill, *Principles of Political Economy*, 174.
3. Yearley, *Mencius and Aquinas*, 203.
4. Wiredu, "How Not to Compare."
5. Halbfass, *India and Europe*, 432.

1 Is There Such a Thing as Comparative Philosophy?

1. Van Norden, "What Should Western Philosophy Learn from Chinese Philosophy?" 225.
2. Quoted in Ching and Oxtoby, *Moral Enlightenment*, 223. I owe the reference to Defoort, "Is 'Chinese Philosophy' a Proper Name?" 626.
3. Hegel, *The Philosophy of History*, 93, 99.
4. Hume, *Political Essays*, 86, note f. For some background on this passage, which Hume later edited, see Immerwahr, "Hume's Revised Racism."
5. Pigliucci, "On the Pseudo-profundity of some Eastern Philosophy."
6. Dotson, "How Is This Paper Philosophy?," 7–8.
7. See Defoort, "Is There Such a Thing as Chinese Philosophy?" 393.
8. Ikuenobe, "The Parochial Universalist Conception of 'Philosophy' and 'African Philosophy,'" 196.
9. Krishna, "Comparative Philosophy," 76.
10. See Schwitzgebel, "Why don't we Know our Chinese Philosophy?" 27.
11. Van Norden, *Taking Back Philosophy*, 108.
12. Interested readers may refer to "2016–2017 SOAS SU Educational priorities," 1–2, which may be accessed at this link: https://soasunion.org/pageassets/education/educationalpriorities/Educational-priorities-2016-17(3).pdf
13. An informative account of the affair can be found in Kenan Malik's article in *The Guardian*, entitled "Are Soas students right to 'decolonise' their

minds from western philosophers?" which readers will find here: https://www.theguardian.com/education/2017/feb/19/soas-philosopy-decolonise-our-minds-enlightenment-white-european-kenan-malik

14. Sabaratnam, "Decolonising the curriculum: what's all the fuss about?"
15. Krishna, "Comparative Philosophy," 72.
16. Birt, "Identity and the Question of African Philosophy," 95.
17. See Bernasconi, "Ethnicity, Culture, and Philosophy," 574–5.
18. Sellars, *Science, Perception and Reality*, 1.
19. Edelglass and Garfield, "Introduction," 3. For a similar view, see Prabhu, "Philosophy in an Age of Global Encounter," 30.
20. For discussion of these problems, see Lao, "On Understanding Chinese Philosophy," 266–7.
21. Defoort, "Is There Such a Thing as Chinese Philosophy?" 401–2.
22. Some of the material in this and the preceding two paragraphs is taken from Connolly, "Chinese Philosophy *qua* Philosophy," 377–8.
23. This definition is taken with slight modifications from Raud, "Philosophies versus Philosophy," 621–2.
24. Wittgenstein, *Philosophical Investigations*, §66.
25. Harrison, *Eastern Philosophy: The Basics*, 5.
26. Ma and van Brakel, *Fundamentals of Comparative and Intercultural Philosophy*, 19.
27. See Ni, "Traversing the Territory of Comparative Philosophy," 23–4.
28. At a 2008 conference sponsored by the International Society for Comparative Studies of Chinese and Western Philosophy, attendees were asked to come up with a statement of the "minimal methodology" of comparative philosophy. The first principle they came up with was that "Openness is fundamental," but to this they added the qualification that "so is the exercise of critical philosophical judgment." See Angle, "The Minimal Definition and Methodology of Comparative Philosophy," 109.
29. Allinson, "The Myth of Comparative Philosophy," 270.
30. Allinson, "The Myth of Comparative Philosophy," 271.

2 The Goals of Comparison

1. Paul Masson-Oursel, "True Philosophy is Comparative Philosophy," 6.
2. Angle, "The Minimal Definition and Methodology," 106, with slight modifications. See also Neville, "Two Forms of Comparative Philosophy," 2; he refers to the two approaches as the "objectivist" and "normative" elements of comparative philosophy, respectively.
3. Botz-Bornstein, "Ethnophilosopy, Comparative Philosophy, Pragmatism," 157.

4. Biderman, *Crossing Horizons*, 7.
5. Balslev, "Philosophy and Cross-Cultural Conversation," 369.
6. Yu, *The Ethics of Confucius and Aristotle*, 4.
7. Brooks, "How Global is Global Justice?" 8.
8. Garfield, *Empty Words*, viii.
9. Littlejohn, "Comparative Philosophy."
10. Kupperman, "The Purposes and Functions of Comparative Philosophy," 26.
11. Smid, *Methodologies of Comparative Philosophy*, 4, with slight modifications.
12. Hall and Ames, *Anticipating China*, 111.
13. Halbfass, *India and Europe*, 433.
14. Henry Rosemont, Jr., as quoted in Silius, "Diversifying Academic Philosophy," 277. A slightly different version of the quote appears in Lin, Rosemont, Jr., and Ames, "Chinese Philosophy," 753.
15. Slingerland, *Confucius: Analects*; the passage is 6.30.
16. Ames and Rosemont, *The Analects of Confucius*.
17. Waley, *The Analects of Confucius*.
18. For these points, see Li, *The Tao Encounters the West*, 6–9.
19. Rhees (ed.), *Recollections of Wittgenstein*, 157.
20. Yu, *The Ethics of Confucius and Aristotle*, 9.
21. Nussbaum, "Non-Relative Virtues," 26–7.
22. Scharfstein, "A Comparative History of World Philosophy," 7.
23. Hansen, "Freedom and Moral Responsibility in Confucian Ethics," 169.
24. Hall and Ames, *Thinking Through Confucius*, 5.
25. Moeller, "Sino-Nietzscheanismus," 51. Quoted in Roetz, "What it Means to Take Chinese Ethics Seriously," 18.
26. For an interesting exploration of this point, see Murphy and Weber, "Confucianizing Socrates and Socratizing Confucius."
27. See Nussbaum, *Cultivating Humanity*, 118 ff.
28. Konings, Maex, and Bogaerts, "From Mount Lu to the Agora," 475.
29. On this point, see Kasulis, *Intimacy or Integrity*, 6 ff.
30. Yearley, *Mencius and Aquinas*.
31. Taylor, "Understanding the Other," 36.
32. Taylor, "Understanding the Other," 34.
33. Taylor, "Understanding the Other," 29.
34. Jullien, *Detour and Access*, 371.
35. On this point, see Struhl, "No (More) Philosophy without Cross-Cultural Philosophy."
36. Raghuramaraju, *Debates in Indian Philosophy*, 2.
37. See Sherratt, *Continental Philosophy of Science*, 200–1.
38. Butnor and McWeeny, "Why Feminist Comparative Philosophy?" 5.

39. Kupperman, "The Purposes and Functions of Comparative Philosophy," 27–8.
40. Van Norden, "What Should Western Philosophy Learn from Chinese Philosophy?" 239.
41. Siderits, *Personal Identity and Buddhist Philosophy*, xiii.
42. Garfield, *Two Truths and Method*, 8.
43. Garfield, *Two Truths and Method*, 8.
44. See Siderits, *Personal Identity and Buddhist Philosophy*, xiii.
45. Aristotle, *Metaphysics*, 993a30-b1. For discussion of this approach to truth in comparative philosophy, see Yu and Bunnin, "Saving the Phenomena," 299 ff.
46. Cline, *Confucius, Rawls, and the Sense of Justice*, 43 ff.

3 The Role of Tradition and Culture

1. Wong, "Comparative Philosophy."
2. Smid, *Methodologies of Comparative Philosophy*, 2.
3. Wang, "Incommensurability and Comparative Philosophy," 14.
4. Garfield, "Two Truths and Method," 3.
5. Garfield, "Just Another Word for Nothing Left to Lose," 174. For additional discussion of the problem of free will in Indian philosophy, see Freschi, "Freedom Because of Duty," 140ff.
6. MacIntyre, *After Virtue*, 221.
7. Ma and van Brakel, *Fundamentals of Comparative and Intercultural Philosophy*, 20.
8. On this point, see Angle, "Piecemeal Progress," 188.
9. Though there are some notable exceptions, e.g., Scharfstein, *A Comparative History of World Philosophy*.
10. Tylor, *Primitive Culture*, 1.
11. Appiah, "Race, Culture, Identity," 83.
12. Benedict, *Patterns of Culture*, 46.
13. Koller, "The Importance of Asian Philosophy in the Curriculum," 15.
14. Hall and Ames, *Anticipating China*, 23.
15. Ekei, "The Challenges of African Moral Heritage," 328.
16. Nussbaum, *Cultivating Humanity*, 127–8.
17. Appiah, "Race, Culture, Identity," 83–4.
18. For this objection, see Vargas, "On the Value of Philosophy," 48 ff.
19. Ikuenobe, "The Parochial Universalist Conception of 'Philosophy' and 'African Philosophy.'" 189.

20. Zhao, "A Defense of Universalism," 124.
21. Zhao, "A Defense of Universalism," 125.
22. Quoted in Zhao, "A Defense of Universalism," 126.
23. Appiah, *Thinking it Through*, 339 ff.
24. Vargas, "On the Value of Philosophy," 49.
25. Appiah, *The Ethics of Identity*, 254.
26. Weber, "Comparative Philosophy and the *Tertium*," 167.
27. Vargas, "On the Value of Philosophy," 34–5.
28. Yu and Bunnin, "Saving the Phenomena," 296.
29. On the connections between African and Western philosophy, see D.A. Masolo, "African Philosophy."
30. Edelglass and Garfield, "Introduction," 4.
31. Edelglass and Garfield, "Introduction," 4.
32. In addition to the work discussed in this section, see Wiredu, "Can Philosophy be Intercultural?" 160–1; and Garfield, "Two Truths and Method," 8.
33. See Ivanhoe, "Moral Tradition Respect," 163.
34. Hansen, "The Normative Impact of Comparative Ethics," 79.
35. Hansen, "The Normative Impact of Comparative Ethics," 79.
36. See Ivanhoe, "Moral Tradition Respect," 165.
37. See Ivanhoe, "Moral Tradition Respect," 167.
38. Smid, *Methodologies of Comparative Philosophy*, 89.
39. Garfield, *Empty Words*, 169.

4 Linguistic Incommensurability

1. Interested students can refer to Havil, *The Irrationals*, 19 ff, for further discussion.
2. The account in this section is informed by Turiel, *The Culture of Morality*, 37 ff.
3. Benedict, *Patterns of Culture*, 45.
4. Benedict, *Patterns of Culture*, 48.
5. Benedict, *Patterns of Culture*, 223.
6. Kuhn, "What are Scientific Revolutions?" 16–17.
7. Kuhn, *The Structure of Scientific Revolutions*, 5.
8. Kuhn, *The Structure of Scientific Revolutions*, 6.
9. Kuhn, *The Structure of Scientific Revolutions*, 149.
10. Kuhn, *The Structure of Scientific Revolutions*, 150.
11. Kuhn, *The Structure of Scientific Revolutions*, 158.
12. Kuhn, *The Structure of Scientific Revolutions*, 150.
13. Sapir, "The Status of Linguistics as a Science," 162.

14. Nietzsche, *Beyond Good and Evil*, §20.
15. Graham, *Disputers of the Tao*, 389.
16. The above table is adapted from Graham, "'Being' in Western Philosophy Compared with *Shih/Fei* and *Yu/Wu* in Chinese Philosophy," 323–9; and Reding, *Comparative Essays in Early Greek and Chinese Rational Thinking*, 171.
17. Graham, "'Being' in Western Philosophy Compared with *Shih/Fei* and *Yu/Wu* in Chinese Philosophy," 343–4.
18. Graham, "'Being' in Western Philosophy Compared with *Shih/Fei* and *Yu/Wu* in Chinese Philosophy," 343–4.
19. Hall and Ames, "Chinese Philosophy," §1.
20. See Swoyer, "The Linguistic Relativity Hypothesis," and Berlin and Kay, *Basic Color Terms*. For a critical discussion of Berlin and Kay's research, refer to Lloyd, *Cognitive Variations*, 9 ff.
21. On this point, see Reding, *Comparative Essays in Early Greek and Chinese Rational Thinking*, 172 ff.
22. Davidson, "On the Very Idea of a Conceptual Scheme," 6.
23. Davidson, "Belief and the Basis of Meaning," 153.
24. MacIntyre, *Whose Justice? Which Rationality?* 378–9.
25. Booth and Eglash, "Jewish Activists want to Pray on Jerusalem's Temple Mount."
26. MacIntyre, "Relativism, Power, and Philosophy," 7.
27. MacIntyre, *Whose Justice? Which Rationality?* 374.
28. Mou, *Cross-Tradition Engagement in Philosophy*, 113; my italics.
29. Mou, *Cross-Tradition Engagement in Philosophy*, 59.
30. Mou, *Cross-Tradition Engagement in Philosophy*,
31. Ma and van Brakel, *Fundamentals of Comparative and Intercultural Philosophy*, 147.
32. Ma and van Brakel, *Fundamentals of Comparative and Intercultural Philosophy*, 148.
33. Ma and van Brakel, *Fundamentals of Comparative and Intercultural Philosophy*, 209.
34. Ma and van Brakel, *Fundamentals of Comparative and Intercultural Philosophy*, 223.
35. Rosemont, Jr., "Against Relativism," 41 n. 11.
36. Cline, *Confucius, Rawls, and the Sense of Justice*, 11 ff.
37. Van Norden, *Virtue Ethics and Consequentialism in Early Chinese Philosophy*, 22.
38. Cline, *Confucius, Rawls, and the Sense of Justice*, 15.
39. Taylor, "Understanding the Other," 34.
40. Hansen, "Response to Bao Zhiming," 421.

41. For a recent discussion of the two principles' uses in comparative philosophy, see Hansen, "Principle of Humanity vs. Principle of Charity."
42. Grandy, "Reference, Meaning, and Belief," 443.
43. Wong, *Moral Relativity*, 113.
44. See McLeod, "Moral Personhood," 27–31.
45. See Angle, *Human Rights in Chinese Philosophy*, 44.
46. Graham, "Conceptual Schemes and Linguistic Relativism," 198.

5 Foundational and Evaluative Incommensurability

1. The unpublished research by Kaiping Peng, John Doris, Shaun Nichols, and Stephen Stich is discussed in Doris and Plakias, "How to Argue about Disagreement," 323 ff.
2. Collingwood, *An Essay on Metaphysics*, 31.
3. Evans-Pritchard, *Witchcraft, Oracles and Magic among the Azande*, 18.
4. Winch, "Understanding a Primitive Society," 321.
5. Wong, *Natural Moralities*, 8–9.
6. For this criticism see Mounce, "Understanding a Primitive Society," 351–3, and Horton, *Patterns of Thought in Africa and the West*, 148. For a helpful discussion of the debate between Winch and his critics, see Burley, "Mounce and Winch on Understanding (or *Not* Understanding) an Indigenous Society."
7. The Daodejing of Laozi (tr. Ivanhoe), Ch. 57.
8. Slingerland, *Analects*, 12.18.
9. For discussion of the "pragmatic" form of justification in classical Chinese texts, see Xiao, "Agency and Practical Reasoning in the *Analects* and *Mencius*," 630 ff.
10. Graham, *Disputers of the Tao*, 3.
11. Hall and Ames, *Anticipating China*, 123 ff.
12. Van Norden, *Virtue Ethics and Consequentialism in Early Chinese Philosophy*, 15.
13. See Ma and van Brakel, *Fundamentals of Comparative and Intercultural Philosophy*, 85-86.
14. See Yu, "The Practicality of Ancient Virtue Ethics."
15. Anscombe, "Modern Moral Philosophy," 17.
16. Zhuangzi, *Basic Writings*, 43.
17. See Wong, "Three Kinds of Incommensurability."
18. MacIntyre, "Incommensurability, Truth, and the Virtues," 109.

19. MacIntyre, "Incommensurability, Truth, and the Virtues," 112.
20. See Wong, "Three Kinds of Incommensurability," 147.
21. See Wong, "Three Kinds of Incommensurability," 154–5.
22. Cook, *Morality and Cultural Differences*, 11.
23. Marglin, "Towards the Decolonization of the Mind," 13.
24. Marglin, "Towards the Decolonization of the Mind," 13.
25. Carens, *Culture, Citizenship, and Community*, 40.
26. Moody-Adams, *Fieldwork in Familiar Places*, 41.
27. For this point, see again Moody-Adams, *Fieldwork in Familiar Places*, 33–4.
28. Doris and Plakias, "How to Argue about Disagreement," 319–20.
29. Luo, *Doing Philosophy Comparatively* [Review], 318–19. For further doubts about this study, see Pölzer, "Moral Reality and the Empirical Sciences," 115 ff.
30. Nussbaum, "Comparing Virtues," 349.
31. For these points, see Wong, *Natural Moralities*, 84–92.
32. MacIntyre, "Incommensurability, Truth, and the Virtues," 117–18.
33. Yu, *The Ethics of Confucius and Aristotle*, 8.
34. Ivanhoe, "Moral Tradition Respect," 169.
35. See Wong, *Natural Moralities*, 93.
36. Winch, "Understanding a Primitive Society," 321.

6 One-Sidedness

1. Rorty, "Rationality and Cultural Difference," 195. I owe the reference to Clarke, *Oriental Enlightenment*, 186.
2. This definition is adapted from Cook, *Morality and Cultural Differences*, 93.
3. Clarke, *Oriental Enlightenment*, 40–1.
4. Voltaire, *A Philosophical Dictionary*, 142.
5. Schopenhauer, *The World as Will and Representation*, 9.
6. Schopenhauer, *The World as Will and Representation*, 416. My italics.
7. Schopenhauer, *The World as Will and Representation*, 416.
8. Tuck, *Comparative Philosophy and the Philosophy of Scholarship*, 7.
9. Shun, "Studying Confucian and Comparative Ethics," 456–7.
10. See for instance Krishna, "What Comparative Philosophy is and What it Ought to Be", and Wiredu, "Toward Decolonizing African Philosophy and Religion."
11. Shun, "Studying Confucian and Comparative Ethics," 473.
12. Said, *Orientalism*, 3, 95.
13. Said, *Orientalism*, 12.
14. For this argument, see Cline, *Confucius, Rawls, and the Sense of Justice*, 38–9.

15. On this point, see Clarke, *Oriental Enlightenment*, 27 ff.
16. Kirloskar-Steinbach and Kalmanson, *A Practical Guide to World Philosophies*, 105–6.
17. Priest, "Where is Philosophy at the Start of the Twenty-First Century?" 99. I owe the reference to Cline, *Confucius, Rawls, and the Sense of Justice*, 37–8.
18. Wong, "Comparative Philosophy."
19. Shen, "Some Thoughts on Intercultural Philosophy and Chinese Philosophy," 360.
20. Wiredu, "Toward Decolonizing African Philosophy and Religion."
21. Denecke, *The Dynamics of Masters Literature*, 335; Libbrecht, "Comparative Philosophy: A Methodological Approach," 31.
22. Shun, "Studying Confucian and Comparative Ethics," 476.
23. Deutsch, "Knowledge and the Tradition Text in Indian Philosophy," 165.
24. Ivanhoe, "Understanding Traditional Chinese Philosophical Texts," 305.
25. Scharfstein, "The Contextual Fallacy."
26. Hall and Ames, *Anticipating China*, xx.
27. Scharfstein, "The Contextual Fallacy."
28. Stalnaker, *Overcoming Our Evil*, 48–9.
29. For this criticism, see McLeod, "Moral Personhood," 66.
30. Ma and van Brakel, *Fundamentals of Comparative and Intercultural Philosophy*, 97.
31. Ma and van Brakel, *Fundamentals of Comparative and Intercultural Philosophy*, 100.
32. Ma and van Brakel, *Fundamentals of Comparative and Intercultural Philosophy*, 223.
33. Yu, *The Ethics of Confucius and Aristotle*, 4.
34. Garfield, *Empty Words*, 169.
35. Thanks to Robin Wang for this example.
36. Dussel, "Bridging the Gaps," 22.
37. Bell and Metz, "Confucianism and *Ubuntu*," 78.
38. Schepen and van Rappard, "African and Chinese Philosophies Compared," 1377–8.
39. Dottin, "Sino-African Philosophy," 50.
40. Silva, "Comparative Philosophy and Decolonial Struggle," 128.
41. See also Shun, "Studying Confucian and Comparative Ethics," 469–70.
42. Hall and Ames, *Thinking Through Confucius*, 41.
43. See Gardner, *The Four Books*, xiii–xiv.
44. See Connolly, *Learning Chinese Philosophy with Commentaries*, for further discussion.
45. I owe this point to an anonymous reader for Bloomsbury.

7 Generalization

1. Rosemont, Jr., and Ames, "On Translation and Interpretation," 56.
2. Nussbaum, *Cultivating Humanity*, 127.
3. For this definition, see Ames, *Confucian Role Ethics*, 27.
4. Plato, *Euthyphro*, 6e.
5. Zakaria, "Culture is Destiny," 114.
6. Bhargava, "Overcoming the Epistemic Injustice of Colonialism," 415.
7. Narayan, "Essence of Cultures and a Sense of History," 491.
8. Clarke, *Oriental Enlightenment*, 10.
9. Huntington, "The Clash of Civilizations?" 25.
10. For these criticisms, see Sen, "Democracy as a Universal Value," especially 15–16.
11. Wong, *Natural Moralities*, 104.
12. See Ames, *Confucian Role Ethics*, 26–7.
13. Feldman, *Trouble in the Middle*, 408, with modifications.
14. Ahlstrom and Bruton, *International Management*, 35, with modifications.
15. Chaney and Martin, *The Essential Guide to Business Etiquette*, 164.
16. Kasulis, *Intimacy or Integrity*, 7.
17. Hall and Ames, *Thinking Through Confucius*, 11.
18. Hall and Ames, *Thinking Through Confucius*, 16.
19. Tanaka, "Davidson and Chinese Conceptual Scheme," 56.
20. Goldin, "The Myth That China Has No Creation Myth."
21. Bell, *Beyond Liberal Democracy*, 52.
22. Puett, *To Become a God*, 25.
23. Goldin, "The Myth That China Has No Creation Myth," 11.
24. Zhang, *Mighty Opposites*, 16–17.
25. As the scholar of Indian philosophy Anindita Balslev writes, "The object of the comparativist is how to generate a creative discourse by doing away with stereotypes about cultures in general and philosophical traditions in particular." One of her examples is the notion that Indian philosophers conceive of time as "cyclic" rather than linear, which in turn perpetuates the stereotype that Indian culture is opposed to progress. If we want to understand Indian philosophy, she argues, we must first dismantle this generalization. See Balslev, "Philosophy and Cross-Cultural Conversation," 361.
26. Stevenson, *The Complete Idiot's Guide to Eastern Philosophy*, 27.
27. On this view of textual interpretation, see Ivanhoe, "Understanding Traditional Chinese Philosophical Texts," 309–10.
28. Hall and Ames, *Anticipating China*, xv.
29. Kasulis, *Intimacy or Integrity*, 8.

30. Nussbaum and Sen, "Internal Criticism and Indian Rationalist Traditions," 302–6.
31. Lewis, *The Construction of Space in Early China*, 20.
32. Ames, "The Meaning of Body in Classical Chinese Philosophy," 163.
33. Raphals, "Embodied Virtue, Self-Cultivation, and Athletics," 143.
34. Slingerland, "Body and Mind in Early China," and more recently, *Mind and Body in Early China*.
35. Slingerland, "Body and Mind in Early China," 23.
36. Hofstede, *Culture's Consequences*.
37. Nisbett, *The Geography of Thought*, 89–92.
38. Nisbett, *The Geography of Thought*, 109.
39. Nisbett, *The Geography of Thought*, 47–9.
40. Appiah, *Ethics of Identity*, 45.
41. See, for example, Greenwood, "Individualism and Collectivism in Moral and Social Thought," 168.
42. Oyserman et al., "Rethinking Individualism and Collectivism."
43. Slingerland, "Body and Mind in Early China," 3–4.
44. Ortner, "East Brain, West Brain."
45. Lloyd, *Cognitive Variations*, 161 ff.
46. See Bunnin and Yu, *The Blackwell Dictionary of Western Philosophy*, s.v. "Individualism."
47. For discussion of this point, see Li, "Comparative Philosophy and Cultural Patterns."
48. Nisbett, *Geography of Thought*, 29–30.
49. Burik, Smid, and Weber, "Epilogue," 248.
50. Mason, "Generalizations, Cultural Essentialism, and Metaphorical Gulfs," 495.
51. Li, "Comparative Philosophy and Cultural Patterns," 544.
52. McLeod and Brown, *Transcendence and Non-Naturalism in Early Chinese Thought*, 193.
53. Berger and Kramer, "Lessons from Intercultural Philosophy," 137.
54. Mason gave me this and many other valuable comments on this section as I was working on the draft version.

8 Universalism

1. Flanagan, *The Bodhisattva's Brain*, ix.
2. Scharfstein, *A Comparative History of World Philosophy*, 7.
3. Schor, *Bad Objects*, 3.
4. Gray, *Enlightenment's Wake*, 187–8.

5. Hall and Ames, "A Pragmatist Understanding of Confucian Democracy," 128–9.
6. Rosemont, Jr., "Whose Democracy?" 68. Quote slightly modified.
7. Dallmayr, "Beyond Monologue," 253.
8. Zhao, "Some Progressive and Problematic Features of Current Philosophy in China," 106.
9. Yu and Bunnin, "Saving the Phenomena," 301.
10. Jaspers, *The Origin and Goal of History*.
11. Jaspers, *The Origin and Goal of History*. Quote slightly modified.
12. Roetz, *Confucian Ethics of the Axial Age*, 5.
13. Roetz, "What It Means to Take Chinese Ethics Seriously," 15.
14. Roetz, "What It Means to Take Chinese Ethics Seriously," 13.
15. *Mencius*, 5B8.
16. Clarke, *Oriental Enlightenment*, 119.
17. Northrop, "The Complementary Emphases of Eastern Intuitive and Western Scientific Philosophy."
18. Radhakrishnan, "On Philosophical Synthesis," 4.
19. Dewey, "On Philosophical Synthesis," 3.
20. Santayana, "On Philosophical Synthesis," 5.
21. The account in this paragraph and the preceding two is indebted to McDermott, "Radhakrishnan's Contribution to Comparative Philosophy," especially 436–7.
22. Hansen, "The Normative Impact of Comparative Ethics," 81.
23. Scharfstein, *A Comparative History of World Philosophy*, 36; Wiredu, *Cultural Universals and Particulars*, 34 ff.
24. Lloyd, *Cognitive Variations*, 5.
25. Nussbaum, "Non-Relative Virtues."
26. Wiredu, *Cultural Universals and Particulars*, 21.
27. See, for instance, Scharfstein, *A Comparative History of World Philosophy*, 34.
28. Scharfstein, *A Comparative History of World Philosophy*, 6.
29. Scharfstein, *A Comparative History of World Philosophy*, 1–4.
30. Wiredu, *Cultural Universals and Particulars*, 29. Zhao Dunhua emphasizes a similarly other-oriented test: a value is universal if it will improve the lives of those who adopt it. This judgment is made not by the person who maintains the value is universal, but from the perspective of those who adopt it. See Zhao, "A Defense of Universalism," 120–1.
31. Wiredu, *Cultural Universals and Particulars*, 70.
32. Krishna, "Comparative Philosophy."
33. *The Daodejing of Laozi* (tr. Ivanhoe), Ch. 11.
34. A concise discussion may be found in their recent paper, "Necessary Preconditions of the Practice of Comparative Philosophy."

35. For this example, see Ma and van Brakel, "Necessary Preconditions of the Practice of Comparative Philosophy," 35. For further discussion, see Wang, "Thing-ing and No-Thing in Heidegger, Kant, and Laozi."

36. Tagore, "On the Concept of World Philosophy," 534.

37. Tagore, "On the Concept of World Philosophy," 538.

9 Pluralism

1. Ivanhoe, "Moral Tradition Respect," 170.

2. Wong, "Comparative Philosophy."

3. Wong calls his view "Pluralistic Relativism" but here I follow Ivanhoe and others in taking it as a case of pluralism (see Ivanhoe, "Pluralism, Toleration, and Ethical Promiscuity," note 1).

4. Wong, *Natural Moralities*, 65.

5. Wong, *Natural Moralities*, 22–3.

6. *Analects* 13.18 (tr. Slingerland).

7. Mencius, 3B9. For discussion, see Connolly, "Friendship and Filial Piety," 74–6.

8. Wong, *Natural Moralities*, 24–5.

9. Wong, *Natural Moralities*, 25.

10. Wong, "A Chinese Virtue is Now the Law."

11. Bell, *Beyond Liberal Democracy*, 77.

12. Wong, "A Chinese Virtue is Now the Law."

13. Wong, *Natural Moralities*, 21.

14. Berlin, "Two Concepts of Liberty," 238.

15. Ivanhoe, "Pluralism, Toleration, and Ethical Promiscuity," 318.

16. Zhuangzi, *Basic Writings*, 28–9. Slight modifications.

17. Ivanhoe, "Pluralism, Toleration, and Ethical Promiscuity," 315.

18. Ivanhoe, "Pluralism, Toleration, and Ethical Promiscuity," 315.

19. See Wong, *Natural Moralities*, 235, and also Connolly, "Perspectivism as a Way of Knowing in the *Zhuangzi*," 501.

20. Ganeri, "A Manifesto for Re:emergent Philosophy," 136.

21. Ganeri, "A Manifesto for Re:emergent Philosophy," 137.

22. Ganeri, "A Manifesto for Re:emergent Philosophy," 141.

23. Ganeri, "A Manifesto for Re:emergent Philosophy," 139.

24. For further discussion, see Ganeri, "Ancient Indian Logic as a Theory of Case-Based Reasoning," 35ff.

25. Wong, "Comparative Philosophy."

26. Quoted in Angle, *Human Rights in Chinese Thought*, 1.

27. Wong, *Agon* and *Hé*.

28. See Kupperman, *Learning from Asian Philosophy*, 144.

29. See Angle, *Human Rights in Chinese Thought*, 68–70.
30. Boghossian, *Fear of Knowledge*, 4.
31. Ganeri, "Reflections on Re:emergent Philosophy," 175.
32. Ganeri, "Why Philosophy Needs Sanskrit, Now More than Ever." 154
33. Panikkar, "What is Comparative Philosophy Comparing?" 116.
34. Hountondji, *African Philosophy*, 165.
35. Hountondji, *African Philosophy*, 167.
36. Ivanhoe, "Moral Tradition Respect," 170.

10 Consensus

1. Rawls, "The Idea of an Overlapping Consensus," 9.
2. Rawls, "The Idea of an Overlapping Consensus," 4.
3. See An-Na'im, "The Cultural Mediation of Human Rights," 153.
4. Taylor, "Conditions of an Unforced Consensus on Human Rights," 130.
5. Chan, "A Confucian Perspective on Human Rights for Contemporary China," 212.
6. Taylor, "Conditions of an Unforced Consensus on Human Rights," 135.
7. Morsink, *The Universal Declaration of Human Rights*, 284–90.
8. Morsink, *The Universal Declaration of Human Rights*, 287.
9. Morsink, *The Universal Declaration of Human Rights*, 289.
10. "The Universal Declaration of Human Rights: History of the Document."
11. An-Na'im, "The Cultural Mediation of Human Rights," 153.
12. Yasuaki, "Toward an Intercivilizational Approach to Human Rights," 122-123.
13. Jiang, *A Confucian Constitutional Order*, 164–6.
14. Parekh, *Rethinking Multiculturalism*, 88.
15. Engelhardt, Jr., "Global Bioethics," 1.
16. Bell, *Beyond Liberal Democracy*, 81.
17. Bell, *Beyond Liberal Democracy*, 80.
18. Angle, *Human Rights in Chinese Thought*, 72–3.
19. Parekh, "Non-Ethnocentric Universalism," 139.
20. Engelhardt, Jr., "Global Bioethics," 3.
21. For this criticism, see Griffin, *On Human Rights*, 139–40.
22. Bell, *Beyond Liberal Democracy*, 83. See his criticisms of the "Universal Declaration of Human Responsibilities" on the preceding page.
23. March, *Islam and Liberal Citizenship*, 20.
24. Parekh, "Non-Ethnocentric Universalism," 138.
25. Parekh, *Rethinking Multiculturalism*, 128.
26. Peerenboom, "Confucian Harmony and Freedom of Thought," 239.
27. Wong, "*Agon* and *Hé*".

28. Hall and Ames, *Democracy of the Dead*, 175–6.
29. Quoted in Li, "The Confucian Ideal of Harmony," 585.
30. Li, "The Confucian Ideal of Harmony," 588.
31. Hall and Ames, *Democracy of the Dead*, 177.
32. Hall and Ames, *Democracy of the Dead*, 179.
33. Wiredu, "State, Civil Society and Democracy in Africa," 1057.
34. Wiredu, "State, Civil Society and Democracy in Africa," 1057.
35. Yasuaki, "Toward an Intercivilizational Approach to Human Rights," 80.

11 Global Philosophy

1. Angle, "Chinese Philosophers and Global Philosophy," 3–4.
2. See especially Angle, "Chinese Philosophers and Global Philosophy";
   Brooks, "How Global is Global Justice?"; Flanagan, *The Bodhisattva's Brain*;
   Mou, "On Constructive-Engagement Strategy of Comparative
   Philosophy"; Siderits, *Personal Identity and Buddhist Philosophy*; and
   Chakrabarti and Weber, "Introduction" to *Comparative Philosophy Without
   Borders*. Angle's paper sets forth his own conception of "global philosophy"
   (that elsewhere he calls "rooted global philosophy") and discusses several
   past and present Chinese philosophers who exemplify this approach.
   Brooks, a political philosopher with a special interest in Indian philosophy,
   also defends a view he calls "global philosophy." Flanagan describes his
   approach as "cosmopolitan"; Siderits and Chakrabarti and Weber use the
   term "fusion philosophy"; and Mou calls his approach "constructive
   engagement." What all these philosophers have in common is that they
   challenge or reject traditional notions of comparative philosophy while at
   the same time calling for openness to learning from other cultural-
   philosophical traditions, focusing especially on how such learning can
   advance contemporary philosophical discussions.
3. Chakrabarti and Weber, "Introduction," 22.
4. Chakrabarti and Weber, "Afterword/Afterwards," 231.
5. Chakrabarti and Weber, "Afterword/Afterwards," 232.
6. Chakrabarti and Weber, "Introduction," 22.
7. Chakrabarti and Weber, "Afterword/Afterwards," 234.
8. Chakrabarti and Weber, "Afterword/Afterwards," 237.
9. Angle, "Chinese Philosophers and Global Philosophy," 5.
10. Fay, *Contemporary Philosophy of Social Science*, 233.
11. Fay, *Contemporary Philosophy of Social Science*, 234.
12. Fay, *Contemporary Philosophy of Social Science*, 234.
13. Mou and Tieszen, *Constructive Engagement of Analytic and Continental
    Approaches in Philosophy*, 1.

14. Fay, *Contemporary Philosophy of Social Science*, 234.
15. Brooks, "How Global is Global Justice?" 4.
16. Littlejohn, "Comparative Philosophy."
17. Mind & Life Institute, "Dialogues."
18. These topics are taken, with slight modifications, from Mind & Life Institute, "Past Conferences."
19. Flanagan, *The Bodhisattva's Brain*, "Acknowledgements."
20. Flanagan, *The Bodhisattva's Brain*, 1.
21. Flanagan, *The Bodhisattva's Brain*, 72–80.
22. Flanagan, *The Bodhisattva's Brain*, 90.
23. Quoted in Zajonc, "Reflections on 'Investigating the Mind,'" 224.
24. Flanagan, *The Bodhisattva's Brain*, 1.
25. Flanagan, *Geography of Morals*, 11–12.
26. Flanagan, *Geography of Morals*, 20–1.
27. Both the case and ensuing questions are taken from Machery et al., "Semantics, Cross-Cultural Style."
28. See among others, Rose et al., "The Ship of Theseus Puzzle," and De Freitas et al., "Consistent Belief in a Good True Self in Misanthropes and Three Interdependent Cultures."
29. Vargas, "On the Value of Philosophy," 37 ff.
30. Parfit, *Reasons and Persons*, 211.
31. Siderits, *Personal Identity and Buddhist Philosophy*.
32. Both of the following examples are taken from Angle and Slote, "Introduction," 5–6.
33. Bruya, "Introduction," xvii.
34. On this general idea of exchange between traditions, see Angle, *Sagehood*, 7.
35. Levine, "Does Comparative Philosophy Have a Fusion Future?" 213.
36. Coquereau, "From Comparative Philosophy to Fusion Philosophy," 153.
37. Angle, "Chinese Philosophers and Global Philosophy," 18.
38. Kalmanson, "The Ritual Methods of Comparative Philosophy."
39. This is adapted from a quote attributed to the Stanford philosopher John Perry, as discussed in Ivanhoe, "Understanding Traditional Chinese Philosophical Texts," 309.
40. See Siderits, *Personal Identity and Buddhist Philosophy*, xii–xiii.
41. Angle and Slote, "Introduction," 6.

Conclusion

1. Littlejohn, "Comparative Philosophy."
2. "American Philosophical Association Statement on the Philosophy Major."
3. Nussbaum, *Cultivating Humanity*, 83.

Bibliography

Ahlstrom, David and Garry Bruton. *International Management: Strategy and Culture in the Emerging World*. Mason, OH: South-Western Cengage Learning, 2010.

Allinson, Robert E. "The Myth of Comparative Philosophy or the Comparative Philosophy Malgré Lui." In *Two Roads to Wisdom? Chinese and Analytic Philosophical Traditions*, edited by Bo Mou. La Salle, IL: Open Court, 2001, 269–92.

American Anthropological Association. "Statement on Human Rights." *American Anthropologist* 49, 4 (1947): 539–43.

"American Philosophical Association Statement on the Philosophy Major." *Proceedings and Addresses of the APA* 80, 5 (2007): 76–89.

Ames, Roger T. "The Meaning of Body in Classical Chinese Philosophy." In *Self as Body in Asian Theory and Practice*, edited by Thomas P. Kasulis, Roger T. Ames, and Wimal Dissanayake. Albany: State University of New York Press, 1993, 157–77.

Ames, Roger T. *Confucian Role Ethics: A Vocabulary*. Hong Kong: Chinese University Press, 2011.

Ames, Roger T. and Henry Rosemont, Jr. (trans.) *The Analects of Confucius: A Philosophical Translation*. New York: Ballantine, 1998.

Ames, Roger T. and Henry Rosemont Jr. "Were the Early Confucians Virtuous?" In *Ethics in Early China: An Anthology*, edited by Chris Fraser, Dan Robins, and Timothy O'Leary. Hong Kong: Hong Kong University Press, 2011, 17–39.

An-Na'im, Abdullahi A. "The Cultural Mediation of Human Rights: The Al-Arquam Case in Malaysia." In *The East Asian Challenge for Human Rights*, edited by Joanne Bauer and Daniel A. Bell. Cambridge: Cambridge University Press, 1999, 147–68.

An-Na'im, Abdullahi A. "Islam and Human Rights: Beyond the Universality Debate." *Proceedings of the annual meeting—American Society of International Law* 94 (2000): 95–103.

Angle, Stephen C. *Human Rights in Chinese Thought: A Cross-Cultural Inquiry*. Cambridge: Cambridge University Press, 2002.

Angle, Stephen C. "中國哲學家與全求哲學 [Chinese Philosophers and Global Philosophy]," 《中國哲學與文化》 [*Chinese Philosophy and Culture*] 1, 1 (2007): 239–56.

Angle, Stephen C. "The Minimal Definition and Methodology of Comparative Philosophy: A Report from a Conference." *Comparative Philosophy* 1, 1 (2010): 106–10.

Angle, Stephen C. "Piecemeal Progress: Moral Traditions, Modern Confucianism, and Comparative Philosophy." In *Ethics in Early China*, edited by C. Fraser, D. Robins, and T. O'Leary. Hong Kong: Hong Kong University Press, 2011, 175–95.

Angle, Stephen C. "Building Bridges to Distant Shores: Pragmatic Problems with Confucian Role Ethics." In *Appreciating the Chinese Difference: Engaging Roger T. Ames on Methods, Issues, and Roles*, edited by Jim Behuniak. Albany: State University of New York Press, 2018, 159–181.

Angle, Stephen C. and Michael Slote. "Introduction." In *Virtue Ethics and Confucianism*, edited by Stephen C. Angle and Michael Slote. New York: Routledge, 2014, 1–11.

Anscombe, G.E.M. "Modern Moral Philosophy." *Philosophy* 33, 124 (1958): 1–19.

Appiah, K. [Kwame] Anthony. "Race, Culture, Identity: Misunderstood Connections." In *Color Conscious: The Political Morality of Race*, edited by K. Anthony Appiah and Amy Gutmann. Princeton, NJ: Princeton University Press, 1996.

Appiah, K. [Kwame] Anthony. *Thinking it Through: An Introduction to Contemporary Philosophy*. New York: Oxford University Press, 2003.

Appiah, K. [Kwame] Anthony. *The Ethics of Identity*. Princeton, NJ: Princeton University Press, 2005.

Aristotle. *Metaphysics*. In *The Complete Works of Aristotle*, edited by Jonathan Barnes. Princeton, NJ: Princeton University Press, 1984.

Bai, Tongdong. *Against Political Equality: The Confucian Case*. Princeton, NJ: Princeton University Press, 2019.

Balslev, Anindita N. "Philosophy and Cross-Cultural Conversation: Some Comments on the Project of Comparative Philosophy." *Metaphilosophy* 28, 4 (1997): 270–359.

Bauer, Joanne R. and Danielle A. Bell. *The East Asian Challenge for Human Rights*. Cambridge: Cambridge University Press, 1999.

Bell, Daniel A. "Which Rights are Universal?" *Political Theory* 27, 6 (1999): 849–56.

Bell, Daniel A. *Beyond Liberal Democracy: Political Thinking for an East Asian Context*. Princeton, NJ: Princeton University Press, 2006.

Bell, Daniel A. *The China Model: Political Meritocracy and the Limits of Democracy*. Princeton: Princeton University Press, 2015.

Bell, Daniel A. and Thaddeus Metz. "Confucianism and *Ubuntu*: Reflections on a Dialogue between Chinese and African Traditions." *Journal of Chinese Philosophy* 38, Supplement (2011): 78–95.

Benhabib, Seyla. *The Claims of Culture: Equality and Diversity in the Global Era.* Princeton, NJ: Princeton University Press, 2002.

Benedict, Ruth. *Patterns of Culture.* Boston: Houghton Mifflin, 1934.

Berger, Douglas and Eli Kramer. "Lessons from Intercultural Philosophy: Getting Over Reductive Comparisons and Attending to Others." *Eidos. A Journal for Philosophy of Culture* 1, 7 (2019): 134–40.

Berlin, Isaiah. "Two Concepts of Liberty." In *The Proper Study of Mankind: An Anthology of Essays.* New York: Farrar, Straus, and Giroux, 1998, 191–241.

Berlin, Brent and Paul Kay. *Basic Color Terms: Their Universality and Evolution.* Berkeley, CA: University of California Press, 1991.

Bernasconi, Robert. "Ethnicity, Culture, and Philosophy." In *The Blackwell Companion to Philosophy*, edited by Nicholas Bunnin and E.P. Tsui-James. Malden, MA: Blackwell, 2003, 567–581.

Bhargava, Rajeev. "Overcoming the Epistemic Injustice of Colonialism." *Global Policy* 4, 4 (2013): 413–17.

Biderman, Shlomo. *Crossing Horizons: World, Self, and Language in Indian and Western Thought*, translated by Ornan Rotem. New York: Columbia University Press, 2008.

Billington, Ray. *Understanding Eastern Philosophy.* New York: Routledge, 1997.

Birt, Robert E. "Identity and the Question of African Philosophy." *Philosophy East and West* 41, 1 (1991): 95–109.

Blackburn, Simon. *Think: A Compelling Introduction to Philosophy.* New York: Oxford University Press, 1999.

Blum, Lawrence. "Human Morality, Naturalism, and Accommodation." In *Moral Relativism and Chinese Philosophy: David Wong and His Critics*, edited by Y. Xiao and Y. Huang. Albany: State University of New York Press, 2014, 33–47.

Boghossian, Paul. *Fear of Knowledge: Against Relativism and Constructivism.* Oxford: Oxford University Press, 2006.

Booth, William and Ruth Eglash. "Jewish activists want to pray on Jerusalem's Temple Mount, raising alarm in Muslim world." *Washington Post*, December 2, 2013.

Botz-Bornstein, Thorsten. "Ethnophilosophy, Comparative Philosophy, Pragmatism: Toward a Philosophy of Ethnoscapes." *Philosophy East and West* 56, 1 (2006): 153–71.

Brooks, Thom. "How Global is Global Justice? Towards a Global Philosophy." In *New Waves in Global Justice*, edited by Thom Brooks. Basingstoke: Palgrave MacMillan, 2014, 228–244.

Brown, Joshua R. and Alexus McLeod. *Transcendence and Non-Naturalism in Early Chinese Thought.* London: Bloomsbury Academic, 2021.

Bruya, Brian. "The Rehabilitation of Spontaneity: A New Approach in Philosophy of Action." *Philosophy East and West* 60, 2 (2010): 207–50.

Bruya, Brian. "Introduction: Chinese Philosophy as a Resource for Problems in Contemporary Philosophy. In *The Philosophical Challenge from China*, edited by Brian Bruya. Cambridge, MA: The MIT Press, 2015.

Bruya, Brian. "Ethnocentrism and Multiculturalism in Contemporary Philosophy." Philosophy East and West 67, 4 (2017), 991–1018.

Burik, Steven, Robert Smid, and Ralph Weber. "Epilogue." In *Comparative Philosophy and Method: Contemporary Practices and Future Possibilities*, edited by Burik Steven Burik, Robert Smid, and Ralph Weber. London: Bloomsbury Academic, 2022.

Bunnin, Nicholas and Jiyuan Yu. *The Blackwell Dictionary of Western Philosophy*. Malden, MA: Blackwell, 2004.

Burley, Mikel. "Mounce and Winch on Understanding (or *Not* Understanding) an Indigenous Society." *Philosophical Investigations* 35, 3–4 (2012): 350–72.

Bussanich, John. *Ethics in Ancient India*. In *Ancient Ethics*, edited by Jörg Hardy and George Rudebusch. Göttingen: V & R unipress, 2014.

Butnor, Ashby and Jen McWeeny. "Why Feminist Comparative Philosophy?" *APA Newsletter on Asian and Asian-American Philosophers and Philosophies* 9, 1 (2009): 4–5.

Carens, Joseph H. *Culture, Citizenship, and Community: A Contextual Exploration of Justice as Evenhandedness*. New York: Oxford University Press, 2000.

Carozza, Paolo G. "From Conquest to Constitutions: Retrieving a Latin American Tradition of the Idea of Human Rights." *Human Rights Quarterly* 25 (2003): 281–313.

Chakrabarti, Arindam and Ralph Weber. "Afterword/Afterwards." In *Comparative Philosophy without Borders*, edited by Arindam Chakrabarti and Ralph Weber. London: Bloomsbury Academic, 2016.

Chakrabarti, Arindam and Ralph Weber. "Introduction." In *Comparative Philosophy without Borders*, edited by Arindam Chakrabarti and Ralph Weber. London: Bloomsbury Academic, 2016.

Chan, Joseph. "A Confucian Perspective on Human Rights for Contemporary China." In *The East Asian Challenge for Human Rights*, edited by Joanne Bauer and Daniel A. Bell. Cambridge: Cambridge University Press, 1999, 212–37.

Chaney, Lillian H. and Jeanette S. Martin. *The Essential Guide to Business Etiquette*. Westport, CT: Praeger Publishers, 2007.

Chen, Xunwu. "The Problem of Mind in Confucianism." *Asian Philosophy* 26, 2 (2016): 166–81.

Cheng, Chung-ying. *New Dimensions of Confucian and Neo-Confucian Philosophy*. Albany: State University of New York Press, 1991.

Ching, J. and W.G. Oxtoby. *Moral Enlightenment: Leibniz and Wolff on China*. Nettetal: Steyler Verlag, 1992.

Clarke, J.J. *Oriental Enlightenment: The Encounter between Asian and Western Thought*. New York: Routledge, 1997.

Cline, Erin M. *Confucius, Rawls, and the Sense of Justice.* New York: Fordham University Press, 2013.

Collingwood, R.G. *An Essay on Metaphysics.* Revised edn. New York: Oxford University Press, 1998.

Connolly, Tim. "Perspectivism as a Way of Knowing in the *Zhuangzi.*" *Dao: A Journal of Comparative Philosophy* 10, 4 (2011): 487–505.

Connolly, Tim. "Friendship and Filial Piety: Relational Ethics in Aristotle and Early Confucianism." *Journal of Chinese Philosophy* 39, 1 (2012): 71–88.

Connolly, Tim. "Learning Chinese Philosophy with Commentaries." *Teaching Philosophy* 35, 1 (2012): 1–18.

Connolly, Tim. "Chinese Philosophy *qua* Philosophy." *Journal of Chinese Philosophy* 40, 3–4 (2013): 477–80.

Connolly, Tim. "Ethics of Compassion: Buddhist *karuna* and Confucian *ren.*" In *Brahman and Dao: Comparative Studies of Indian and Chinese Philosophy and Religion*, edited by Ithamar Theodor and Zhihua Yao. Lanham, MD: Lexington Books, 2013, 107–18.

Connolly, Tim. "Sagehood and Supererogation in the *Analects.*" *Journal of Chinese Philosophy* 40, 2 (2013): 269–86.

Cook, John W. *Morality and Cultural Differences.* New York: Oxford University Press, 1999.

Coquereau, Elise. "From Comparative Philosophy to Fusion Philosophy." *Journal of World Philosophies* 1 (2016): 152–4.

Coutinho, Steve. "Mutual Openness and Global Justice: Learning from Ancient Chinese Philosophy." *Journal of World Philosophies* 6 (2021): 105–9.

Dallmayr, Fred. "Beyond Monologue: For a Comparative Political Theory." *Perspectives on Politics* 2 (2004): 249–57.

Davidson, Donald. "On the Very Idea of a Conceptual Scheme." *Proceedings and Addresses of the American Philosophical Association* 47 (1973–4): 5–20.

Davidson, Donald. "Belief and the Basis of Meaning." In *Inquiries into Truth and Interpretation.* New York: Oxford University Press, 1984, 141–54.

De Freitas, Julian, Hagop Sarkissian, George E. Newman, Igor Grossman, Felipe De Brigard, Andres Luco, and Joshua Knobe. "Consistent Belief in a Good True Self in Misanthropes and Three Interdependent Cultures." *Cognitive Science* (2017): 1–27.

Defoort, Carine. "Is There Such a Thing as Chinese Philosophy? Arguments of an Implicit Debate." *Philosophy East and West* 51, 3 (2001): 393–413.

Defoort, Carine. "Is 'Chinese Philosophy' a Proper Name? A Response to Rein Raud." *Philosophy East and West* 56, 4 (2006): 625–60.

Denecke, Wiebke. *The Dynamics of Masters Literature: Early Chinese Thought from Confucius to Han Feizi.* Cambridge, MA: Harvard University Asia Center, 2011.

Deutsch, Eliot. "Knowledge and the Tradition Text in Indian Philosophy." In *Interpreting across Boundaries: New Essays in Comparative Philosophy*, edited by Gerald James Larson and Eliot Deutsch. Princeton, NJ: Princeton University Press, 1988, 165–73.

Deutsch, Eliot. (ed.), *Culture and Modernity: East-West Philosophic Perspectives*. Honolulu: University of Hawaii Press, 1991.

Dewey, John. "On Philosophical Synthesis." *Philosophy East and West* 1, 1 (1951): 3.

Doris, John M. and Alexandra Plakias. "How to Argue about Disagreement: Evaluative Diversity and Moral Realism." In *Moral Psychology, Vol. 2: The Cognitive Science of Morality: Intuition and Diversity*, edited by Walter Sinnott-Armstrong. Cambridge, MA: MIT Press, 2008, 303–31.

Dotson, Kristie. "How Is This Paper Philosophy?" *Comparative Philosophy* 3, 1 (2012): 3–29.

Dottin, Paul A. "Sino-African Philosophy: A Re-'Constructive Engagement.'" *Comparative Philosophy* 10, 1 (2019): 38–66.

Dussel, Enrique. "Bridging the Gaps: The Voices of Non-Western Philosophies in Global Polylogue." In *Intercultural Dialogue: In Search of Harmony in Diversity*, edited by Edward Demenchonok. Newcastle upon Tyne, UK: Cambridge Scholars Publishing, 2014.

Edelglass, William and Jay L. Garfield. "Introduction." In *The Oxford Handbook of World Philosophy*, edited by Jay L. Garfield and William Edelglass. New York: Oxford University Press, 2011.

Ekei, John Chukwuemeka. "The Challenges of African Moral Heritage: The Igbo Case." In *African Philosophy and the Hermeneutics of Culture: Essays in Honour of Theophilus Okere*, edited by J.Obi Oguejiofor and Godfrey Igwebuike Onah. New Brunswick, NJ: Transaction Publishers, 2005.

Engelhardt, Jr., H. Tristram. "Global Bioethics: An Introduction to The Collapse of Consensus." In *Global Bioethics: The Collapse of Consensus*. Salem, MA: M & M Scrivener Press, 2006, 1–17.

Evans-Pritchard, E.E. *Witchcraft, Oracles and Magic among the Azande*. New York: Oxford University Press, 1976.

Fay, Brian. *Contemporary Philosophy of Social Science: A Multicultural Approach*. Cambridge, MA: Blackwell, 1996.

Feldman, Steven P. *Trouble in the Middle: American-Chinese Business Relations, Culture, Conflict and Ethics*. New York: Routledge, 2013.

Flanagan, Owen. *The Bodhisattva's Brain: Buddhism Naturalized*. Cambridge, MA: MIT Press, 2011.

Flanagan, Owen. *The Geography of Morals: Varieties of Moral Possibility*. Oxford: Oxford University Press, 2016.

Flanagan, Owen. "Confucian Excellence." In *Self-Transcendence and Virtue: Perspectives from Philosophy, Psychology, and Theology*, edited by Jennifer A. Frey and Candace Vogler. New York, Routledge, 2019.

Freschi, Elisa. "Freedom Because of Duty: The Problem of Agency in Mīmāṃsā." In *Free Will, Agency, and Selfhood in Indian Philosophy*, edited by Matthew R. Dasti and Edwin F. Bryant. Oxford: Oxford University Press.

Frisina, Warren G. "Thinking Through Hall and Ames: On the Art of Comparative Philosophy." *Dao: A Journal of Comparative Philosophy* 15 (2016): 563–74.

Gadamer, Hans-Georg. *Truth and Method*. 2nd edn, translated by Joel Weinsheimer and Donald G. Marshall. New York: Crossroad, 1992.

Ganeri, Jonardon. "Ancient Indian Logic as a Theory of Case-Based Reasoning." *Journal of Indian Philosophy* 31 (2003): 33–45.

Ganeri, Jonardon. "A Manifesto for Re:emergent Philosophy." *Confluence: An Online Journal of World Philosophies* 4 (2016): 134–41.

Ganeri, Jonardon. "Reflections on Re:emergent Philosophy." *Confluence: An Online Journal of World Philosophies* 4 (2016): 164–86.

Ganeri, Jonardon. "Why Philosophy Needs Sanskrit, Now More than Ever." In *Comparative Philosophy and Method: Contemporary Practices and Future Possibilities*, edited by Steven Burik, Robert Smid, and Ralph Weber. London: Bloomsbury Academic, 2022.

Gardner, Daniel K. *The Four Books: The Basic Teachings of the Later Confucian Tradition*. Indianapolis, IN: Hackett, 2007.

Garfield, Jay L. *Empty Words*: Buddhist Philosophy and Cross-Cultural Interpretation. New York: Oxford University Press, 2002.

Garfield, Jay L. "Just Another Word for Nothing Left to Lose: Freedom, Agency and Ethics for Mādhyamikas." In *Free Will, Agency, and Selfhood in Indian Philosophy*, edited by Matthew R. Dasti and Edwin F. Bryant. New York: Oxford University Press, 2014.

Garfield, Jay L. "Two Truths and Method." In *The Finger, Not the Moon: Buddhism, Logic and Analytic Philosophy*, edited by Yasup Deguchi, Jay L.Garfield, Graham Priest, and Koji Tanaka. New York: Oxford University Press, 2014.

Garfield, Jay L. and Bryan W. Van Norden. "If Philosophy Won't Diversify, Let's Call It What It Really Is." *New York Times*, May 11, 2016.

Goldin, Paul R. "The Myth that China has no Creation Myth." *Monumenta Serica* 56 (2008): 1–22.

Gowans, Christopher C. "Naturalism, Relativism, and the Authority of Morality." In *Moral Relativism and Chinese Philosophy: David Wong and His Critics*, edited by Yang Xiao and Yong Huang. Albany: State University of New York Press, 2014.

Graham, A.C. *Disputers of the Tao: Philosophical Argument in Ancient China*. La Salle, IL: Open Court, 1989.

Graham, A.C. "'Being' in Western Philosophy Compared with *Shih/Fei* and *Yu/ Wu* in Chinese Philosophy." In *Studies in Chinese Philosophy and Philosophical Literature*. Albany: State University of New York Press, 1990, 322–59.

Graham, A.C. "Conceptual Schemes and Linguistic Relativism in Relation to Chinese." In *Culture and Modernity: East-West Philosophic Perspectives*, edited by Eliot Deutsch. Honolulu: University of Hawaii Press, 1991, 193–212.

Grandy, Richard. "Reference, Meaning, and Belief." *Journal of Philosophy* 70 (1973): 439–52.

Gray, John. *Enlightenment's Wake: Politics and Culture at the Close of the Modern Age*. New York: Routledge, 1995.

Greenwood, John. "Individualism and Collectivism in Moral and Social Thought." In *The Moral Circle and the Self: Chinese and Western Approaches*, edited by Kim-chong Chong, Sor-hoon Tan, and C.L. Ten. La Salle, IL: Open Court, 2003, 163–73.

Griffin, James. *On Human Rights*. New York: Oxford University Press, 2008.

Halbfass, Wilhelm. *India and Europe: An Essay in Understanding*. Albany: State University of New York Press, 1988.

Halbfass, Wilhelm. *Tradition and Reflection: Explorations in Indian Thought*. Albany: State University of New York Press, 1991.

Hall, David L. and Roger T. Ames. *Thinking Through Confucius*. Albany: State University of New York Press, 1987.

Hall, David L. and Roger T. Ames. *Anticipating China: Thinking Through the Narratives of Chinese and Western Culture*. Albany: State University of New York Press, 1995.

Hall, David L. and Roger T. Ames. *The Democracy of the Dead: Dewey, Confucius, and the Hope for Democracy in China*. La Salle, IL: Open Court, 1999.

Hall, David L. and Roger T. Ames. "A Pragmatist Understanding of Confucian Democracy." In *Confucianism for the Modern World*, edited by Daniel A. Bell and Hahm Chaibong. Cambridge: Cambridge University Press, 2003, 124–60.

Hall, David L. and Roger T. Ames. "Chinese Philosophy." In the *Routledge Encyclopedia of Philosophy*. Accessed October 29, 2021. http://www.rep.routledge.com/article/G001

Hansen, Chad. "Freedom and Moral Responsibility in Confucian Ethics." *Philosophy East and West* 22, 2 (1972): 169–86.

Hansen, Chad. "Response to Bao Zhiming." *Philosophy East and West* 35, 4 (1985): 419–24.

Hansen, Chad. "The Normative Impact of Comparative Ethics: Human Rights." In *Confucian Ethics: A Comparative Study of Self, Autonomy, and Community*, edited by Kwong-loi Shun and David B. Wong. Cambridge: Cambridge University Press, 2004, 72–99.

Hansen, Chad. "Principle of Humanity vs. Principle of Charity." In *Moral Relativism and Chinese Philosophy: David Wong and His Critics*, edited by

Yang Xiao and Yong Huang. Albany: State University of New York Press, 2014, 71–101..

Harrison, Victoria S. *Eastern Philosophy: The Basics*. New York: Routledge, 2013.

Havil, Julian. *The Irrationals: A Story of the Numbers You Can't Count On*. Princeton, NJ: Princeton University Press, 2012.

Hegel, G.W.F. *The Philosophy of History*, translated by J. Sibree. Mineola, NY: Dover, 2004.

Hing, Bill Ong. *To Be an American: Cultural Pluralism and the Rhetoric of Assimilation*. New York: New York University Press, 1997.

Hofstede, Geert. *Culture's Consequences: Comparing Values, Behaviors, Institutions, and Organizations across Nations*. 2nd edn. Thousand Oaks, CA: Sage Publications, 2001.

Horton, Robin. *Patterns of Thought in Africa and the West: Essays on Magic, Religion and Science*. Cambridge: Cambridge University Press, 1993.

Hountondji, Paulin J. *African Philosophy: Myth and Reality*. Bloomington: Indiana University Press, 1996.

Huang, Yong. "Confucius and Mencius on the Motivation to be Moral." *Philosophy East and West* 60, 1 (2010): 65–87.

Huang, Yong. *Why be Moral? Learning from the Neo-Confucian Cheng Brothers*. Albany: State University of New York Press, 2014.

Hume, David. *Political Essays*, edited by Knud Haakonssen. Cambridge: Cambridge University Press, 1994.

Huntington, Samuel P. "The Clash of Civilizations?" *Foreign Affairs* 72, 3 (1993): 22–49.

Ikuenobe, Polycarp. "The Parochial Universalist Conception of 'Philosophy' and 'African Philosophy.'" *Philosophy East and West* 47, 2 (1997): 189–210.

Ikuenobe, Polycarp. *Philosophical Perspectives on Communalism and Morality in African Traditions*. Lanham, MD: Lexington Books, 2006.

Immerwahr, John. "Hume's Revised Racism." *Journal of the History of Ideas*, 53, 3 (1992): 481–6

Ivanhoe, Philip J. "Pluralism, Toleration, and Ethical Promiscuity." *Journal of Religious Ethics* 37, 2 (2009): 311–29.

Ivanhoe, Philip J. "Moral Tradition Respect." In *Ethics in Early China*, edited by Chris Fraser, Dan Robins, and Timothy O'Leary. Hong Kong: Hong Kong University Press, 2011, 161–74.

Ivanhoe, Philip J. "Understanding Traditional Chinese Philosophical Texts." *International Philosophical Quarterly* 52, 3 (2012): 303–14.

Jaspers, Karl. *The Origin and Goal of History*, translated by Michael Bullock. New Haven, CT: Yale University Press, 1953.

Jiang, Qing. *A Confucian Constitutional Order: How China's Ancient Past Can Shape Its Political Future*, translated by Edmund Ryden. Princeton, NJ: Princeton University Press, 2012.

Jiang, Xinyan. "Zhang Dongsun: Pluralist Epistemology and Chinese Philosophy." In *Contemporary Chinese Philosophy*, edited by Chung-ying Cheng and Nicholas Bunnin. Malden, MA: Blackwell, 2002.

Jullien, François. *Detour and Access: Strategies of Meaning in China and Greece*, translated by Sophie Hawkes. New York: Zone Books, 2000.

Kalmanson, Leah. "The Ritual Methods of Comparative Philosophy." *Philosophy East and West* 67, 2 (2017): 399–418.

Kalmanson, Leah. *Cross-Cultural Existentialism: On the Meaning of Life in Asian and Western Thought*. London: Bloomsbury Academic, 2020.

Kasulis, Thomas P. *Intimacy or Integrity: Philosophy and Cultural Difference*. Honolulu: University of Hawaii Press, 2002.

Kim, Richard. "Human Nature and Moral Sprouts: Mencius on the Pollyanna Problem." *Pacific Philosophical Quarterly* 99, 1 (2018): 140–62.

King, R.A.H. (ed.). *The Good Life and Conceptions of Life in Early China and Graeco-Roman Antiquity*. Berlin: De Gruyter, 2015.

King, R.A.H. and Dennis Schilling (eds). *How Should One Live? Comparing Ethics in Ancient China and Greco-Roman Antiquity*. Berlin: De Gruyter, 2011.

Kirloskar-Steinbach, Monika and Leah Kalmanson. *A Practical Guide to World Philosophies: Selves, Worlds, and Ways of Knowing*. London: Bloomsbury Academic, 2021.

Klausen, Jimmy Casas. "Civilization and Culture in Anticolonial and Comparative Political Theory." In *The Oxford Handbook of Comparative Political Theory*, edited by Leigh K. Jenco, Murad Idris, and Megan C. Thomas. Oxford: Oxford University Press, 2020.

Koller, John M. "The Importance of Asian Philosophy in the Curriculum." In *Asian Texts—Asian Contexts: Encounters with Asian Philosophies and Religions*, edited by David Jones and E.R. Klein. Albany: State University of New York Press, 2010.

Konings, P., E. Maex, and G. Bogaerts. "From Mount Lu to the Agora: Returning to the Marketplace." *Philosophy East and West* 45, 4 (1995): 475–80.

Krausz, Michael (ed.). *Relativism: Interpretation and Confrontation*. Notre Dame, IN: Notre Dame University Press, 1989.

Krishna, Daya. "Comparative Philosophy: What it is and What it Ought to Be." In *Interpreting across Boundaries: New Essays in Comparative Philosophy*, edited by Gerald James Larson and Eliot Deutsch. Princeton, NJ: Princeton University Press, 1988, 71–83.

Krishna, Daya. "Thinking versus Thought: Strategies for Conceptual Creativity." In *Contrary Thinking: Selected Essays of Daya Krishna*, edited by Nalini Bhushan, Jay L. Garfield, and Daniel Raveh. Oxford: Oxford University Press, 2011.

Kuhn, Thomas S. *The Structure of Scientific Revolutions*, 2nd edn. Chicago: University of Chicago Press, 1970.

Kuhn, Thomas S. "What are Scientific Revolutions?" In *The Road Since Structure: Philosophical Essays, 1970–1993, with an Autobiographical Interview*, edited by James Conant and John Haugeland. Chicago: The University of Chicago Press, 2000.

Kupperman, Joel. *Learning from Asian Philosophy*. Oxford: Oxford University Press, 1999.

Kupperman, Joel. "The Purposes and Functions of Comparative Philosophy." *APA Newsletter on Asian and Asian-American Philosophers and Philosophies* 2, 1 (2002): 26–9.

Lacertosa, Massimiliano. "For a philosophy of comparisons: the problems of comparative studies in relation with Daoism." *Asian Philosophy* 27, 4 (2017): 324–39.

Lai, Karyn. "Confucian Reliability and Epistemic Agency: Engagements with Feminist Epistemology." In *Feminist Encounters with Confucius*, edited by Mathew Foust and Sor-hoon Tan. Boston: Brill, 2016.

Lao, Sze-Kwang. "On Understanding Chinese Philosophy: An Inquiry and a Proposal." In *Understanding Chinese Thought: The Philosophical Roots*, edited by Robert E. Allinson. Hong Kong: Oxford University Press, 1989.

Laozi. *Tao Te Ching*, translated by D.C. Lau. New York: Penguin, 1963.

Laozi. *The Way of Lao Tzu (Tao-te ching)*, translated by Wing-Tsit Chan. New York: Bobbs-Merrill, 1963.

Laozi. *The Daodejing of Laozi*, translated by Philip J. Ivanhoe. Indianapolis, IN: Hackett, 2002.

Laozi. *Daodejing: A Philosophical Translation*, translated by Roger T. Ames and David L. Hall. New York: Ballantine Books, 2003.

Laozi. *Daodejing*, translated by Hans-Georg Moeller. La Salle, IL: Open Court, 2007.

Larson, Gerald James and Eliot Deutsch (eds). *Interpreting across Boundaries: New Essays in Comparative Philosophy*. Princeton, NJ: Princeton University Press, 1988.

Levine, Michael. "Does Comparative Philosophy Have a Fusion Future?" *Confluence: An Online Journal of World Philosophies* 4 (2016): 208–37.

Lewis, Mark Edward. *The Construction of Space in early China*. Albany: State University of New York Press, 2012.

Li, Chenyang. "Shifting Perspectives: Filial Morality Revisited." *Philosophy East and West* 47, 2 (1997): 211–32.

Li, Chenyang. *The Tao Encounters the West: Explorations in Comparative Philosophy*. Albany: State University of New York Press, 1999.

Li, Chenyang. "The Confucian Ideal of Harmony." *Philosophy East and West* 56, 4 (2006): 583–603.

Li, Chenyang. "Comparative Philosophy and Cultural Patterns." In *Dao: A Journal of Comparative Philosophy* 15 (2016): 53–46.

Li, Zehou. *A History of Classical Chinese Thought*, translated by Andrew Lambert. New York: Routledge, 2020.

Libbrecht, Ulrich. "Comparative Philosophy: A Methodological Approach." *Einstein Meets Magritte* 10 (2009): 31–67.

Lin, Tongqi, Henry Rosemont, Jr., and Roger T. Ames. "Chinese Philosophy: A Philosophical Essay on the 'State-of-the-Art.'" *The Journal of Asian Studies* 54, 3 (1995), 727–58.

Littlejohn, Ronnie. "Comparative Philosophy." In the *Internet Encyclopedia of Philosophy*. Accessed October 29, 2021. http://www.iep.utm.edu/comparat/

Liu, JeeLoo. "Confucian Moral Realism." *Asian Philosophy* 17, 2 (2007):167–84.

Liu, Xiaogan. "The Notion of *Wu* or Nonbeing as the Root of the Universe and a Guide for Life." In *Nothingness in Asian Philosophy*, edited by JeeLoo Liu and Douglas L. Berger. New York: Routledge, 2014.

Lloyd, G.E.R. *The Ambitions of Curiosity: Understanding the World in Ancient Greece and China*. Cambridge: Cambridge University Press, 2002.

Lloyd, G.E.R. *Ancient Worlds, Modern Reflections: Philosophical Perspectives on Greek and Chinese Science and Culture*. New York: Oxford University Press, 2004.

Lloyd, G.E.R. *Cognitive Variations: Reflections on the Unity and Diversity of the Human Mind*. New York: Oxford University Press, 2007.

Lloyd, G.E.R. *Disciplines in the Making: Cross-Cultural Perspectives on Elites, Learning, and Innovation*. New York: Oxford University Press, 2009.

Luo, Shirong. *Doing Philosophy Comparatively* [Review]. *Philosophy East and West* 68, 1 (2018): 316–21.

Ma, Lin, and Jaap van Brakel. *Fundamentals of Comparative and Intercultural Philosophy*. Albany: State University of New York Press, 2016.

Ma, Lin, and Jaap van Brakel. "Necessary Preconditions of the Practice of Comparative Philosophy." In *Comparative Philosophy and Method: Contemporary Practices and Future Possibilities*, edited by Steven Burik, Robert Smid, and Ralph Weber. London: Bloomsbury Academic, 2022.

MacIntyre, Alasdair. "Relativism, Power and Philosophy." *Proceedings and Addresses of the American Philosophical Association* 59, 1 (1985): 5–22.

MacIntyre, Alasdair. *Whose Justice? Which Rationality?* Notre Dame, IN: University of Notre Dame Press, 1988.

MacIntyre, Alasdair. "Incommensurability, Truth, and the Conversation Between Confucians and Aristotelians about the Virtues." In *Culture and Modernity: East-West Philosophic Perspectives*, edited by Deutsch. Honolulu: University of Hawaii Press, 1991, 104–22.

MacIntyre, Alasdair. *A Short History of Ethics: A History of Moral Philosophy from the Homeric Age to the 20th Century*, 2nd edn. New York: Routledge, 1998.

MacIntyre, Alasdair. *After Virtue: A Study in Moral Theory*, 3rd edn. Notre Dame, IN: University of Notre Dame Press, 2008.

McDermott, Robert A. "Radhakrishnan's Contribution to Comparative Philosophy." *International Philosophy Quarterly* 10, 3 (1970): 420–40.

McLeod, Gustavus Alexus. "Moral Personhood in Confucius and Aristotle." PhD diss., University of Connecticut, 2009.

Machery, Edouard, Ron Mallon, Shaun Nichols and Stephen P. Stich. "Semantics, Cross-Cultural Style." *Cognition* 92 (2004): 1–12.

Malik, Kenan. "Are SOAS students right to 'decolonise' their minds from western philosophers?" *The Guardian*, February 19, 2017. https://www.theguardian.com/education/2017/feb/19/soas-philosopy-decolonise-our-minds-enlightenment-white-european-kenan-malik.

March, Andrew F. *Islam and Liberal Citizenship: The Search for an Overlapping Consensus*. New York: Oxford University Press, 2011.

Marglin, Stephen A. "Towards the Decolonization of the Mind." In *Dominating Knowledge: Development, Culture, and Resistance*, edited by Frédérique Appfel Marglin and Stephen A. Marglin. New York: Oxford University Press, 2001, 1–28.

Masolo, D.A. "African Philosophy: A Historical Overview." In *A Companion to World Philosophies*, edited by Eliot Deutsch and Ron Bontekoe. Malden, MA: Blackwell, 1997.

Mason, Joshua. "Generalizations, Cultural Essentialism, and Metaphorical Gulfs." *Dao: A Journal of Comparative Philosophy* 17 (2018): 479–97.

Masson-Oursel, Paul. "True Philosophy is Comparative Philosophy." *Philosophy East and West* 1, 1 (1951): 6–9.

Mencius. *Mencius*, translated by Irene Bloom. New York: Columbia University Press, 2009.

Metz, Thaddeus. "*Ubuntu* as a moral theory and human rights in South Africa." *African Human Rights Law Journal*, 11, 2 (2011): 532–59.

Mika, Carl. "Counter-Colonial and Philosophical Claims: An indigenous observation of Western philosophy." *Educational Philosophy and Theory*, 47, 11 (2015): 1136–42.

Mill, John Stuart. *Principles of Political Economy with Some of Their Applications to Social Philosophy*, edited by Stephen Nathanson. Indianapolis, IN: Hackett, 2004.

Mind & Life Institute. "Dialogues." Accessed August 6, 2014. http://www.mindandlife.org/dialogues/

Mind & Life Institute. "Past Conferences." Accessed August 6, 2014. http://www.mindandlife.org/dialogues/past-conferences/

Moeller, Hans-Georg. "Sino-Nietzscheanismus: Eine geistesgeschichtliche Analyse." *Minima Sinica* 2 (2000): 38–54.

Moeller, Hans-Georg, and Paul J. D'Ambrosio. *Genuine Pretending: On the Philosophy of the Zhuangzi*. New York: Columbia University Press, 2017..

Moody-Adams, Michele. *Fieldwork in Familiar Places: Morality, Culture, and Philosophy*. Cambridge, MA: Harvard University Press, 1997.

Morsink, Johannes. *The Universal Declaration of Human Rights: Origins, Drafting, and Intent*. Philadelphia, PA: University of Pennsylvania Press, 1999.

Mou, Bo. "On Constructive-Engagement Strategy of Comparative Philosophy: A Journal Theme Introduction." *Comparative Philosophy* 1, 1 (2010): 1–32.

Mou, Bo (ed.), *Two Roads to Wisdom? Chinese and Analytic Philosophical Traditions*. La Salle, IL: Open Court, 2001.

Mou, Bo. *Cross-Tradition Engagement in Philosophy: A Constructive-Engagement Account*. New York: Routledge, 2020.

Mou, Bo and Richard Tieszen (eds), *Constructive Engagement of Analytic and Continental Approaches in Philosophy: From the Vantage Point of Comparative Philosophy*. Leiden: Brill, 2013.

Mou, Zongsan. *Nineteen Lectures on Chinese Philosophy*, translated by Julie Lee Wei. Accessed September 13, 2021. https://nineteenlects.org

Mounce, H.O. "Understanding a Primitive Society." *Philosophy* 48, 186 (1973): 347–62.

Murphy, Tim and Ralph Weber. "Confucianizing Socrates and Socratizing Confucius: On Comparing *Analects* 13:18 and the *Euthyphro*." *Philosophy East and West* 60, 2 (2010): 187–206.

Narayan, Uma. "Essence of cultures and a sense of history: A Feminist Critique of Cultural Essentialism." In *The African Philosophy Reader*, 2nd edn, edited by P.H. Coetzee and A.P.J. Roux. New York: Routledge, 2003.

Neville, Robert. "Two Forms of Comparative Philosophy." *Dao: A Journal of Comparative Philosophy* 1, 1 (2001): 1–13.

Ni, Peimin. "Traversing the Territory of Comparative Philosophy." *Society for Asian and Comparative Philosophy Forum* 23, 46 (2006): 17–34.

Ni, Peimin. "Deliberate One-Sidedness as a Method of Doing Philosophy: Reflections on Rosemont's View of the Person." *Comparative Philosophy* 9, 1 (2018): 110–17.

Nietzsche, Friedrich. *Beyond Good and Evil: Prelude to a Philosophy of the Future*, translated by Walter Kaufmann. New York: Vintage, 1966.

Nisbett, Richard. *The Geography of Thought: How Asians and Westerners Think Differently . . . and Why*. New York: The Free Press, 2003.

Northrop, F.S.C. "The Complementary Emphases of Eastern Intuitive and Western Scientific Philosophy." In *Philosophy—East and West*, edited by Charles A. Moore. Princeton, NJ: Princeton University Press, 1944, 168–234.

Nuccetelli, Susana. *Latin American Thought: Philosophical Problems and Arguments*. Boulder, Colorado: Westview Press, 2002.

Nuccetelli, Susana. "Latin American Philosophy: Metaphilosophical Foundations." *Stanford Encyclopedia of Philosophy.* Accessed October 24, 2021. https://plato.stanford.edu/entries/latin-american-metaphilosophy/

Nussbaum, Martha C. "Non-Relative Virtues: An Aristotelian Approach." *Wider Working Papers* 32 (1987): 1–37.

Nussbaum, Martha C. "Comparing Virtues." *Journal of Religious Ethics* 21, 2 (1993): 345–67.

Nussbaum, Martha C. *Cultivating Humanity: A Classical Defence of Reform in Liberal Education.* Cambridge, MA: Harvard University Press, 1997.

Nussbaum, Martha C. and Amartya Sen. "Internal Criticism and Indian Rationalist Traditions." In *Relativism: Interpretation and Confrontation,* edited by Michael Krausz. Notre Dame, IN: Notre Dame University Press, 1989, 299–325.

Orosco, José-Antonio. "The Philosophical Gift of Brown Folks: Mexican American Philosophy in the United States." *APA Newsletter on Hispanic/ Latino Issues in Philosophy,* 15 (2016): 23–8.

Ortner, Sherry. "East Brain, West Brain." *New York Times,* April 20, 2003.

Oyserman, Daphna, Heather M. Coon, and Markus Kemmelmeier. "Rethinking Individualism and Collectivism: Evaluation of Theoretical Assumptions and Meta-Analyses." *Psychological Bulletin* 128, 1 (2002): 3–72.

Pang-White, Ann A. (ed.). *The Bloomsbury Research Handbook of Chinese Philosophy and Gender.* London: Bloomsbury Academic, 2016.

Panikkar, Raimundo. "What is Comparative Philosophy Comparing?" In *Interpreting across Boundaries: New Essays in Comparative Philosophy,* edited by Gerald James Larson and Eliot Deutsch. Princeton, NJ: Princeton University Press, 1988, 116–36.

Parekh, Bhikhu. "Non-Ethnocentric Universalism." In *Human Rights and Global Politics,* edited by Tim Dunne and Nicholas J. Wheeler. Cambridge: Cambridge University Press, 1999, 128–59.

Parekh, Bhikhu. *Rethinking Multiculturalism: Cultural Diversity and Political Theory.* Cambridge, MA: Harvard University Press, 2002.

Parfit, Derek. *Reasons and Persons.* New York: Oxford, 1984.

Peerenboom, Randall. "Confucian Harmony and Freedom of Thought: The Right to Think Versus Right Thinking." In *Confucianism and Human Rights,* edited by W.T. de Bary and Tu Weiming. New York: Columbia University Press, 1998, 234–60.

Pereda, Carlos. "On Mexican Philosophy, For Example." *Comparative Philosophy* 10, 1 (2019): 192–207.

Perry, John, Michael Bratman, and John Martin Fischer (eds.). *Introduction to Philosophy: Classic and Contemporary Readings, 7th edition.* New York: Oxford University Press, 2015.

Pigliucci, Massimo. "On the pseudo-profundity of some Eastern philosophy." *Rationally Speaking* (blog). May 23, 2006. http://www.rationallyspeaking. blogspot.com/2006/05/on-pseudo-profoundity-of-some-eastern.html

Plato. *Euthyphro*. In *Plato: Complete Works*, edited by John M. Cooper. Indianapolis: Hackett, 1997.

Pölzer, Thomas. *Moral Reality and the Empirical Sciences*. New York: Routledge, 2018.

Prabhu, Joseph. "Philosophy in an Age of Global Encounter." *APA Newsletters* 100, 3 (2001): 29–31.

Priest, Graham. "Where is Philosophy at the Start of the Twenty-First Century?" *Proceedings of the Aristotelian Society* (New Series) 103 (2003): 85–99.

Puett, Michael J. *To Become a God: Cosmology, Sacrifice, and Self-Divinization in Early China*. Cambridge, MA: Harvard University Press, 2004.

Radhakrishnan, S. "On Philosophical Synthesis." *Philosophy East and West* 1, 1 (1951): 4.

Raghuramaraju, A. *Debates in Indian Philosophy: Classical, Colonial, and Contemporary*. New Delhi: Oxford University Press, 2006.

Raphals, Lisa. "Embodied Virtue, Self-Cultivation, and Ethics." In *Ethics in Early China*, edited by Chris Fraser, Dan Robins, and Timothy O'Leary. Hong Kong: Hong Kong University Press, 2011, 143–57.

Raud, Rein. "Philosophies versus Philosophy: In Defense of a Flexible Definition." *Philosophy East and West* 56, 4 (2006): 618–25.

Rawls, John. "The Idea of an Overlapping Consensus." *Oxford Journal of Legal Studies* 7, 1 (1987): 1–25.

Reding, Jean-Paul. *Comparative Essays in Early Greek and Chinese Rational Thinking*. Burlington, VT: Ashgate, 2004.

Reiff, Mark R. "Incommensurability, Cultural Relativism, and the Fundamental Presuppositions of Morality." In *The Routledge Handbook of Philosophy of Relativism*, edited by Martin Kusch. New York: Routledge, 2020.

Rhees, Rush (ed.), *Recollections of Wittgenstein*. New York: Oxford University Press, 1984.

Roetz, Heiner. *Confucian Ethics of the Axial Age: A Reconstruction under the Aspect of the Breakthrough toward Postconventional Thinking*. Albany: State University of New York Press, 1993.

Roetz, Heiner. "What It Means to Take Chinese Ethics Seriously." In *Taking Confucian Ethics Seriously: Contemporary Theories and Applications*, edited by Kam-por Yu, Julia Tao, and Philip J. Ivanhoe. Albany: State University of New York Press, 2010.

Rorty, Richard. "Rationality and Cultural Difference." In *Truth and Progress: Philosophical Papers*. Cambridge: Cambridge University Press, 1998, 186–201.

Rorty, Richard. *Philosophy and the Mirror of Nature, Thirtieth-Anniversary Edition*. Princeton, NJ: Princeton University Press, 2009.

Rose, David, Edouard Machery, et al. "The Ship of Theseus Puzzle." *Oxford Studies in Experimental Philosophy, Volume 3*, edited by Tania Lombrozo, Joshua Knobe, and Shaun Nichols. Oxford: Oxford University Press.

Rosemont, Jr., Henry. "Against Relativism." In *Interpreting across Boundaries: New Essays in Comparative Philosophy*, edited by Gerald James Larson and Eliot Deutsch. Princeton, NJ: Princeton University Press, 1988, 36–70.

Rosemont, Jr., Henry. "Whose Democracy? Which Rights? A Confucian Critique of Modern Western Liberalism." In *Confucian Ethics: A Comparative Study of Self, Autonomy, and Community*, edited by Kwong-loi Shun and David B. Wong. Cambridge: Cambridge University Press, 2004, 49–71.

Rosemont, Jr., Henry. *Against Individualism: A Confucian Rethinking of the Foundations of Morality, Politics, Family, and Religion*. Lanham, MD: Lexington Books, 2015.

Rosemont, Jr., Henry and Roger T. Ames. "On Translation and Interpretation (with Special Reference to Classical Chinese)." In *Eastwards: Western Views on East Asian Culture*, edited by Frank Kraushaar. Bern: Peter Lang, 2010, 39–58.

Said, Edward. *Orientalism*. New York: Pantheon Books, 1978.

Rosenlee, Li-Hsiang Lisa. *Confucianism and Women: A Philosophical Interpretation*. Albany: State University of New York Press, 2006.

Sabaratnam, Meera. "Decolonising the curriculum: what's all the fuss about?" *SOAS Blog*. Jan. 18, 2017. https://study.soas.ac.uk/decolonising-curriculum-whats-the-fuss/

Santayana, George. "On Philosophical Synthesis." *Philosophy East and West* 1, 1 (1951): 5.

Santideva. *The Bodhicaryāvatāra*, translated by Kate Crosby and Andrew Skilton. New York: Oxford University Press, 1995.

Sapir, Edward. "The Status of Linguistics as a Science." In *Selected Writings in Language, Culture, and Personality*, edited by David G. Mandelbaum. Berkeley, CA: University of California Press, 1949.

Scharfstein, Ben-Ami. "The Contextual Fallacy." In *Interpreting across Boundaries: New Essays in Comparative Philosophy*, edited by Gerald James Larson and Eliot Deutsch. Princeton, NJ: Princeton University Press, 1988, 84–97.

Scharfstein, Ben-Ami. *A Comparative History of World Philosophy: From the Upanishads to Kant*. Albany: State University of New York Press, 1998.

Schepen, Renate and Hans van Rappard. "African and Chinese Philosophies Compared: A Dialogue Between East and South." *Philosophy East and West* 68, 4 (2018): 1369–79.

Schopenhauer, Arthur. *The World as Will and Representation*. Vol. 1, translated by Judith Norman, Alistair Welchman, and Christopher Janaway. Cambridge: Cambridge University Press, 2010.

Schor, Naomi. *Bad Objects: Essays Popular and Unpopular*. Durham, NC: Duke University Press, 1995.

Schwitzgebel, Eric. "Why don't we know our Chinese Philosophy?" *APA Newsletter on the Status of Asian & Asian-American Philosophers & Philosophies* 1 (2001): 26–7.

Sellars, Wilfred. *Science, Perception and Reality*. London: Routledge, 1963.

Sen, Amartya. "Democracy as a Universal Value." *Journal of Democracy* 10, 3 (1999): 3–17.

Shen, Vincent. "Some Thoughts on Intercultural Philosophy and Chinese Philosophy." *Journal of Chinese Philosophy* 30, 3–4 (2003): 357–72.

Sherratt, Yvonne. *Continental Philosophy of Social Science*. Cambridge: Cambridge University Press, 2005.

Shun, Kwong-Loi. "Studying Confucian and Comparative Ethics: Methodological Reflections." *Journal of Chinese Philosophy* 36, 3 (2009): 455–78.

Shun, Kwong-loi and David B. Wong (eds). *Confucian Ethics: A Comparative Study of Self, Autonomy, and Community*. Cambridge: Cambridge University Press, 2004.

Siderits, Mark. *Personal Identity and Buddhist Philosophy: Empty Persons*. Burlington, VT: Ashgate, 2003.

Siderits, Mark. "Comparison or Confluence in Philosophy?" In *The Oxford Handbook of Indian Philosophy*, edited by Jonardon Ganeri. New York: Oxford University Press, 2017.

Silius, Vytis. "Diversifying Academic Philosophy: The Post-Comparative Turn and Transculturalism." *Asian Studies*, 8, 2 (2020): 257–80.

Silva, Grant J. "Comparative Philosophy and Decolonial Struggle: The Epistemic Injustice of Colonization and Liberation of Human Reason." *The Southern Journal of Philosophy* 57, Supplement (2019), 107–34.

Sim, May. *Remastering Morals with Aristotle and Confucius*. Cambridge: Cambridge University Press, 2007.

Slingerland, Edward. (trans.). *Confucius: Analects, with Selections from Traditional Commentaries*. Indianapolis, IN: Hackett, 2003.

Slingerland, Edward. "The Situationist Critique and Early Confucian Virtue Ethics," *Ethics* 121, 2 (2011): 390–419.

Slingerland, Edward. "Body and Mind in Early China: An Integrated Science-Humanities Approach." *Journal of the American Academy of Religion* 81, 1 (2013): 1–50.

Slingerland, Edward. *Mind and Body in Early China: Beyond Orientalism and the Myth of Holism*. Oxford: Oxford University Press, 2019.

Smid, Robert W. *Methodologies of Comparative Philosophy: The Pragmatist and Process Traditions*. Albany: State University of New York Press, 2002.

Solomon, Robert C. and Kathleen M. Higgins (eds), *The Big Questions: A Short Introduction to Philosophy, 8th Edition*. Belmont, CA: Wadsworth Cengage Learning, 2010.

Stalnaker, Aaron. *Overcoming Our Evil: Human Nature and Spiritual Exercises in Xunzi and Augustine*. Washington, DC: Georgetown University Press, 2006.

Stevenson, Jay. *The Complete Idiot's Guide to Eastern Philosophy*. Indianapolis: Alpha Books, 2000.

Struhl, Karsten J. "No (More) Philosophy without Cross-Cultural Philosophy." *Philosophy Compass* 5, 4 (2010): 287–95.

Swoyer, Chris. "The Linguistic Relativity Hypothesis." In *The Stanford Encyclopedia of Philosophy*. Accessed October 29, 2021. https://stanford. library.sydney.edu.au/archives/spr2015/entries/relativism/supplement2.html

Tagore, Saranindranath. "On the Concept of World Philosophy." *Philosophy East & West* 67, 2 (2017): 531–44.

Tan, Kok-Chor. "Globalizing Cosmopolitanism." *Journal of World Philosophies* 6 (2021): 99–138.

Tan, Sor-hoon. *Confucian Democracy: A Deweyan Reconstruction*. Albany: State University of New York Press, 2003.

Tan, Sor-hoon. (ed.). *The Bloomsbury Research Handbook of Chinese Philosophy Methodologies*. London: Bloomsbury Academic, 2016.

Tanaka, Koji. "Davidson and Chinese Conceptual Scheme." In *Davidson's Philosophy and Chinese Philosophy*, edited by Bo Mou. Leiden: Brill, 2007, 55–71.

Taylor, Charles. "Conditions of an Unforced Consensus on Human Rights." In *The East Asian Challenge for Human Rights*, edited by Joanne Bauer and Daniel A. Bell. Cambridge: Cambridge University Press, 1999, 124–44.

Taylor, Charles. "Understanding the Other: A Gadamerian View on Conceptual Schemes." In *Dilemmas and Connections: Selected Essays*. Cambridge, MA: Harvard University Press, 2011.

Tuck, Andrew P. *Comparative Philosophy and the Philosophy of Scholarship: On the Western Interpretation of Nagarjuna*. New York: Oxford University Press, 1990.

Turiel, Elliot. *The Culture of Morality: Social Development, Context, and Conflict*. Cambridge: Cambridge University Press, 2002.

Tylor, Edward B. *Primitive Culture: Researches into the Development of Mythology, Philosophy, Religion, Art, and Custom*. London: John Murray, 1871.

"The Universal Declaration of Human Rights: History of the Document." Accessed March 25, 2014. http://www.un.org/en/documents/udhr/history. shtml

Van Norden, Bryan W. "What Should Western Philosophy Learn from Chinese Philosophy?" In *Chinese Language, Thought and Culture: Nivison and His Critics*, edited by Philip J. Ivanhoe. La Salle, IL: Open Court, 1996.

Van Norden, Bryan W. *Virtue Ethics and Consequentialism in Early Chinese Philosophy*. Cambridge: Cambridge University Press, 2007.

Van Norden, Bryan W. *Taking Back Philosophy: A Multicultural Manifesto*. New York: Columbia University Press, 2017.

Vargas, Manuel. "On the Value of Philosophy: The Latin American Case." *Comparative Philosophy* 1, 1 (2010): 33–52.

Voltaire. *A Philosophical Dictionary*. Vol. 2. London: John and H.L. Hunt, 1824.

Waley, Arthur (trans.). *The Analects of Confucius*. New York: Vintage, 1989.

Wang, Qingli James. "Thing-ing and No-Thing in Heidegger, Kant, and Laozi". *Dao: A Journal of Comparative Philosophy* 15 (2016): 159–74.

Wang, Robin R. "Yinyang Gender Dynamics: Lived Bodies, Rhythmical Changes, and Cultural Performances." In *The Bloomsbury Research Handbook of Chinese Philosophy and Gender*, edited by Ann A. Pang-White, London: Bloomsbury Academic, 2016.

Wang, Xinli. "Incommensurability and Comparative Philosophy." Keynote address, "Incommensurability 50," Taipei, Taiwan, June 1–3, 2013.

Wang, Xinli. *Incommensurability and Cross-Language Communication*. New York: Routledge, 2016.

Warburton, Nigel. *Philosophy: The Basics, 3rd Edition*. New York: Routledge, 1999.

Wawrytko, Sandra A. "Buddhist Nondualism: Deconstructing Gender and Other Delusions of the Discriminating Mind through Awareness." In *The Bloomsbury Research Handbook of Chinese Philosophy and Gender*, edited by Ann A. Pang-White. London: Bloomsbury Academic, 2016.

Weber, Ralph. "A Stick Which may be Grabbed on Either Side: Sino-Hellenic Studies in the Mirror of Comparative Philosophy." *International Journal of the Classical Tradition* 20, 1–2 (2013): 1–14.

Weber, Ralph. "'How to Compare?'—On the Methodological State of Comparative Philosophy." *Philosophy Compass* 8, 7 (2013): 593–603.

Weber, Ralph. "Comparative Philosophy and the *Tertium*: Comparing What with What, and in What Respect?" *Dao: A Journal of Comparative Philosophy* 13, 2 (2014): 151–71.

Whorf, B.L. "Science and Linguistics." *Technology Review* 42, 6 (1940): 229–31, 247–8.

Winch, Peter. "Understanding a Primitive Society." *American Philosophical Quarterly* 1, 4 (1964): 307–24.

Wiredu, Kwasi. *Cultural Universals and Particulars: An African Perspective*. Bloomington: Indiana University Press, 1996.

Wiredu, Kwasi. "Can Philosophy be Intercultural? An African Viewpoint." *Diogenes* 184, 4 (1998): 147–67.

Wiredu, Kwasi. "Toward Decolonizing African Philosophy and Religion." *African Studies Quarterly* 1, 4 (1998), http://www.asq.africa.ufl.edu/v1/4/3.htm

Wiredu, Kwasi. "How Not to Compare African Traditional Thought with Western Thought." In *African Philosophy: An Anthology*, edited by Emmanuel Chukwudi Eze. Malden, MA: Blackwell, 1998.

Wiredu, Kwasi. "State, Civil Society and Democracy in Africa." In *Reclaiming the Human Sciences and Humanities through African Perspectives, Vol. II*, edited by Helen Lauer and Kofi Anyidoho. Ghana: Sub-Saharan Publishers, 2012, 1055–66.

Wittgenstein, Ludwig. *Philosophical Investigations*, translated by G. E. M. Anscombe. Malden, MA: Blackwell, 2003.

Wong, David B. *Moral Relativity*. Berkeley, CA: University of California Press, 1984.

Wong, David B. "Three Kinds of Incommensurability." In *Relativism: Interpretation and Confrontation*, edited by Michael Krausz. Notre Dame, IN: Notre Dame University Press, 1989, 140–59.

Wong, David B. *Natural Moralities: A Defense of Pluralistic Relativism*. New York: Oxford University Press, 2006.

Wong, David B. *Agon and Hé*: Contest and Harmony". In *Ethics in Early China*, edited by C. Fraser, D. Robins, and T. O'Leary. Hong Kong: Hong Kong University Press, 2011, 197–216.

Wong, David B. "Comparative Philosophy: Chinese and Western." In *The Stanford Encyclopedia of Philosophy*. Accessed October 29, 2021. https://plato.stanford.edu/entries/comparphil-chiwes/

Wong, Edward. "A Chinese Virtue is Now the Law." *New York Times*, July 2, 2013.

Xiao, Yang. "Agency and Practical Reasoning in the *Analects* and *Mencius*." *Journal of Chinese Philosophy* 36, 4 (2009): 629–41.

Xiao, Yang and Yong Huang (eds). *Moral Relativism and Chinese Philosophy: David Wong and His Critics*. Albany: State University of New York Press, 2014.

Xie, Ming. *Conditions of Comparison: Reflections on Comparative Intercultural Inquiry*. New York: Continuum, 2011.

Yang, Guorong. *Philosophical Horizons: Metaphysical Investigation in Chinese Philosophy*, translated by Paul J. D'Ambrosio, Daniel Sarafinas, Sharon Small, Ady van den Stock, and Stefano Gandolfo. Leiden: Brill, 2019.

Yao, Xinzhong. "Self-Construction and Identity: The Confucian Self in Relation to Some Western Perceptions." *Asian Philosophy* 6, 3 (1996): 179–95.

Yao, Xinzhong. *An Introduction to Confucianism*. Cambridge: Cambridge University Press, 2000.

Yasuaki, Onuma. "Toward an Intercivilizational Approach to Human Rights." In *The East Asian Challenge for Human Rights*, edited by Joanne Bauer and Daniel A. Bell. Cambridge: Cambridge University Press, 1999, 103–23.

Yearley, Lee H. *Mencius and Aquinas: Theories of Virtue and Conceptions of Courage*. Albany: State University of New York Press, 1990.

Yu, Jiyuan. "The Language of Being: Between Aristotle and Chinese Philosophy." *International Philosophical Quarterly* 39, 4 (1999): 439–54.

Yu, Jiyuan. *The Ethics of Confucius and Aristotle: Mirrors of Virtue*. New York: Routledge, 2007.

Yu, Jiyuan. "The Practicality of Ancient Virtue Ethics: Greece and China." *Dao: A Journal of Comparative Philosophy* 9, 3 (2010): 289–302.

Yu, Jiyuan and Nicholas Bunnin. "Saving the Phenomena: An Aristotelian Method in Comparative Philosophy." In *Two Roads to Wisdom? Chinese and Analytic Philosophical Traditions*, edited by Bo Mou. La Salle, IL: Open Court, 2001, 293–312.

Zajonc, Arthur. "Reflections on 'Investigating the Mind,' One Year Later." In *The Dalai Lama at MIT*, edited by Anne Harrington and Arthur Zajonc. Cambridge, MA: Harvard University Press, 2008.

Zakaria, Fareed. "Culture Is Destiny: A Conversation with Lee Kuan Yew." *Foreign Affairs* 73, 2 (1994): 109–26.

Zea, Leopoldo. "The Actual Function of Philosophy in Latin America." In *Latin American Philosophy in the Twentieth Century*, edited by J.J.E. Gracia. Buffalo: Prometheus Books, 1986.

Zhang, Longxi. *The Tao and the Logos: Literary Hermeneutics, East and West*. Durham, NC: Duke University Press, 1992.

Zhang, Longxi. *Mighty Opposites: From Dichotomies to Differences in the Comparative Study of China*. Stanford, CA: Stanford University Press, 1998.

Zhao, Dunhua. "Some Progressive and Problematic Features of Current Philosophy in China." In *Dialogue of Philosophies, Religions and Civilizations in the Era of Globalization (Chinese Philosophical Studies XXV)*, edited by Zhao Dunhua. Washington, DC: Council for Research and Values in Philosophy, 2007, 99–110.

Zhao, Dunhua. "A Defense of Universalism: With a Critique of Particularism in Chinese Culture." *Frontiers of Philosophy in China* 4, 1 (2009): 116–29.

Zhuangzi. *Zhuangzi: Basic Writings*, translated by Burton Watson. New York: Columbia University Press, 2003.

Index